Tatra

THE LEGACY OF HANS LEDWINKA
FULLY REVISED AND UPDATED NEW EDITION

Ivan Margolius and John G Henry

TATRA T30 RACER WITH JOSEF VEŘMIŘOVSKÝ AND CO-DRIVER JALŮVKA ATTENDING THE SCHWABENBERG HILLCLIMB, BUDAPEST, OCTOBER 25TH, 1926. DRAWING BY ROY WHITE.

TATRA T77 AT HRADČANY CASTLE,
PRAGUE IN 1934 AND IN 2014.
(COURTESY PAVEL KASÍK, KAREL THÉR,
DALIBOR LUPÍK)

UPDATED & ENLARGED COLLECTOR'S EDITION OF 1500 COPIES

Tatra

THE LEGACY OF HANS LEDWINKA

IVAN MARGOLIUS & JOHN G HENRY

CONTENTS

FOREWORD

About 30 years ago I discovered the Tatra T87 saloon in the Deutsches Museum in Munich, and it was love at first sight.

Then I did not know about the designer, a brilliantly innovative engineer named Hans Ledwinka (1878-1967), who had gifted it to the museum (originally it was a retirement gift to him from Felix Wankel, the inventor of the rotary engine). The reason the vehicle remained in my memory was simply because I was so deeply impressed by the scale of its presence and the beauty of its flowing lines.

Now, so many years later, I am the proud owner of an almost identical model, and for me this vehicle still has the same power of attraction. Perhaps like a work of art or architecture which is radical in its period; that same quality endures into the future and becomes even more prized with the passage of time.

If today people stop and stare when I drive by in the Tatra, try to imagine the public impact in 1934, the year of its birth, in the form of the earlier T77. The voluptuous steel body with its sculpted air intakes and striking dorsal fin is continually described as 'futuristic,' and I enjoy the affinities of this automobile with the artistic movement of Italian Futurism. For example, the figure by Umberto Boccioni, 'Unique Forms of Continuity in Space' (1913), looks as if it had been sculpted in the slipstream of a wind tunnel, and seems to anticipate the embodiment of speed in a new generation of automobiles, still two decades away from realisation.

The Tatra is one of a handful of such streamlined vehicles that defined this new generation and there are interesting connections which link them together. This explains why I group together a particular selection of cars and models in my garage. Under the same roof as the Tatra there is the Dymaxion of Buckminster Fuller, and the Chrysler Airflow saloon, both of 1934. Then there are the models – the Chrysler Building and the Citroën Traction Avant – again creations of the same period. Nearby is a khaki coloured 1944 KdF-Wagen, modified for military use. Designed by Ferdinand Porsche, it is the origin of the iconic post-war VW Beetle. Next to it is a Porsche 356 Coupé (a rare pre-A split screen example from 1950, the first year of production at Stuttgart). Over time this would evolve into the now familiar Porsche 911.

So what are the themes that weave through these objects and culturally link them together? As is so often the case they can be traced back to the role of individuals. One dominant figure, Paul Jaray (1889-1974), is closely linked to the design of the Tatra. He was the father of streamlining, and pioneered the concept through wind tunnel studies, airships, prototype cars and patents. Jaray's connection is clear. He set up the 'Stromlinien-Karosserie-Gesellschaft' to market his European patents in 1927. Tatra was one of the licensees, and Jaray worked with Ledwinka on the initial designs for the T77.

Through many experiments, Paul Jaray created an ideal form, which looks uncannily like the artist Constantin Brancusi's minimally abstract sculpture titled 'Fish' (1926). Perhaps the auto which most closely follows the ultimate teardrop shape pioneered by Jaray is Fuller's Dymaxion, co-authored with Starling Burgess, the yacht designer, and artist Isamu Noguchi. It is difficult to believe that this fish-like form is made from the same standard components as the boxy Ford sedan of the time – their use made possible by the generosity of Fuller's friend, Henry Ford, who heavily discounted the cost to Fuller of any Ford parts.

Jaray also set up the 'Jaray Streamline Corporation' in New York City in 1932, to market the aerodynamic patents he had been granted in the US in 1927. In May 1935 it served legal papers on Chrysler after it launched the 'Airflow,' and the dispute was resolved by Chrysler acknowledging its debt to Jaray, and agreeing to the payment of royalties.

The 'Airflow' was another legendary attempt to reinvent the auto. It was conceived in a wind tunnel with the help of Wilbur Wright, and among its many firsts was the unification of the chassis and body into one integrated structure to provide greater strength and safety. Technically its many innovations anticipated the modern day saloon, whilst visually its detailing, from bumpers and tail lights to interior furniture, echoed the Art Deco architecture of the time – especially the steel pinnacle of Van Alen's Chrysler Building – both the car and building were conceived in 1927.

All of these vehicles stretched the technology of the day and one individual rises to prominence – Edward G

Budd (1870-1946) – whose enterprise, The Budd Company, was at the cutting-edge of translating these design dreams into reality. It was Budd whose heroic presses stamped out the body panels for the Airflow. He also found a kindred spirit in André Citroën, to make possible the Avant Traction, another first in terms of monocoque construction, this time using spot-welding as a new technique. Again, the year is 1934, which stretches the bounds of coincidence. Sometimes the connections across the continents of North America and Europe are tangible with collaborations which are declared. At other times industrial espionage and dirty tricks are hinted at through legal confrontations. In one of these explorations of the past we discover that Budd's chief engineer, Joseph Ledwinka, was possibly a relative of the Tatra's co-designer Hans Ledwinka.

Any published reference to the Tatra eventually links into another contemporary designer, Ferdinand Porsche (1875-1951), and his role in the birth of the VW Beetle and a line of similarly rear-engined sports cars. There are two issues, which are rarely discussed in any of the many documents on these marques. First was the role of the Jewish engineer Josef Ganz in the evolution of the KdF-Wagen or 'People's car,' a Hitler initiative which was the genesis of the VW Beetle. Recent research suggests that Ganz was sidelined for the credit in favour of Porsche, and was fortunate to escape with his life. The second fact is that Tatra sued Porsche, through the VW enterprise, for infringement of patents, eventually receiving one million Deutsche Marks in an out of court settlement in 1965. Its first attempt in 1939 through the international court was thwarted by the onset of the Second World War. At the end of the war both Porsche and Ledwinka were imprisoned on charges of collaboration.

The intrigue behind the innovation and beauty of the Tatra enlarges its appeal from the aesthetic to the intellectual. It is also a reminder that all great artists, architects, engineers, and designers feed off each other, whether or not they choose to admit that reality. It does not necessarily compromise the individuality of any of their works. The Tatra may have been an influence on generations of rear-engined Porsche sports cars and historians may ponder this possibility. It is, however, a matter of celebration that there is only one Tatra and in our current age where every auto looks the same, the Tatra stands out as a proud individual – head and shoulders above the herd.

My personal Tatra was restored by Ecorra, a company based in Kopřivnice, Moravia, the home town of the Tatra factory. It is pristine, in gloss black – its original colour with continuity of metal and finish inside and out. Like all really interesting classic cars, the detailing craves for close-up photography to capture its delightful originality. But the Tatra is more than a museum piece. Despite the folklore of mishaps in its historic past, this vehicle today is totally at home on any high speed motorway, and is as much a joy to drive as it is to contemplate.

Norman Foster
London

1948 TATRA T87 OWNED BY NORMAN FOSTER. T87S MADE BETWEEN 1947 AND 1950 HAD HEADLAMPS SET INTO THE FRONT OF THE BODY. (COURTESY NIGEL YOUNG)

MY FATHER

The history of the early age of automobile production was based on the achievements of a handful of designers and inventors, individuals of great talent and vision whose contribution to the development of the motor car has not yet been fully appreciated. Nowadays, unlike some of the other marques, the people of the Western world are hardly ever confronted with the Tatra marque. However, in the first half of the 20th century, Tatra motor cars were among the best known and most sought-after automobiles in Europe. The man behind this success was their designer Hans Ledwinka, whose entire life and work became an integral part of the history of the modern motor car.

In 1878, when my father Hans Ledwinka was born, the horse-drawn carriage was the only means of passenger transportation. During his lifetime, the automobile, probably more than any other machine, has changed the way of life of the whole world. After the early years, when it was chiefly a plaything of the rich and adventurous, it has become an everyday necessity for millions of people. In all this, Hans Ledwinka played an important role.

My father was in his late teens when he came to the Nesselsdorfer wagon factory, which later became the Tatra company. The year was 1897, and the management of the plant decided to launch the construction of the first automobile. This was, at the time, a brave venture which required keen foresight and uncommon initiative. Hans immediately became interested in this project, eager to take part in such a bold undertaking. From this first encounter with the construction of the automobile, it became clear that he had found his true vocation.

Throughout his long life he remained faithful to the automobile industry. He was above all an outstanding designer, while his prowess in technical engineering and management was equally remarkable. His designs and constructions, brilliant in their simplicity and expediency, became milestones in the development of motor cars as we see them today. Besides his extraordinary talent, it was my father's total dedication to his work, his intuition and persistent attention to detail, which led to his many successes.

Shortly after the First World War, he became aware of the broad popular interest in the automobile and

popular in all Europe and influenced car design for many years to come.

My father's career with the Tatra company was not without difficulties, but it bought fame and recognition to both the designer and the factory. In 1928 the German magazine *Motor-Kritik* called him "the greatest master of the art of European automobile design." It is unfortunate that this fruitful collaboration ended in personal tragedy for this talented and dedicated man. In 1945, at a time when he was the technical director of the factory, he was made responsible for the unavoidable involvement of the Tatra company in Wehrmacht arms production. He was incarcerated for six years, and lost all his fortune as well as the results of his lifelong endeavour – several hundred patents. After his release he received a number of awards and distinctions, but rehabilitation from the Czechoslovak government never came. (For update see: Ledwinka's Great Contribution, page 153).

Our world tends to take the blessings of technological progress too much for granted, and forgets the enormous trials of the pathfinders who made it all possible. I hope this book will contribute to a revival of interest in the life and work of one of the greatest of these pathfinders, my father, Dr techn. h.c. Hans Ledwinka.

Prof Dipl Ing Dr techn **Erich Ledwinka**
Car Designer, Závody Tatra as (1930-37)
Chief Engineer, Bücker-Flugzeugbau, Berlin (1937-40)
Chief Car Designer and Development Manager, Ringhoffer-Tatra-Werke AG (1940-45)
Chief Car Designer and Technical Director, Steyr-Daimler-Puch AG (1950-75)

Graz, May 1989

understood, well ahead of his time, the need for a dependable, affordable, small car which people could use for their everyday transportation. He also realised that for the construction of such a vehicle, a totally new concept was necessary – and not merely a reduction in the size of the existing large motor car. His revolutionary solution to this problem gave birth to the famous Tatra T11. It was a simple, inexpensive, sturdy little car which became immensely

NESSELSDORFER WAGENBAU. CONTEMPORARY ADVERTISEMENT FOR NESSELSDORFER AUTOMOBILE SHOWING THE FACTORY COMPLEX, PUBLISHED IN *ALLGEMEINE AUTOMOBIL-ZEITUNG*, JANUARY 14TH, 1900.

INTRODUCTION

The Tatra company, based in Kopřivnice, Czechoslovakia (now the Czech Republic, consisting of principal regions Bohemia and Moravia), has been in continuous automotive vehicle production since 1897, and as such belongs to the exclusive group of the oldest car manufacturers in the world. Its survival throughout the turmoil of the 20th century is due to the great technical mastery and talent of the people of Central Europe, and one man in particular, Dr Hans Ledwinka (1878-1967). Tatra is an extraordinary marque with a reputation mainly established by this forgotten engineering genius, one of the most inventive and prolific of automobile pioneers.

Although these avant-garde cars and their visionary maker made a significant contribution to European automobile design and production in the first half of the 20th century, neither the cars nor their designer have been adequately acknowledged. Apart from the first edition of this book in 1990, no other major substantial work on this subject matter has been published in English speaking countries since. Ledwinka, whose revolutionary cars reached an original level of technical inventiveness similar to his contemporary Ferdinand Porsche, who has been celebrated many times over, deserves better recognition.

Ledwinka's Tatra car designs and proposals were greatly influential in his most productive time, affecting many of the principles that later initiated the development of cars powered by air-cooled engines and the concepts of German Volkswagen. He paved the way for the use of swing half-axles, independent suspension, and forced air-cooling, along with front and rear positioned engines, backbone frame chassis, and monoblock engine assemblies. The majority of these elements were combined and incorporated into the courageous initiation of the serial production of truly streamlined, aerodynamic cars. However, until now these Tatra designs have never been fully appreciated, having remained almost totally neglected and overshadowed by

▲

UNE

VOITURE

D'AVANT-GARDE

LA TATRA

77

▼

TATRA T77's GRAPHIC DESCRIPTION IN
FRENCH MAGAZINE *OMNIA*, NOVEMBER 1934.

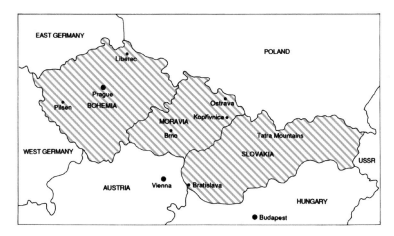

MAP OF CZECHOSLOVAKIA AFTER 1945.

other famous marques. The time has surely come again to redress this imbalance and shed more light on both Tatra and Ledwinka.

The main reason for this gap in our knowledge is possibly because the Tatra passenger motor cars were manufactured and driven in a rather confined locality, having been cut off from the Western world for many years behind the Iron Curtain. This partly explains why Tatras are not familiar to the present general public outside their home country of origin. It follows that the same can unfortunately be said of their creator Ledwinka. Only car enthusiasts recall his original, highly advanced designs which have occasionally been illustrated in motoring books and magazines.

Nowadays, seeing a Tatra on the streets of Western European towns, excepting German and Austrian cities, is a near impossibility. This is true especially in the United Kingdom where they were never imported in large numbers, the British getting their only glimpse of Tatra cars when Czechoslovak diplomats made occasional speedy trips through London streets. Although, since the first edition of this book, this situation has somewhat improved: the Tatra Register UK had been founded with over 90 members owning around 65 Tatra cars.

The Tatra company built its reputation on a number of significant models. One of the most influential of the

TATRA T54 STEERING WHEEL.
(COURTESY DAVID YANDO,
LANE MOTOR MUSEUM)

TATRA T87, THE BEST KNOWN TATRA
CAR, ADMIRED BY CROWDS AT A PRAGUE
AUTOSALON.

Tatra range was the model T11/12. This was one of the first real people's cars, with its radical, flexible central tubular chassis structure and an independent suspension system using swing half-axles. This simple concept incorporating a front air-cooled, overhead valve, twin-cylinder engine, was committed to paper in 1921 – preceding the first Volkswagen prototypes by over ten years. The soundness of this design has been confirmed by the fact that T11/12s were still on the road in Czechoslovakia, Austria and Germany until the latter part of the 20th century, often with half a million kilometres on the clock.

The next major landmark in Tatra design was the T77 – one of the first rear engine automobiles with a truly aerodynamic streamlined body in serial factory production.

This magnificent motor car with an air-cooled eight-cylinder engine placed behind the rear half-axles was generally acknowledged as the outstanding vehicle of the decade. The T77, and later the T87 (known as the Autobahn car) together with the earlier T11/12, as well as the air-cooled diesel trucks with independent suspension were the crowning achievements of the Tatra factory production output.

The Tatra company started its existence as Schustala & Comp, which was incorporated in 1891 as the Nesselsdorfer Wagenbau-Fabriks (Nesselsdorfer Wagon Works) and was well regarded abroad for the high level of craftsmanship, long-lasting quality and the most up-to-date design. The factory was located in the small village of Nesselsdorf, in Czech Kopřivnice, meaning Nettle Village, near a town called Neutitschein (Nový Jičín) in Eastern Moravia just below the Beskydy section of the Carpathian Mountain chain. The highest peaks in this range are called the Tatra Mountains.

At the beginning of the development of the NW 'Nesselsdorfer Automobile' marque (NW – sometimes nicknamed nur weg, fast getaway), Leopold Sviták (1856-1931), a locally born Czech, was the leading factory personality. As chief mechanic and production manager he headed the team which pioneered the manufacture of the first 100 Nesselsdorfer automobiles. The later history of the marque, which was renamed Tatra in 1919, is inseparably connected with the innovative designer Dr Hans Ledwinka.

It may come as a surprise to some to learn that such innovation came from what is now regarded as a fairly remote area of the European continent. However, between the World Wars, Czechoslovakia had a truly democratic constitution and attempted to become one of the first genuinely humane welfare states. As a nation it had also established itself as one of the most highly educated and industrialised in Europe. Within this industrialisation Tatra came to play an important role, as the Czech population possessed increasingly large numbers of locally made as well as imported motor vehicles.

The specific region of Moravia, which before the First World War was part of the Austro-Hungarian Empire, can also boast of being a birthplace of a large number of famous people. The founder of psychoanalysis, Sigmund Freud, was born in Freiberg (Příbor), modernist architect Adolf Loos and mathematician Kurt Gödel in Brünn (Brno), physicist Ernst Mach in Brünn-Chirlitz, the founder of genetic science Gregor Mendel in Heinzendorf (Hynčice), and the Secessionist architect Josef Hoffmann in Pirnitz (Brtnice). Also composer Leoš Janáček was born in Hukvaldy, the Art Nouveau painter Alfons Mucha in Ivančice, philosopher Edmund Husserl, the inventor of contact lenses Otto Wichterle in Prossnitz (Prostějov), and the famous long-distance runner Emil Zátopek in Kopřivnice itself.

Ledwinka himself was not born in Moravia but in the Austrian part of the Empire near Vienna, although his father Anton came from the same Moravian town as Josef Hoffmann. However, Hans spent the main portion of his life living in Moravia and working for Nesselsdorfer (Kopřivničan)/ Tatra. By 1914, Ledwinka had already been designing motor cars which technically surpassed the average conventional automobile concept. His four- and six-cylinder engines, with hemispherical combustion chambers and slanted valves with an overhead camshaft, formed one block with the gearbox. These features of the engine, together with the introduction of a four-wheel braking system, were milestones found only in Nesselsdorfer automobiles at the time. These innovations were not all created by Ledwinka, but he had the vision and courage to introduce them into a serial factory production. He later became the chief technical director of Tatra and was also devoted to heavy truck, railway wagon and railcar design, and many of his innovations appeared in these modes of transport as well.

Ledwinka was a modest man who shunned publicity, and, as such, was not as interested in sports and racing cars as other contemporary designers such as Porsche. However, much of the attention given to car design in the last century has been increasingly linked with achievements in motorsport, and it is not perhaps surprising that the latter's name now has much higher public profile. Ledwinka's skills were directed more towards the exploration of all aspects of motor vehicle design and production. This less

LINE-UP OF SOME OF THE TATRAS IN STREAMLINED TATRA CLASS AT THE PEBBLE BEACH CONCOURS D'ELEGANCE, 2014. (COURTESY DAVID J RUSSEL)

conspicuous approach nevertheless contributed many progressive proposals for Nesselsdorfer/Tatra. Ledwinka introduced cars and goods vehicles for people of modest means, which always kept up to date with the current trends in technology and fashion.

The comparison with Porsche is an inevitable one; the two men obviously compared notes from time to time. However, as the Tatra and Ledwinka story unravels itself, it is clear that Ledwinka's subsequent influence on Porsche's development of the Volkswagen is one of automobile history's best kept secrets.

The history of the Tatra company is also fascinating for the general versatility of its production and for the depth of its endeavours. All modes of transport were explored, improved, reconstructed and produced, from simple horse drawn traps and carriages to motor cars and racing cars. Development extended to railway wagons and carriages, electric and petrol driven railcars, light and heavy trucks, buses, military vehicles, trams, agricultural and refrigeration machinery, trolleybuses, and even aeroplanes.

Apart from Tatra, only five car factories can make the claim of having uninterrupted automobile production since the 19th century. Daimler/Mercedes-Benz, Peugeot, Renault, Ford, and Fiat are the only other companies that belong to this select group of the oldest automobile manufacturers.

GATHERING OF BRITISH REGISTERED TATRAS AT THE SLOVAK EMBASSY, LONDON, JUNE 2011: 1970 T2-603, 1938 T97, 1946 T87, 1952 T600 AND 1990 T613-3.

TATRA T77A AND THE PRÄSIDENT POSED FOR THE 40TH ANNIVERSARY OF TATRA CAR PRODUCTION IN 1937.

To this day, although it continued to produce passenger cars up to 1999, the Tatra commercial trucks are better known mainly due to their successes in Dakar rallies, where they won outright in 1988, 1994, 1995, 1998, 1999 and 2001. Therefore, even though the Tatra marque is now little known 'on the road,' it deserves a distinguished and fully recorded place in automobile history.

In recent years, where car design has been subjected to the rigours of economy, uniform styling, sharing of car parts and components and everyday practicality, it is not surprising that there has been an increasing revival of interest in the classic car designs of bygone eras. The Tatra-Freunde International, which is based in Brunn am Gebirge, Austria, and has members in many countries, organises rallies to promote and develop interest in these classic cars. In May 1988, Tatra cars from all over Europe arrived in the South of England for a ten day tour, observed along their way by scores of fascinated and inquiring onlookers. Further public exposure of Tatra cars came when an agency for Löwenbräu lager made the 'Gently Does It' advertisement which ran on ITV and Channel 4 in the UK, featuring the Tatra T603 as its centrepiece. The interest in Tatra cars was highlighted further by trailers for the film *Autoerotic*, shown on Channel 4 in 1995. A 1938 T87, borrowed from Die Neue Sammlung collection in Munich, was a star exhibit at the 2006 Victoria & Albert Museum 'Modernism: Designing a New World 1914-1939' show in London, and a special Tatra T2-603 B5/6 participated in Goodwood Revival races in 2008 and 2012. A 1948 T87 is on permanent display as artwork at the Minneapolis Institute of Arts. The readers of *The New York Times* selected a 1941 Tatra T87 as the '2010 Collectible Car of The Year;' a 1937 Tatra T77a was awarded the 'Car of the Show' at the 2010 NEC Classic Motor Show, and a special Streamlined Tatra class was staged at the 2014 Pebble Beach Concours d'Elegance, California, with nine Tatra cars present, from T77 up to T2-603. Nowadays many Tatra clubs exist in the United Kingdom, Germany, the Netherlands, Austria and the Czech Republic.

The objective of this book is to provide a comprehensive and illustrated guide to Tatra's history in the English language. We have focused on the Tatra motor car manufacturing output, describing in detail several famous and significant automobiles that left the gates of the factory.

By doing this, we hope to fill an important gap in the history of automobile production, not only by illustrating the background to the Tatra company, but also demonstrating the legacy left to the annals of automobile design by its principal designer, Dr Hans Ledwinka.

1930s RINGHOFFER–TATRA ADVERTISEMENT SHOWING THE
LARGE RANGE OF THE COMPANY'S PRODUCTS.

Dedicated to JUDr Rudolf Margolius (who was driven in a Tatraplan, was arrested in a Tatraplan, and whose ashes were scattered under a Tatraplan), and Robert Patrick Henry.

Schustala & Comp.

EARLY DAYS

Schustala & Comp.

In the middle of 1850, a 28 year old Czech, Ignaz Schustala (Ignác Šustala 1822-1891), a saddler by trade, started his own business manufacturing horse-drawn carts, traps, brakes, coaches and carriages. In those days saddlers acted as entrepreneurs of carriage building. They organised the co-operation of all the trades involved; the wheelwrights, the smiths, the carpenters, the upholsterers and the saddlers. Schustala had gained useful experience in the construction of carriages while previously employed by the Emperor's appointed coachbuilder, Philipp Koller, in Vienna. Ignaz set up his workshop on his brother Jan's land, in Nesselsdorf. It was situated in a hilly, mainly agricultural region of Moravia in the heart of the European continent, then a part of the Austro-Hungarian Empire, where the official language was German.

For centuries this part of Central Europe had been affected by a turbulent history. In Moravia and Bohemia, Czech settlers displaced the Celtic population during the first centuries AD. Apart from a brief domination by the Magyars, these two kingdoms were governed by native rulers, until 1526 when the Czech crown passed on to the head of Habsburg House and Ferdinand I became the joint ruler of the Czech lands which formed the triple federal alliance with Austria and Hungary.

In 1620, after the defeat of the Protestant Bohemian forces at the White Mountain, Czech freedom ended totally with the direct establishment of the Catholic Austrian rule which governed until 1918. The Czech lands were subjected to rigorous Germanisation. In general, the rural population remained Czech, but the larger towns became almost fully German in culture and language, especially in Moravia.

Bohemia and Moravia formed a small part of the Austro-Hungarian Empire, which also included Austria, Hungary, Slovakia, Ruthenia, Transylvania, Croatia and Slavonia, Dalmatia, Trieste, Austrian Silesia, Galicia and Bukowina,

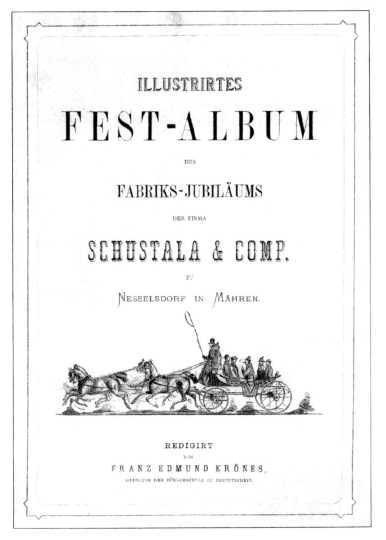

1873 SCHUSTALA & COMP CATALOGUE OF 12 COACHES OFFERED BY THE COMPANY AND EXHIBITED AT THE VIENNA WORLD FAIR.

and later Bosnia and Herzegovina. All these provinces combined into a large empire in Central Europe. After the First World War, the Austro-Hungarian monarchy dissolved into independent countries. Czechoslovakia, consisting of Bohemia, Moravia, Slovakia and Ruthenia, became one of the new states with full restoration of its rights after four centuries of rule by other nations, and established Czech

OPEN HUNTING COACH TYPE 231 BY SCHUSTALA & COMP.

and Slovak as its official languages. After the Second World War, Ruthenia was annexed to the Soviet Union. From January 1st, 1993, the former Czechoslovakia split into two independent states: the Czech Republic and Slovakia.

On December 15th, 1852, Schustala obtained permission from the local council in the city of Olmütz (Olomouc) to erect new factory premises, and in 1853 he began building, starting with a brick-built smith's forge. Once established, the factory complex, together with carriage production, grew quickly.

A year later the first stationary steam engine of 6bhp was bought. It was used to power lathes, saws and grinders. By then the production process was already so advanced that it was possible to supply all the necessary parts for the manufacture of carriages from the Nesselsdorf factory. The quality of factory products, which was much admired, was achieved because Schustala was personally able to oversee all the stages of manufacture. In 1858, to strengthen the financial base of the company, Schustala accepted Adolf Raška and Karel Mosler as partners, and the firm of Schustala & Comp was thus founded. Schustala himself looked after manufacture; Raška and Mosler managed the financial side.

By the early 1870s, Schustala & Comp employed 150 workers. Conveyances of all kinds were produced, not only for local distribution, but also export to Prussia, and as far afield as the Balkans and Turkey. Its best known carriage was called 'Neutitscheinka' and was exhibited together with another 11 Schustala vehicles at the Vienna World Fair in 1873. The company received first prize and a gold medal. As production grew, the firm's agencies became more numerous, located in Lemberg (Galicia), Ratibor and Breslau (Prussia), Vienna, Prague and Berlin.

In 1867, after the defeat of Emperor Franz Josef in the Austro-Prussian War at Königgrätz (Hradec Králové) in Bohemia, the Austrian Empire became Austria-Hungary, a

IGNAZ SCHUSTALA.

LEOPOLD SVITÁK.

dual monarchy. These political changes, however, did not adversely affect the company. Towards the end of 1870s, yearly production reached almost 1200 vehicles of various kinds, and by then the firm had been appointed as royal coachbuilders by Friedrich Karl of Prussia. However, in 1877 Raška died; his death caused a short-term financial crisis which was only resolved when Schustala received a bank loan.

On December 18th, 1881, the village of Nesselsdorf was included in the growing railway network, becoming one of the stops on the Stauding-Stramberg (Studénka-Štramberk) line. This significant event gave the company new possibilities for expansion. The production of railway coaches and wagons started the following year and lasted, without interruption, until 1951. Initially, only open freight wagons were made; later covered wagons were produced, and from 1887 passenger railway carriages appeared.

HUGO FISCHER VON RÖSLERSTAMM.

Ignaz Schustala had little experience in the manufacture of railway rolling stock and needed an expert, preferably from Wiener Neustadt, which was the centre of the Austro-Hungarian railway wagon industry. Finally, he hired Leopold Sviták, the son of a local business friend Josef Sviták. Leopold was born in 1856, in Frankstadt (Fernštát pod Radhoštěm), Moravia, where he had been apprenticed as a locksmith. Between 1878 and 1884 he worked as a master, foreman and shop floor manager in the wagon works at Wiener Neustadt. In 1884, after a three-month trial period at Schustala & Comp, Sviták became foreman of the three main shops involved in the new wagon production.

To help further with the overall supervision of the manufacture of the new railway stock business, Schustala engaged a Viennese railway engineer, Hugo Fischer von Röslerstamm (1856-1917), as director in charge in 1890. Fischer was representative of the new Viennese dynamism in the originally Czech enterprise, but for some time sharp conflicts followed because Fischer's modernising attitudes were hardly compatible with the family-style running of the huge factory by self-made men like Schustala and his sons.

In 1891, in order to acquire a large financial base to support the sudden expansion of the carriage business into railway wagon manufacture, the factory directors accepted the advice of David von Guttmann and incorporated Schustala & Comp. The issue of shares brought in capital of 2 million Austrian crowns. This broadened financial base enabled the company to purchase modern manufacturing equipment and to increase production. The company's name now became 'Nesselsdorfer Wagenbau-Fabriks-Gesellschaft A. G. vormals k.k. priv. Wagenbau-Fabrik Schustala & Comp.' Due to the superb quality of workmanship, in a very short time Nesselsdorfer became a supplier of luxury and saloon railway coaches to the heads of states in Europe and Asia. Orders also came from Canada, Australia, South America, and Russia.

After Ignaz Schustala's death in Vienna on January 29th, 1891, Fischer and Ignaz's son Adolf became directors of what was then a predominantly rail rolling stock manufacturing business. The production of railway wagons and coaches

VIEW OF THE NESSELSDORFER FACTORY COMPLEX, IN THE 1890s.

grew so fast that Nesselsdorfer Wagenbau soon became the largest enterprise of this kind in the Austro-Hungarian Empire, and subsequently Czechoslovakia. At this time in Germany significant steps were taken toward the development of the motor car which would dictate the future emphasis of the Nesselsdorfer company.

However, it continued to manufacture railway rolling stock through the turn of the century, leading to the production of motor driven railcars and coaches which began in 1920. It culminated in 1936 with the 'Slovenská Strela' (Slovak Arrow), a Tatra M290 four-axle, 72-seat railcar, of which two were made, that ran on a scheduled

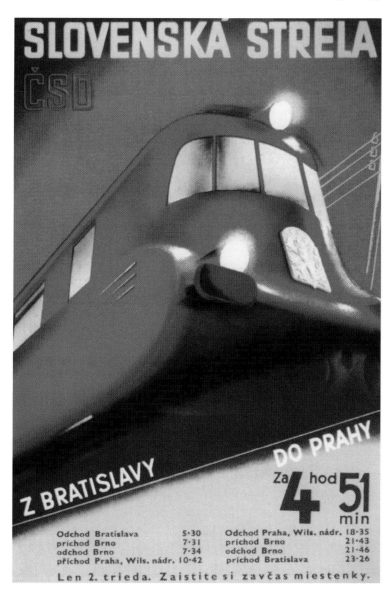

SLOVENSKÁ STRELA

ČSD

Z BRATISLAVY DO PRAHY Za 4 hod 51 min

Odchod Bratislava	5·30	Odchod Praha, Wils. nádr.	18·35
príchod Brno	7·31	príchod Brno	21·43
odchod Brno	7·34	odchod Brno	21·46
príchod Praha, Wils. nádr.	10·42	príchod Bratislava	23·26

Len 2. trieda. Zaistite si zavčas miestenky.

CONTEMPORARY POSTER ADVERTISING THE SLOVAK ARROW RAILCAR (TATRA M290) ROUTE FROM BRATISLAVA TO PRAGUE, 1936.

route Prague-Bratislava with a maximum speed of 150kph, shortening the journey time from 7 hours to 4 hours 18 minutes – the fastest achieved.

The self-propelled railcar was powered by two six-cylinder 165bhp petrol engines, one in each bogie. The initial use of diesel engines after testing was rejected due to excessive noise and vibration. The engines fed an electro-mechanical gearing, which used a torque converter up to the maximum speed, whereupon the electrical system cut out; the drive then became mechanical and direct. While the technical concept was established by Ledwinka, the aerodynamic, streamlined body of the Strela was designed, based on Paul Jaray's principles, by architect Vladimír Grégr, who also proposed the interior. The model of the railcar was tested at a wind tunnel at the Military and Aircraft Research Institute at Letňany, Prague.[1] After the war the Strela was still in special service on the Prague-Nürnberg track, taking Czechoslovak officials to the trial of the Third Reich leadership, and Allied Armies members to the Czech spas. During the 70 years of manufacture, more than 70,000 railway wagons, coaches and other rail vehicles left the Nesselsdorfer/Tatra factory.

NOTES

1 Karel Zeithammmer, 'Slovenská strela,' in Jana Pauly a Petr Kožíšek, *100. Výročí zahájení automobilové výroby v Tatře Kopřivnice*, Praha: NTM, 1997, p 94.

THE PRÄSIDENT

The next stage of development was one of the most crucial for the future of the company. In summer 1888, a very important technical exhibition took place near the Isator in Munich. At the Kraft und Arbeitsmaschinen Ausstellung für das Deutsche Reich, Karl Benz presented his new Benz-Patent-Motorwagen, Benz's second type. The first three-wheeler type had been shown to the public in Mannheim on July 3rd, 1886, but there was little interest in this noisy, unreliable vehicle.

The earliest motor car with a combustion engine to reach the kingdom of Bohemia and Moravia was Benz's new type, Victoria (now in the collection of the National Technical Museum, Prague), which had a 2.9-litre one-cylinder engine of 3bhp, and was capable of a maximum speed of 25kph. The car arrived at Reichenberg (Liberec) from Mannheim in autumn 1893. It was being delivered to a rich young textile manufacturer, Theodor Freiherr von Liebieg (1872-1939), who was only the third man in the world to own a Benz automobile; the first and second being Benz's sales representative Emile Roger of Paris, and the painter Eugen Zardetti of Bregenz. The Bohemian customs officers did not know what to make of this new machine, and shrewdly decided to impose import duty on the carriage and the motor separately.

Soon, Liebieg obtained a driver's licence from the Reichenberg authorities – the first in Bohemia, and possibly in the whole Austro-Hungarian Empire. Between July 16th and 22nd, 1894, one week before the famous 142km long Paris-Rouen race, Liebieg, with his friend Dr Franz Stránský, drove the Benz on one of the first ever long distance car journeys from Reichenberg to Gondorf (Germany) via Mannheim, visiting his mother and Karl Benz on the way. From there they went for an excursion to Etain, Verdun, Clermont and Reims; the travelling distance to Gondorf was 939km, or 69 hours of driving. The return journey was 970km and took 57 hours.

In 1895, Ignaz Schustala's sons, Adolf, Josef, Jan, and Ignaz Junior, had, under pressure, sold their shares in the business to the current directors. Schustala's influence in all the decision making ceased to exist, leaving Fischer as the director in charge of the wagon works and, from 1899, of the whole concern.

The number of new vehicle owners grew quickly, and the sharp increase of interest in the new transportation created a demand for an Austro-Hungarian product, alerting the former producers of horse-drawn carriages to new commercial opportunities. Fischer realised his chance, and in 1895 decided to establish an experimental automobile shop. It was Liebieg, who was on friendly terms with Karl Benz, that suggested setting up automobile production in Nesselsdorf. On his recommendation, the directors started to negotiate with Benz & Company Rheinische Gasmotoren-Fabrik in Mannheim to obtain its licence.

By 1896, it was necessary to speed things up because Nesselsdorfer's chief potential competitor, the carriage manufacturer, Ludwig Lohner of kuk Hofwagenfabrik Jakob Lohner & Co in Vienna, was trying to acquire the patents from Daimler-Motoren-Gesellschaft in Cannstatt. In the end this deal fell through because Lohner refused to employ a Daimler agent directly into his firm. While waiting for the situation to resolve itself, he decided, with his young new recruit, Bohemian born Ferdinand Porsche, to develop an electromobile because of its simple construction and quiet operation. Then, in November 1896, Lohner's study engine, a petrol two-cylinder 4-6bhp Pygmée, arrived from Lefèbre-Fessard, France.

In the winter of 1896-7, the Nesselsdorfer directors sent their chief machinist Franz Cáhel to Mannheim to buy the licence to enable them to manufacture Benz automobiles in Nesselsdorf. His mission was also to

A RECONSTRUCTION OF THE BUILDING OF THE PRÄSIDENT FOR THE OCCASION OF THE MAY 1898 TRIP TO VIENNA, SHOWING THE PRINCIPAL PARTICIPANTS. SVITÁK IS IN THE DRIVER'S SEAT. LEDWINKA IS KNEELING IN FRONT OF THE CAR.

learn how to drive. He was taught by the Benz driving instructor, Hans Thum, who later became a racing driver. There Cáhel bought a new Benz Phaeton. The Phaeton and a spare two-cylinder Benz engine arrived at the Neutitschein railway station on March 7th, 1897. Leopold Sviták and Cáhel picked up the single-cylinder car and drove it to Nesselsdorf. This car was named 'Instruktor,' as in those days it was the custom for each individual car to be given a name.

Having thoroughly studied the Benz, and using the technical information received from Mannheim, Sviták, with his young talented mechanic, Jan Kuchař, began the manufacture of the first Nesselsdorfer car in the summer

of 1897, which extended over several months. The car was subsequently called Präsident. A name chosen as a friendly gesture towards the newly elected president of the Österreichische Automobil-Club, Count Gustav von Pötting-Persing.

Hans Ledwinka joined the wagon shop at the Nesselsdorfer factory in September 1897 at Fischer's instigation. Hans was born on February 14th, 1878, in Klosterneuburg, near Vienna, the son of Anton Ledwinka (1840-1903), born in Pirnitz-Brtnice in Moravia, a barracks canteen manager, and Leopoldine (née Weissmann, 1843-1923). Hans' technical talent was developed by his uncle when the young Ledwinka worked as a metal machinist apprentice in his workshop. Later he studied at Technische Fachschule für Maschinenbau in Vienna. Even in his early years, Ledwinka was already displaying an excellent instinct for technical design and proper use of materials in development and production techniques.

Ledwinka moved to Moravia in the middle of his 19th year, heralding the start of a long involvement with the Nesselsdorfer company. In the future he would dedicate his prodigious design talent and most productive years almost exclusively to this single firm. Initially, Fischer had engaged him especially to design railway coaches, but Ledwinka was soon involved with the Präsident, which had grown in a corner of the shop floor and was already showing considerable improvement upon the Benz.

The Präsident's design was based on the luxury Mylord-type coach. The body had a so-called 'American,' collapsible leather roof which enveloped all four seats. The water-cooled 6.5bhp Benz engine had two opposed cylinders of 2.714-litre total capacity, with 120mm bore and 120mm stroke, placed behind the rear axle. The transmission was based on the Benz Victoria's two-speed

THE FIRST NESSELSDORFER MOTOR VEHICLE, THE PRÄSIDENT, BUILT IN 1897.

leather belt drive, and the gear changing was actioned by pushing the steering column forward and pulling back for higher gear; the neutral lay in the middle.

This car may also have had the world's first front bumper, which later formed the basis for several subsequent patent disputes. The Präsident was also the first factory produced automobile in the Austro-Hungarian Empire.[1] The production cost came to 400,000 gulden (florins, 1 florin = 2 shillings) including all the materials, design drawings, models, salaries and wages. In those days this was a colossal sum, considering that one gulden could buy 60 eggs. In 1933, the same amount of purchasing power could buy 250 Steyr Typ XXX cars!

Ledwinka had not performed a very important part in the first Nesselsdorfer car. The assembly of the Präsident had been directed by the master mechanic Sviták. Apart from the mechanic Kuchař there had been other personalities involved, among them engineer Edmund Rumpler, who later worked for Adler and was the designer of the Tropfen-Auto (1921-25). Also involved was engineer Karl Sage. The young Ledwinka, who had already shown great skill in preparing detailed engineering sketches, was

THE NESSELSDORFER AUTOMOBILE WORKSHOP IN 1899.

THE PRÄSIDENT BEFORE ITS JOURNEY TO VIENNA. FISCHER VON RÖSLERSTAMM IS DRIVING WITH COUNT PÖTTING-PERSING; AT THE BACK ARE BARON LIEBIEG AND W E HARDY, ON MAY 21ST, 1898.

chiefly employed in clarifying doubtful points in the working drawings.

On May 21st, 1898, the Präsident accomplished its first long distance journey, 328km from Nesselsdorf to Vienna. The journey lasted a total of 24 hours and 15 minutes, with 14.5 hours of actual driving time. The drivers were Count Pötting-Persing, the president of the newly founded Österreichische Automobil-Club (on February 6th, 1898), his vice-president Baron Theodor von Liebieg, an American, W E Hardy, and Hugo Fischer von Röslerstamm, the director of the Nesselsdorfer factory. The Benz Instruktor driven by Sviták, Rumpler, Sage and Cáhel, accompanied the Präsident all the way to Vienna. Ledwinka followed part of the way on his bicycle.

The daily *Neue Wiener Abendblatt* of May 17th, 1898, announced the drive, and requested the cycling clubs' help because the cars might scare horses and cause other similar problems in rural regions. They hoped that the cyclists would ride from village to village at a certain distance in front of the cars and warn the citizens that automobiles were approaching their community. On May 24th, the same newspaper reported that the ride had been accomplished successfully; apart from a village in Hanakia region (Hanácko) where, "the cyclists, who rode ahead of the cars in the role of éclaireurs (heralds) and performed a very valuable service to the long distance drivers, were attacked and insulted by stone throwing villagers ..."

The Präsident had participated in the grand assembly of Austrian-built automobiles in Vienna in celebration of the Emperor Franz Josef's 50th jubilee. Jubiläums-Gewerbe-Ausstellung was open from May 7th until October 1st, 1898, and was held in the Prater Park.

There were only four cars shown. One was a then dated 1875 vehicle, with a 0.57-litre single-cylinder horizontal 1bhp

THE BENZ INSTRUKTOR READY FOR THE SAME JOURNEY. L SVITÁK WITH E RUMPLER AT THE FRONT, BEHIND THEM K SAGE AND F CÁHEL.

VIENNESE ARISTOCRATIC LADIES ENJOYING A DRIVE IN THE VERSUCHER, 1899.

engine designed by Siegfried Marcus. (The manufacture of this car has been attributed now to Messrs Märky, Bronovský and Schulz of Prague at Adamsthal, Moravia, and not in Vienna in 1875, as claimed in 1898. The Austrian automobile historian Hans Seper published an article in the official ÖAMTC magazine *Auto-Touring* on March 15th, 1969, in which he confirmed that, on the basis of newly discovered authentic documents, the four-stroke Marcus car had been made in 1888-89); k.u.k. Hofwagenfabrik Jacob Lohner & Co of Vienna contributed one petrol car fitted with the French Lefèbre-Fessard engine, and one electric motor car. The fourth was the Präsident. After the exhibition the Präsident was donated to the Österreichische Automobil-Club to help in training new drivers.

The Nesselsdorfer firm thus became established as a serious automobile manufacturer. The first steps were made towards what was to become a long tradition in the manufacture of commercial vehicles in Nesselsdorf in 1898, when a prototype of a goods wagon of 2.5 tonnes

carrying capacity was produced under Sviták's supervision. The goods wagon did not survive but there are photographs and drawings, and a description published in *Neue Wiener Tagblatt* of March 19th, 1899. Behind its rear axle this vehicle had a four-cylinder engine which originated by combining a pair of two-cylinder Benz engines, similar to the one used in the Präsident. With this power unit the wagon reached a speed of between 15-20kph, and could overcome gradients of 12 per cent. The goods wagon could be powered by only one of the built-in two-cylinder engines if necessary. The engines were connected together by using a toothed clutch. On a level road, or when driving without load, only one engine was used; this helped to conserve fuel consumption.

The *Neue Wiener Tagblatt* acknowledged that this automobile achieved a truly high international standard. No serial production of commercial vehicles followed from this prototype, because the capacity of the factory shop floor did not allow it at the time. Between 1974 and 1977, a replica of the Präsident was carried out in Kopřivnice,

THE FIRST NESSELSDORFER TRUCK, 1898.

followed in 1977-79 by a repeated production of the goods wagon.

With the Präsident's durability now fully proven, Nesselsdorfer started a small serial production of passenger cars. All the elements used were made in-house, except the engines, which were still supplied by Benz. A new spacious hall for the automobile manufacture was erected, but the production line only allowed for a small series and for a limited number of cars, about five, to be made at the same time. About 20 cars were produced in a year, while one new prototype a year was under construction as well. When approved for production, the prototype model appeared in a slightly modified series during the next year.

The automobile journalist Adolf Schmal-Filius, who visited the factory in spring 1899, wrote an encouraging article in the *Neue Wiener Tagblatt*, wrongly predicting that Nesselsdorfer would soon produce 300 automobiles a year. However, at the time such optimism seemed justified.

The factory order book dating back to that time has been preserved, and we know almost all the names of the patrons of the early NW cars, even though its first pages are rather unclear. All these cars are based closely in design on the Präsident prototype. Most of the customers were Viennese aristocrats.

The first eight automobiles with flat two-cylinder Benz engines were:

- Präsident, number 50: now in the National Technical Museum, Prague.
- Meteor, number 51: delivered to C Klein, Siebenbürgen on June 21st, 1899.
- Nesselsdorf, number 52: for Count Gustav von Pötting-Persing on July 30th, 1899.
- Wien, number 53: for Baron Theodor von Liebieg, in Vienna on August 10th, 1899.
- Bergsteiger, number 54: delivered on August 25th, 1899.
- Versucher, number 55: details unknown.
- Auhof, number 56: sold on October 19th, 1899 to Ludwig von Bernd, Wiener Neustadt for 3726 Austrian crowns.
- Spitzbub, number 57: delivered to J G Marquart in Vienna on December 19th, 1899.

THE NESSELSDORFER WEIGHT TEST. L SVITÁK WITH BARON LIEBIEG ON THE FRONT SEAT, A SCHMAL-FILIUS LEANING FORWARD, H LEDWINKA LAST ON RIGHT.

THE INAUGURAL AUSTRIAN MOTOR CAR RACE IN THE VIENNESE PRATER PARK, OCTOBER 22ND, 1899. THE NESSELSDORFER CARS CLAIMED FIRST AND SECOND PRIZES.

The next series produced were called Alter Vierer (Old Four-seaters) or type A, and were not individually named. They were expensive but commercially successful, mainly because the cars were well designed for the heavy Central European terrain, which had rather poor roads. The type A cars had engines equipped with a Simms-Bosch low tension magneto ignition, a very modern feature at that time. Chains had replaced belts for the final drive. There were four forward speeds in the Ledwinka-designed gearbox, selected by the shifting handlebar steering column. Initially, Rumpler and Sage were instructed to design the new gearbox, but their efforts did not come to anything. Ledwinka was then asked to take over, and Rumpler and Sage left the Nesselsdorfer factory.

The type A series had the engine positioned in the rear of the chassis. In the first few cars the Benz engines were still used. Later they were replaced by motors designed and supplied by the American William E Hardy, who lived in Vienna and had the Hardy Brothers motor factory there. The first type A car with a 9bhp Hardy engine, product number 71, was made on July 24th, 1900. On the later type A models the Hardy engines were substituted by engines wholly designed and manufactured by Nesselsdorfer Wagenbau. With pneumatic tyres the NW type A cost 8440 Austrian crowns.

The factory was also to become successful in automobile races. On August 27th, 1899, Count Pötting-Persing with the Nesselsdorf (factory number 52) was third in the 10km Semmering hillclimb in Austria, behind the 24bhp Daimler driven by Emil Jellinek, and the 7bhp Daimler driven by Count Gyulai.

Baron Liebieg in his Wien won first prize in the inaugural 5500m long Austrian automobile race, which took place on October 22nd, 1899 on the Trabrennbahn in Prater Park in Vienna. Again, second place went to the Nesselsdorf borrowed from Count Pötting-Persing and driven by Hugo Fischer von Röslerstamm. In third place was Dr E Suchánek in the 6bhp Bollée.

More successes for the Moravian marque quickly followed. On March 29th, 1900, Baron Liebieg with the Spitzbub was first in the hillclimb at La Turbie in France, and second in a distance trial, Nice-Draguignan-Nice, held on March 26th to 27th, 1900.

NOTES

1 In some publications there are claims that the first car was made in 1898. However, in Ing Jaroslav Sviták's (Leopold Sviták's son) 'The Bohemian Veterans,' (in Ivan Sviták, *The Freedom Machine: Absurdity on Wheels*, Chico, 1986) page 49, he says: 'The first Nesselsdorfer veteran automobile was built in summer 1897 and in fall 1897 it was already running, because the children of Leopold Sviták remember how their father took them for a drive with this new horseless carriage." Also in Miroslav Gomola's *Historie automobilů Tatra 1850-1997*, Brno: AGM-Gomola, 1997, page 47, the author quotes Sviták's contemporary Jan Smudl, confirming that he started working on the first car on 20.6.1897 and he remembered the date because it was a day before his wedding.

THE RENNZWEIER

The handlebar column was changed to a steering wheel fixed onto a slanting rod. Into the rear of the car Sviták and Ledwinka fitted a 4.25-litre, two-cylinder, 12bhp Mannheim engine with which the car reached 82.5kph. The car was completed on May 22nd, 1900 at 10.12 in the morning.

On June 1st and 2nd, 1900 on the Salzburg-Linz-Vienna trial, Liebieg in the Rennzweier came second to Richard Ritter von Stern driving a 5.5-litre, four-cylinder, 24bhp

There were lessons to be learned from the very early motor car races. When Wilhelm Bauer, a Daimler driver, lost his life in the Nice-La Turbie hillclimb, it became obvious that racing cars must be built specifically for their purpose; as powerful vehicles designed with a low centre of gravity and a long-wheelbase. With these principles in mind Sviták and Ledwinka started to build the first Austro-Hungarian racing car at the request of Baron Liebieg.

Within six weeks, during April and May 1900, a special racing car, Rennzweier, with a two-seater chassis, factory number 63, was constructed without body panels to decrease weight. The designers had finally freed themselves from the concept of the automobile as a horseless carriage.

THE RENNZWEIER, 1900.

BARON THEODOR VON LIEBIEG.

MAY 22ND, 1900: THE RENNZWEIER IS LEAVING THE FACTORY WITH BARON LIEBIEG DRIVING.

Daimler; he ran second again to a De Dietrich of much greater power in the Frankfurt-Köln trial on July 29th, 1900.

The *Allgemeine Automobil-Zeitung* wrote about the Salzburg-Linz-Vienna trial on June 10th, 1900:

"The most interesting car was certainly the one driven by Baron Theodor von Liebieg. The car was built by Nesselsdorfer especially for this race and its body consisted only of a narrow high seat for the driver and a lower positioned mechanic's seat, which was placed by the driver's feet in order to minimise the amount of surfaces facing the oncoming airflow (!). This pure racing car did not appear at all like a carriage but looked totally like a driving machine. In front of the seats was placed a sloping steering column and before it the petrol tank. Right in front of the car was the radiator for cooling of water, thus allowing it full access by the airflow. Behind the driver's seat was the water tank in the shape of a steam engine funnel. On the good straight horizontal road this car, whose weight was 970kg including all equipment, should reach 92kph and overcome a 12 per cent ascent with the speed of 25kph."

THE FIRST NESSELSDORFER RACING CAR IN ITS CURRENT CONDITION: THE RENNZWEIER, AFTER MODIFICATIONS TO ACCOMPANY BARON LIEBIEG AND HIS BRIDE, MARIA IDA BLASCHKA, ON THEIR 2000KM HONEYMOON JOURNEY.

On May 1st, 1900, tragedy struck right at the home of Nesselsdorfer cars. Whilst testing the brakes on a steep hill near the village of Rychaltice, something went wrong, and the car, probably factory number 60, overturned. The driver, Sviták, was crushed under the automobile, whilst his friend, Jan Kuchař, who sat next to him, lost his life. One passenger, locksmith Bajer, was badly wounded, but the fourth member of the expedition, draughtsman Brauner, escaped without serious injury. The most probable explanation for the accident was that the main driving chain broke and the car became uncontrollable. Sviták underwent surgery and lost his right leg.

After a few months' convalescence he returned to the factory to continue the supervision of the automobile shop.

Later, during the legal proceedings regarding the death of Kuchař, Liebieg gave a sworn testimony to the court that he knew Sviták to be a careful driver, and therefore believed that Sviták should not be held responsible for the accident. However, the development of the NW racing car still cost one human life and the loss of Sviták's leg.

Two racing victories were earned in the distance trial, Baden-Graz-Baden, for regular touring cars, by Rudolf Struhatschek and Karl Ritter von Škoda driving a 9bhp Nesselsdorfer on June 8th and 9th, 1900. An unrecorded triumph also took place in Prague on April 1st, 1900, when, on a Phaeton factory number 59, Franz Ringhoffer, the future owner of the Nesselsdorfer company, successfully negotiated a very steep climb through the Royal Road (now Nerudova Street) up to the Hradčany Castle, which, together with the St Vitus Cathedral, towers majestically over this beautiful city.

The Nesselsdorfer production continued with the Tourenwagen factory number 64, which was finished on May 22nd, 1900, and supplied to Mr Erdödym in Hungary. This car was built at the same time as the Rennzweier and had a flat two-cylinder 9bhp Benz engine.

A steam omnibus using a De Dion-Bouton two-cylinder engine of 30bhp output was completed on May 23rd, 1900. Weighing 8.5 tonnes this vehicle was capable of carrying 12 passengers and their luggage. The omnibus carried a 120kg supply of coke and 400 litres of water, and could achieve a distance of 35km without stopping. This vehicle was exhibited at the Österreichische Automobil-Club spring salon in Vienna in 1900. Despite certain promising results, the Nesselsdorfer directors chose not to proceed further with steam powered engines, arguing that this mode of power had no long-term future.

After the steam omnibus, two electromobiles, numbers 77 and 83 were built: each had 2 EAG electric motors of 2x3bhp output, capable of achieving a maximum speed of 21kph. The cars were delivered to the Elektrizitäts AG, (Elektrotechnická akciová společnost dříve Kolben a spol.) in Prague, which supplied the motors, in December, 1900 and March, 1901.

NESSELSDORF.

THE TYPE B WAS MANUFACTURED BETWEEN 1902 AND 1904 IN MANY BODY VERSIONS, FROM OPEN TWO- TO FOUR-SEATERS, TO PHAETONS, COUPÉS AND BRAKES.

The development of the car manufacturing industry in the village of Nesselsdorf brought considerable and unaccustomed pressure on the local tracks and roads, as some of the testing was carried out in the locality. This activity raised much disapproval from the nearby town of Neutitschein. In September 1901, after many complaints were reported about the Nesselsdorfer cars, the Neutitschein council leader Rosner issued a local 'highway code.'

In this code, speed in towns was to be restricted to a horse's gentle trot: a slightly faster speed, similar to a gait, was permissible outside habitable areas, but only on wide, straight and relatively empty roads. On bends and during market days vehicle movement was to be held to a pedestrian's pace. Coach drivers were directed to keep a tight rein on their horses when a motor car was seen, and even to dismount and hold the bridle. The motor car drivers themselves were not permitted to leave their automobiles while the engine was running, or to allow a non-driver to start it.

By 1901, Ledwinka with two young assistants and under Sviták's general supervision, was already establishing Nesselsdorfer motor car production founded on the principle of achieving outstanding quality through the use of the most up-to-date technology and ideas. It was then that the final transformation from the carriage form of the early Nesselsdorfer vehicle towards the conventional automobile form was made.

Between 1901 and 1906 Nesselsdorfer Wagenbau built six new models starting with the Neuer Vierer (New four-seater) or Type B. This type had been produced in several series, altogether totalling 36 vehicles with variations of bodywork and engines, including a delivery van. There were many innovations, such as locating the stronger 12bhp Nesselsdorfer engine in the middle of the chassis, a radiator positioned at the front, and a new carburettor. Some of these innovations were patented in the name of the factory. The handlebar steering column was replaced by a steering wheel, and further modernisation saw the flywheel and other engine parts covered under a liftable car body. The great disadvantage though, of the centrally positioned engine, was that during a breakdown passengers had to alight to enable the body to be hinged up in order to obtain access to the power unit.

On April 12th, 1901, Liebieg received delivery of a new Nesselsdorfer type B Dreier, factory number 85, with a collapsible 'American' roof, just before his marriage on May 6th. Subsequently Liebieg drove his new acquisition on his honeymoon trip from Reichenberg to Villach, Venice, Milan and back through Gotthard and Arlberg Alpine passes – some 2000km in total. On the trip he and his bride, Maria Ida Blaschka, were followed by Fritz Haban in the Nesselsdorfer Rennzweier racing car, modified mainly by the reconfigured rear water tank to allow carriage of the luggage of the newlyweds.

On June 27th, 1901, 102 automobiles started in the international Paris-Berlin race – 1196km in eight days. Less than half of them arrived in Berlin. With considerable worldwide competition, the Nesselsdorfer racing car, driven by Haban, came 11th in its category, achieving an average speed of 38.4kph. The winner was Henri Fournier in a heavy, specially-built Mors, with an average speed of 74kph. The disappointing difference between the average speed of the two cars led the Nesselsdorfer directors to a wrong decision – to give up racing. Karl Benz made the same decision at about this time.

CRISIS IN THE AUTOMOBILE INDUSTRY

A serious worldwide crisis in the automobile industry followed at the beginning of the new century. At that time there were over 500 makes of cars in existence, and competition became fierce. It was obvious that only the best marques and large factories could survive. In the end, the Nesselsdorfer concern overcame the difficulties because its automobile shop remained a marginal activity, and was, from the financial point of view, an investment in the technical future. The large, prosperous production of railway wagons, which was the main business of the company, had not suffered in the current crisis, and could easily absorb the losses of its small automobile department. The problems continued until about 1909; the situation was not helped by a serious strike in the factory from May 5th to June 11th, 1906, with workers demanding trade union recognition. These difficulties were compounded by a large fire which destroyed several workshops in 1907.

The automobile workshop inevitably now had to look for new markets outside the circle of the Viennese rich, whose favourite car at the time was the excellent 1901 Austro-Daimler. This was the car used by the Archduke Franz Ferdinand and his wife, Sophie, and the Austrian aristocracy tended to follow the court's taste. One of the solutions suggested by factory directors was to develop a contact with the Austro-Hungarian army. Sviták became an expert advisor at the meetings of the army automobile

NW TYPE C/D, 1904.

committee. The newly designed type C, with a horizontally opposed four-cylinder, 24bhp engine placed in the centre of the car under the floor, and a similar type D, were offered free of charge for military use and were positively evaluated in 1903 and 1904, but no orders followed. This policy only paid off a decade later when large army supplies were agreed.

The second move to counter the difficulties in the Austrian market was the development of the next prototype, later becoming the type G, a small locomotive for the nearby Ostrau (Ostrava) coal mine, for decades the best customer of the factory. Three different series of the mine locomotives with combustion engines were produced in 1904 and 1905.

In September 1902 Ledwinka left the Nesselsdorfer company because his own interest in steam power was not shared by the rest of the firm, and because the crisis in the automobile industry at the time made the Nesselsdorfer operation very small. He joined the Alexander Friedmann company in Vienna to work on the design of steam powered cars. He worked there under Richard Knoller, a well-known theorist and later a professor at the Vienna Technical College. Their first joint venture was to fit the Friedmann steam automobiles with front wheel brakes. However, these brakes kept locking with large understeer, caused by a combination of the pedal system used for the front brakes, and a hand lever for the rear pair of brakes. The local motor press commented that any car with front brakes must inevitably turn over; Ledwinka remained undeterred, as he did with the temporary setback of the locking brakes.

At that time, Ledwinka's long fascination with small car proposals began when he got interested in the design of the Gräf brothers' front wheel-driven Kleinwagen, which had a De Dion-Bouton engine with three-speed transmission. Ledwinka also applied then for his first patents on behalf of the newly founded Gräf & Stift (Austrian patents 24876 and 25738, submitted on October 21st, 1904).

Weyher & Richemond of Patin near Paris, France, was building a steam car under licence from Friedmann, and this gave Ledwinka an opportunity to visit France. He stayed there for nine months during 1905, and, on December 1st, he returned directly to the Nesselsdorfer factory to initiate the development of its models S, T and U.

On March 22nd, 1903, *Allgemeine Automobil-Zeitung*, in which, incidentally, the Nesselsdorfer factory neglected to advertise in the previous two years, published an article sharply critical of the Moravian company:

"Since the Paris-Berlin automobile race in 1901, the Nesselsdorfer factory has not taken part in any public competition. We are therefore unable to draw any conclusions about the performance of its cars. Obviously, a company which does not enter competitions and neglects the only available opportunity to present its products to the public view does not create the best impression. At the III Internationale Automobil-Ausstellung which was held from March 14th-28th, 1903 in Vienna, this factory introduces as a novelty a 24/28bhp car [type C]; in the press release it is described as having a 'four-cylinder engine of horizontal construction ... on the basis of the hitherto very favourable experience, the factory has maintained the horizontal construction of the engine in its newest model as well ...' It is clear that the Nesselsdorfer factory – with a perseverance worthy of a more deserving cause – continues to favour the horizontal engine and now it even manufactures a horizontal four-cylinder just because of the 'hitherto favourable experiences.' In this car the engine is again placed in the middle of the chassis; it is necessary to lift up the mousetrap seats to reach the engine – and all that is a result of those favourable experiences ... The world uses vertical forward situated engines, the whole world has accepted this construction as standard. It is no wonder – considering this incomprehensible perseverance with an obsolete conception – why Nesselsdorfer Wagenbau, a company that could today be at the head of the Austrian car industry, is falling so far behind. And for this failure, the factory keeps blaming the good God himself, the world, the whole automobile industry, poor Austria and, above all, the nasty, nasty press – but it never finds fault with itself."

NW TYPE E OPEN FOUR-SEATER. THIS MODEL WAS ALSO PRODUCED WITH MORE TRADITIONAL BODIES, 1904-06.

NW TYPE J LANDAULET, 1906.

NW TYPE K FIRE ENGINE, 1911.

Since this criticism was not isolated, the board of directors at Nesselsdorfer realised that there was no future in manufacturing passenger cars of basically the same design and construction in small numbers; and that construction of other vehicle types and engine variations had to be considerably increased if its automobile manufacture was to survive. During Ledwinka's leave of absence, a decision was made to develop new luxurious models, produced later as types E, F, J and L.

The type E of 1904 still had an underfloor, 3.8-litre horizontal two-cylinder, engine and was one of the few remaining vehicles which still retained the horseless carriage elements. Only five cars of the next unsuccessful four-cylinder type F were made. However, this four-cylinder model F, despite the criticism, was deceptively versatile, and

the automobile would virtually sail up a steep hill in Vienna used for driving tests. The examiner, who rode in the car promptly asked to see the engine, gazed in wonder at the huge red-painted cylindrical muffler which was the only thing visible, and exclaimed, "I cannot believe that a single-cylinder machine can climb such gradients!" He could not see that the horizontal engine had four cylinders and was placed under the floor.[1]

The directors further hired two engineers, Kronfeld and Lang, giving them separate briefs to design new, vertical, front-mounted engines to be built into standard and special vehicles developed for the army.

Kronfeld's and Lang's efforts resulted in the conception of models named J, K, and L. The type J, of which 22 cars were made from 1906-11, had a vertical, Kronfeld designed, water-cooled four-cylinder, rather heavy engine placed between the front wheels. Initially it was supplied with a 30-35bhp engine, which was later increased to 40bhp and finally to 45bhp. The cylinders were separately cast with an overall capacity of 5.878 litres. In this type sparkplugs were used by Nesselsdorfer company for the first time. Chain drives acted independently on each of the rear wheels. The maximum speed of this luxury car was 80kph.

The commercial type K car had Kronfeld's vertical, 5-litre, T-head, four-cylinder engine with chain drive. Lang's type L car was a vertical, 4.5-litre L-head, side-valve engine with four cylinders cast in pairs, magneto ignition and shaft drive. This model was manufactured in a passenger version and as an omnibus. The type K, of which only one was produced, had army fire truck body. Together with the Nesselsdorfer railway wagons, it was exhibited in December 1910 at a jubilee exhibition of transport technology in Buenos Aires. Three products from Nesselsdorfer Wagenbau received the main prizes.

Then followed types M and O. The type M was an army searchlight vehicle with a vertical 4.5-litre engine. Five cars were manufactured with small body variations, the type M1 having a two-wheel trailer. The type O was a 20-passenger omnibus with the 4.5-litre and later 5-litre engines. Three omnibuses were delivered to the Viennese transport authority in February 1907.

The directors were not satisfied with the last series of models, which were underpowered and heavy. Kronfeld and Lang left the factory and the crisis continued.

NOTES

1 Testimony of Antonín Klička, see Miroslav Gomola, *Automobily Tatra – Závodní a sportovní vozy z Kopřivnice*, Brno: AGM CZ, 2003, p 29.

LEDWINKA'S FIRST COMPLETE CARS

HANS LEDWINKA WITH HIS FIRST WIFE,
MARIE, AND SECOND SON, ERICH, IN 1915.

Ledwinka's absence from Nesselsdorfer Wagenbau lasted until December 1905, when he was asked by Fischer von Röslerstamm to return and was appointed, at the age of 27, director of the automobile section. It was hoped that this change would bring new thinking and ideas into the Nesselsdorfer production. Sviták, who, due to his disability, was unable to carry on effectively on the shop floor, was made co-ordinating technical director of all the manufacturing shops.

Ledwinka was now given the task of designing a totally new model. The resulting passenger car became the model S, which included many revolutionary innovations, and was far enough ahead of its time to establish the Moravian company securely in the automobile business, and finally solved the financial difficulties of that division.

The model type S, which Ledwinka started to develop in late 1905, had four cylinders cast in pairs because of foundry limitations, with hemispherical combustion chambers (some 15 years before Harry Ricardo, the combustion engineer, used them), and a single vertically driven overhead camshaft arrangement. The crankshaft was inserted into a barrel crankcase where it rode on three main roller bearings, while the cam was driven by a vertical shaft, and a belt from a pulley on the camshaft-nose turned the fan. The valves in screw-in cages were at an angle of 45 degrees to the cylinder axis. The basic four-cylinder engine had a bore of 90mm, and a stroke of 130mm, giving a capacity of 3.3 litres with 20bhp and later 30bhp output at 2200rpm. The maximum speed was 80-90kph with six passengers.

The engine rested on only three fixing points. A further innovation in this model was the direct attachment of gearbox to engine. The gearbox, with planet gears, together with the engine, then created a massive monoblock. Ledwinka also used his newly designed, oil-bathed, cast iron cone clutch. The preference for engine and gearbox monoblock was to be carried through most of the subsequent Nesselsdorfer/Tatra cars and trucks.

Initially Ledwinka, helped by his assistant Antonín Klička, started to produce the design for this model at home. Their drawings and proposals proceeded very quickly, and the first prototype was ready and being tested even before the directors had a chance to approve the concept. While the decisions on the future moves of the automobile production at Nesselsdorfer Wagenbau were being made, a further ten type S cars were quickly built and sold in advance of completion.

The model S4 went into full production in 1910. Later on, Ledwinka added another pair of cylinders to create a six-cylinder model, the 5-litre type S6 40/50. This he did at the instigation of Fritz Hückel, an industrialist and hat-maker from Neutitschein.

ANNOUNCEMENT OF PRIZES RECEIVED IN THE 1911 1450KM INTERNATIONAL ALPINE TRIAL IN WHICH THE S6 PROTOTYPE WAS, UNIQUELY, DRIVEN BY LEDWINKA, AND THE TYPE S4 BY HÜCKEL.

THE VERY SUCCESSFUL SIX-CYLINDER TYPE S6 WHICH FINALLY ESTABLISHED NESSELSDORFER AS A SERIOUS AUTOMOBILE MANUFACTURER.

On June 4th, 1912, under supervision of Österreichische Automobil-Club, Schlesische Automobil-Club Breslau and Kaiserliche Automobil-Club Berlin, Hückel, accompanied by Karl Habig and Eduard Schlosser, drove the new S6 with the gearbox purposely fixed in fourth gear from Vienna, via Breslau and Berlin, to Stettin. He covered a distance of 1021km in seven minutes under the prescribed 24 hours and won a substantial bet. Hückel's aim was to prove the car's ruggedness and flexibility. The gentle engagement of the oil-bathed clutch helped greatly in achieving this exploit. As a consequence of this feat, the Nesselsdorfer directors agreed to a serial production of the type S.

Many versions with various body options of the basic model S were made, such as the S4 16/20, S4 16/24, and S4 20/30. 65 vehicles of these successful type S4s were produced.

In the prototype for the model T, which appeared in 1909 and went into production in 1914, Ledwinka fitted rod-operated four-wheel brakes, and all four engine cylinders were cast in one block. In 1908, type 4R-Jaguár tow truck, equipped with a winch, and an undersquare – at that time a very unusual proposal – four-cylinder engine of 13.6-litre capacity and 80bhp output, was designed. This vehicle had both axles powered, the first such car from Nesselsdorfer, but only a drawing survives and there is no proof that this model was actually constructed.

From May 9th until October 17th, 1912, a strike paralysed the factory: the workers demanded higher wages and better

NW S 20/30
TITANIC, SPECIAL
18-SEAT OPEN CAR
MADE FOR FACTORY
STAFF OUTINGS
WITH LEDWINKA AT
THE WHEEL IN 1912.

TYPE T, 1922. THIS MODEL HAD EXTERNAL
GEAR AND HANDBRAKE LEVERS WHICH,
IN LATER VERSIONS, WERE LOCATED
INSIDE THE CAR.

working conditions. The strike lasted 23 long weeks due to the directors' unyielding stand against demands. Finally, the dispute ended in a compromise, but Fischer's and the other directors' positions were severely shaken. Fischer left Nesselsdorfer on August 1st, 1913, and died in Vienna in 1917. Sviták, together with several other long-standing factory officials, also retired in November 1912.

In the next stage of development Ledwinka, now fully in charge of the automobile shop, fitted small truck bodies to the S and T chassis, with little modification other than a change of final drive ratios. The last notable design in this series was the model U, which was first marketed in 1915 as a six-cylinder, 65bhp version with brakes on all four wheels. Later, in 1921, it appeared with a water-cooled 5.3-litre, six-cylinder, 68bhp engine in a six-seater aluminium body. It was called the Tatra type 10, and was selling, without tyres, for 165,000 Czechoslovak crowns.

After the beginning of the First World War, the Austro-Hungarian army mainly required the manufacture of commercial vehicles. Initially, the Nesselsdorfer firm supplied the army with two-tonne platform trucks of type

JOSEF VEŘMIŘOVSKÝ IN A TYPE T AFTER GAINING SECOND PLACE AT 1921 ECCE HOMO HILLCLIMB, ŠTERNBERK.

OPEN TYPE U, 1917. THIS MODEL COULD REACH 120KPH, CONSUMING 15-17 LITRES PER 100KM.

HANS LEDWINKA IN 1917.

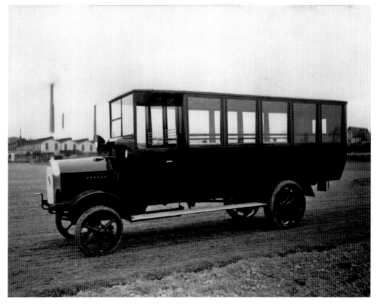

TYPE TL4 OMNIBUS PHOTOGRAPHED IN 1925:
34BHP AND A MAXIMUM SPEED OF 25KPH.

TL2, with engines derived from the passenger model T cars. From 1916 a 4 tonne truck was built and called type TL4. The chassis of these two types supported many different styles of bodies; two-sided dump trucks, tow trucks, omnibuses, box trucks, tipper trucks, etc.

In the heavy winter of 1917, Austro-Hungarian army trucks of other makes were found to be practically useless in the deep snow of the Italian Alps – their rear chains and axles breaking, their engine blocks cracking – so the Nesselsdorfer trucks were called to the rescue. Every truck in the empire was requisitioned and sent to the southern front to carry supplies there, and bring back the wounded.

Nesselsdorfer car production increased steadily with the coming of the First World War, and Ledwinka asked the directors for a new building to be put up, to house the expanding automobile division. But when Erhard Köbel, the new factory director, used the already approved sum of money to build a new rail coach shed instead, Ledwinka accepted an offer to go to Österreichische-Waffenfabriks-Gesellschaft AG, at Steyr in Austria, to establish its own automobile division. In 1916 Ledwinka left together with several good engineers and mechanics from the group he had built up in Moravia. This was the second and last time Ledwinka was to leave the Nesselsdorfer company.

VISIT VELOCE ON THE WEB – WWW.VELOCE.CO.UK
All current books • New book news • Special offers • Gift vouchers • Forum

STEYR

The directors of the arms manufacturing company Österreichische Waffenfabriks-Gesellschaft, formerly Josef und Franz Werndl & Co, and later known as Steyr-Werke AG, located at the confluence of the Enns and Steyr rivers had hoped to produce its first automobile by the year 1916. The company wished to diversify its manufacturing base should the armaments orders cease. This eventually happened after the end of the First World War in 1918. However, even with Ledwinka's help it was not until 1920 that the first car rolled out of the gates of the works.

Steyr was in a favourable position for new and successful automobile production because the factory had the expertise to manufacture all the basic components needed for the making of motor cars, having been a weapons producer since 1864. For that purpose the directors of Steyr started the production of ball bearings, a casting shop was introduced, and a car body shop for design and manufacture was founded. With all these preparations a basis had been built which would allow the Steyr company complete independence from the outside supply and ancillary industries. It was under these circumstances that Ledwinka began work there in 1916.

Almost immediately after Ledwinka arrived, he managed to design a modern and powerful motor car which, in a fairly short time, established Steyr as one of

LEFT AND PAGES 54 & 55: THE DESIGN OF THE STEYR WAFFENAUTO TYPE II, 1923 WAS BASED ON NW TYPES T AND U.

the larger European car manufacturers. The car that he designed, a Waffenauto Type II (12/40), a family tourer, had a six-cylinder engine of 3.3-litre capacity and 40bhp output. The design of this model was based on the Nesselsdorfer types T and U and theoretically was very similar to them. The Waffenauto had such up-to-date features as a barrel crankcase, overhead camshaft and, typical of Ledwinka's concept, the engine was constructed in one unit with the gearbox. The three-piece camshaft was flanged together with a ball bearing at each joint, the engine had a removable cylinder head, and included the screw-in cages for the overhead valves. The gearbox was equipped with a four-speed gate change; a laminated clutch was used for the first time.

He dropped the four-wheel brakes but they were used later on the model Type VI.

By 1925 approximately 3000 Steyr cars had been built displaying the distinctive pointed radiators and type numbers which had become a familiar sight on European roads. Further types followed based on Ledwinka's designs: the Type VI Sport had a four-litre, six-cylinder, 60-90bhp, twin carburettor engine and reached 140kph. However, sporting enthusiasts preferred the model that had the more powerful 145bhp Klausen engine. The Steyr Type VI Klausen Sport, with a longer stroke 4.9-litre engine came third in the Targa Florio race of 1923.

The number IV was given to a smaller car with a side valve 1.8-litre, four-cylinder, 23bhp engine and a bell gearbox of which 950 were made over four years and it indicated Ledwinka's early interest in small, rugged motor cars. The following models Type V and VII were very successful and again proved their original creator's extraordinary skill and ingenuity.

At Steyr, Ledwinka also built trucks with a carrying capacity of up to 2.5 tonnes, having the same six-cylinder engines used in the passenger cars. In this way he established Steyr as one of the best heavy vehicle manufacturers in Austria.

At the beginning of 1921, Ledwinka, on one of his business trips during which he liked to travel fast, was being driven by a young man from Steyr. Near Linz, on a sharp bend, the driver lost control of the car. The long automobile with a somewhat narrow wheelbase, the precise model cannot now be ascertained, ended upside down in a ditch. Ledwinka, was slightly injured, he broke his wrist and was taken to a Linz hospital for treatment.[1]

Due to his painful wrist, he could not sleep and his thoughts turned towards an idea which had occupied his mind for some time since his earlier involvement with Gräf & Stift. This idea was to develop and construct a small and robust Kleinwagen, a 'people's car,' which would be based on a completely new construction principle. It was a revolutionary idea at a time when all European car production was geared towards the manufacture of large, high-performance, expensive, luxury automobiles with four- to six-cylinder engines.   Ledwinka was convinced there was a need for a small car designed with comfort and reliability in mind, but also with a ruggedness and simplicity, which would be affordable for the vast majority of the general public.

On returning from the hospital to Steyr, he mentioned this possible new project to the firm's directors. They could not see any future in Ledwinka's new venture, arguing that there was no demand for small cars, and hence they did not propose to back it financially. However, Ledwinka persevered with his idea. Shortly afterwards he was approached by the director of the newly named Tatra marque company, Ing Leopold Pasching, after Ledwinka's previous colleague, Max Peschel, pushed through the construction of 15,000m^2 building for the new automobile shop in 1920, as Ledwinka had previously requested. Pasching offered full support for Ledwinka's new project. On April 30th 1921 Ledwinka left Steyr and returned to Moravia for good.

With Ledwinka gone, Steyr worked for a long time on the ideas and concepts he had left behind. In fact, Ledwinka's new Tatra contract allowed him to continue to design cars for Steyr, which he did until 1926. For instance, in 1925 when Steyr needed a lower-priced car to maintain sales volume and keep the plant busy, Ledwinka helped by designing an elegant, small 30bhp, six-cylinder engine of 1.56-litre capacity in a car with a low frame and swing half-axles. It went into production in 1926 as the Type XII.

Ledwinka's last contribution to Steyr was an updated car using the Typ VI chassis, renamed Typ XVI and manufactured in 1928-29. Between 1920 and 1928 Steyr had produced 4190 cars based on the Ledwinka's designs. When Porsche took over at the Steyr in 1929 the designs he inherited were all Ledwinka's original proposals. This explains the great similarity between Steyr and Tatra cars. It was said at the time that Porsche went there with the purpose of learning from ideas left behind by Ledwinka. However, it was Ledwinka himself who actually recommended Porsche as his successor at Steyr.

NOTES

1 Hans-Heinrich von Fersen, *Klassische Wagen I*, Bern: Hallwag Verlag, 1978, p 197.

THE TATRA REVOLUTION

At the end of the First World War the Austro-Hungarian Empire was dissolved into several independent national states: Austria, Hungary, Czechoslovakia, Romania and Yugoslavia. Trieste and Trentino were annexed to Italy, and the village of Nesselsdorf in Moravia now belonged to the new Czechoslovak Republic. Its original Czech name Kopřivnice was restored, and the company was now called 'Kopřivnická vozovka as' (Kopřivnice Wagon Works Ltd).

In the winter of 1918-19, three prototypes of the six-cylinder, 65bhp type 'U's in open phaeton bodies, with

brakes on all four wheels, drove eastwards out of the factory. Behind the steering wheels sat men in heavy fur coats. The wind was blowing hard and the weather was cold. Their destination was far away – the Tatra Mountains. While there, they were to test the new four-wheel brakes which had been causing considerable problems. The expedition included the factory director, Josef Novák, who also participated in the new brake construction proposals. He urged them to drive along the worst possible routes.

The cars climbed over stones, the wheels fell into ditches. When the type Us approached the mountains, their tyres started to sink into the deep fresh snow. Snow chains were put on, and the cars proceeded past Štrba toward Tatranská Lomnica. During this section of the journey they overtook a sleigh pulled by mountain horses. The locals, seeing the cars in the mountains for the first time, could not believe the automobiles would overcome the snowdrifts on the way. When the expedition arrived at the main square in Lomnica, the sleigh driver, who by now had also reached the square, exclaimed that they must be devils, not humans, to get to Lomnica through all that snow. From the group

TL4 TRUCK WITH THE FIRST TATRA LOGO PAINTED ON THE CABIN DOOR, MARCH 1919.

of people surrounding the snow-covered cars someone remarked: "This would be a car for the Tatras!"

During the evening meal Novák remembered that statement, and agreed that it was a wonderful idea. From then on the Kopřivnice cars would be called Tatras. When the expedition returned from the mountains, a new diamond-shaped plate, later changed to a roundel, with the name Tatra was made, and from then on affixed to all products coming from Kopřivnická vozovka.[1] The first vehicle with the Tatra marque painted on its cabin was the TL4 truck, which left the factory on March 29th, 1919.[2]

The change of name was in accord with general nationalistic feeling in the new republic, and with the endeavour to erase all previously-used German names. As well as Tatra there were other established car manufacturers in Czechoslovakia: Laurin & Klement (later bought by Škoda Works in 1925), Praga, and Walter. In 1924, NK (Enka) was founded, and then taken over by Aero in 1929. From 1923 there was Z (Zbrojovka), and the luxury and sports car manufacturer Wikow. In 1934 the motorcycle manufacturer Jawa also started car production. All these firms brought a healthy competitive spirit into the Czechoslovak motor industry.

In 1920 3372 passenger cars were produced in Czechoslovakia, including military vehicles, 2143 trucks and buses, 194 special vehicles and 1676 motorcycles and three-wheelers. By 1929 the following numbers of locally made cars drove along the Czechoslovak roads: 8454 Praga cars, 5034 Tatra cars, 4158 Škodas, 1500 Walters and 1083 Zs. The numbers of imported cars on the roads were: 2371 Fiat cars, 662 Renaults, 642 Fords, 557 Steyrs, 501 Studebakers, 411 Opels, Chevrolet and Chrysler with 371 cars each, 332 Overland-Whippets, 313 Austro-Daimlers, 300 Mathis cars, 121 Belgian Minervas and 23 Morris motor cars. In the same year 12,000 passenger cars, and 3000 trucks and buses were produced in Czechoslovakia. By the end of 1945 the numbers were to increase to 150,150 passenger cars, 53,400 trucks and 2284 buses.

In 1921, within a few days of returning to Tatra from Steyr, Antonín Klička recalled that Ledwinka provided all

THE BRILLIANTLY SIMPLE T11 CHASSIS FIRMLY ESTABLISHED THIS CONCEPT FOR FUTURE APPLICATION IN TATRA PASSENGER AND COMMERCIAL VEHICLE PRODUCTION. THE DESIGN DATE OF 1921 BECAME A MAJOR STAGING POST FOR THE TATRA COMPANY TIMELINE. (COURTESY PAUL SCHILPEROORD, JOSEF GANZ ARCHIVES)

the detailed drawings of his new project for the radical innovative 'people's car,' later called the model Tatra Type (T) 11.[3] Production started in 1923, when the new automobile shop building was completed. Ledwinka solved the problem of living in Moravia where most people now spoke Czech, a language which he never learnt, by taking with him a number of Steyr people. These comprised both the original Nesselsdorfer men who had followed him to Austria in 1916, and later followers. As his collaborators spoke more German than Czech, at that time all Tatra automobile construction drawings were captioned in both languages.

The new Tatra T11 car had to be simple in construction, and modest in maintenance, servicing and fuel consumption. Ledwinka was sure that a good, small, light car could never be simply scaled down from a larger model, particularly in view of the poor state of the roads in Bohemia and Moravia in the '20s.

The design of the T11 consisted, in principle, of an air-cooled, front-positioned, horizontally opposed, 1.06-litre, overhead-valve, two-cylinder engine of 12bhp. The

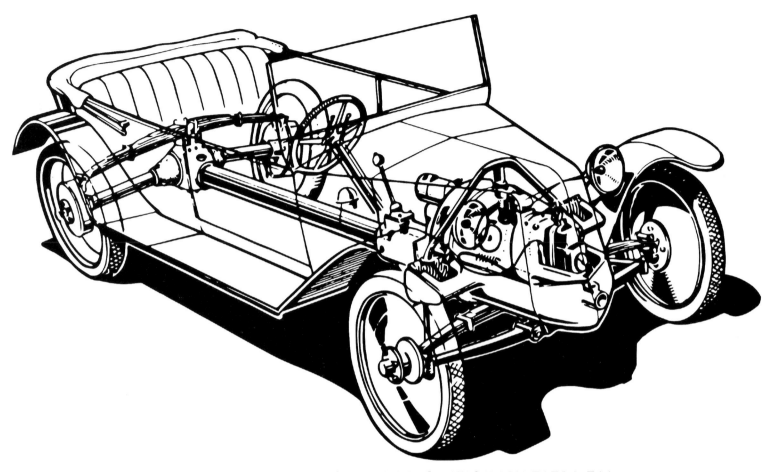

SCHEMATIC DIAGRAM OF THE REVOLUTIONARY TATRA T11.

cylinders were partially covered to control airflow from the flywheel, which doubled as a fan. The engine and the gearbox formed one monoblock, which, together with the central tubular chassis and the axle-drive, comprised a structure of great torsional stiffness, resistant to all distortion. The central tube was bolted to the engine-gearbox monoblock, and had a diameter of 110mm and 3mm thick wall. The tube served as the carrier of the car body, and at the same time provided a protection cover for the jointless driveshaft which powered the rear swing axles. The driveshaft ended in a spur-wheel differential, and in two spiral-tooth concentric pinion shafts engaging crown wheels of differing diameter, but identical tooth count.

These were fixed to the swing half-axles which moved around the pinions in a vertical plane, thus dispensing with the need for universal joints. When either of the rear wheels rose or fell, the corresponding crown wheel simply rolled around the pinion by which it was driven. A later modification set one road wheel and its half-axle slightly behind the other, allowing for equal-size pairs of crown wheels and pinions. This differential system was retained for subsequent models, such as the T57 and even the large Tatra trucks. The highly-placed transverse leaf spring was bolted to the top of the differential, and fixed by its ends to the flexible swing half-axles. The front axle was sprung by means of a cross leaf spring which was attached to the

ABOVE AND RIGHT: T11S ON TEST AND TRIAL
DRIVES IN THE VICINITY OF KOPŘIVNICE.

engine block. The rear-wheel unit, with spring and final drive, could be readily detached from the central tube, as could the front-wheel unit, comprising the engine, suspension, gearbox and steering gear. The steering was effected by a worm and nut mechanism at the base of the steering column geared to the steering arms.

The ignition was initiated by the Bosch magneto. The Solex carburettor was placed above the engine and connected to cylinders via slanting suction tubing. Oil was pumped under pressure and kept in a container outside the engine unit. There were four forward gears and a reverse gear, the gearlever was fitted onto the central tubular frame. The clutch was single plate dry.

The coach body was carried on cross-bearers fitted to the central tube and was therefore safeguarded from any distortion; the total weight of the car was 680kg. There were a number of body variations. The original car had an open four-seater body; later saloon, coupé, Normandie, and cabriolet versions were added. The T11's front bonnet solid mask form, without the need of openings for a radiator,

reduced drag and had great influence on the subsequent proposals for small, air-cooled rear engine cars by other manufacturers.

Ledwinka had not hesitated to patent his chassis idea. A few days after Ledwinka's return to Tatra, Oskar Florian, a long-term friend of Ledwinka and director of Tatra central sales office, under whose name some of Tatra/Ledwinka patents were submitted, placed a patent application for a 'chassis-less automobile' concept in May 1921 in Germany and a year later in France. The concept

1924 T11 SALOON.

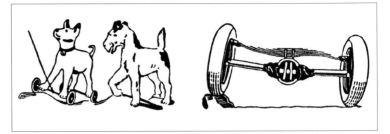

THE LEVEL OF COMFORT THE INDEPENDENT SUSPENSION PROVIDES IN POOR ROAD CONDITIONS IS IMMEDIATELY APPARENT; THIS IS THE PRINCIPLE OF REAR SWING HALF-AXLES.

T11 ROADSTER, 1924. THE T11'S CENTRAL TUBULAR CHASSIS SUPPORTED A VARIETY OF BODY VERSIONS. THE LIGHTWEIGHT BODIES WERE MADE OF METAL, PLYWOOD AND WEATHER-PROOFED FABRIC, STRETCHED ON A TIMBER FRAME.

indicated a backbone frame with front engine, rear swing axles, and cross leaf spring over the rigid front axle. The idea of the backbone frame was not Ledwinka's alone, as Edmund W Lewis had already used this construction in 1904 with his first 8bhp Rover, but Ledwinka designed his tubular frame with greater technical foresight, and more elegance. Although similar small car designs – such as the 1908 Ford Model T, 1922 Austin Seven, and 1921

Citroën 5CV – were also available at that time, none had such revolutionary construction as the T11. In concept the T11, this 'people's car,' was an extraordinary forerunner of Porsche's air-cooled, rear-engined Volkswagen, and even more closely, of P-J Boulanger's air-cooled front-wheel drive Citroën 2CV. Needless to say, both of these cars followed years later.

The small and light Tatra which resulted from Ledwinka's ideas became one of the most famous and revolutionary automobile construction designs in the history of the motor industry. The T11 was the centrepiece of Ledwinka's career. The chassis and suspension, the front air-cooled engine, and the very simple elegant body shape formed a perfect automobile concept. The T11 established the forced air-cooling tradition at Tatra as a viable and marketable proposition. Additionally, the reliability of the engine mechanics and the stability of the central tubular chassis placed this automobile in car history books as a prime example of a visionary and workable design concept which was, and still is, fully recognised by T11 drivers.

The T11 was introduced first to the general public at the Prague autosalon held between April 28th and May 6th, 1923. The magazine *Český svět* reported that the exhibit caused great excitement, the basic four-seater cost 39,600Kč and was a type of 'people's car' of great practicality, suitable for medical doctors, architects, farmers, and businessmen.[4]

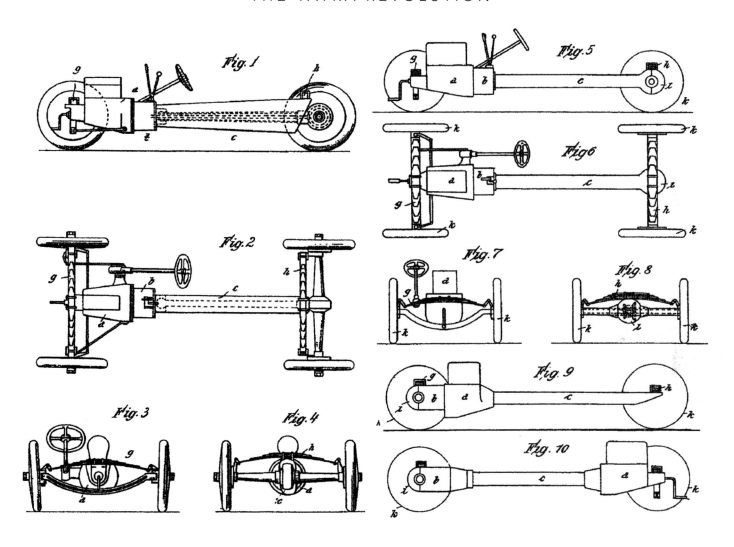

ILLUSTRATION ATTACHED TO TATRA FRENCH PATENT NO 550.924, DATED MAY 1922,
FOR VOITURE AUTOMOBILE SANS CHASSIS ENTERED UNDER THE NAME OF TATRA SALES
DIRECTOR, OSKAR FLORIAN.

Ledwinka never wavered to test his designs personally but did not confine his driving solely to the prototypes. Into one of the serially produced T11 four-seaters he packed his wife Maria (née Fabig 1879-1926) and two sons Fritz (1902-1989) and Erich (1904-1992), and covered nearly 9500km of Austria, Italy, Switzerland and France. Ledwinka drove the whole journey himself, though on business trips he usually preferred to be driven by a chauffeur – and it had to be fast.

The basic T11 design – the backbone chassis, independent suspension and air-cooled engine – was carried on further in the manufacture of future series of Tatra passenger and commercial vehicles of various tonnage and body arrangements. The long and successful

T12 PICK-UP OF 1927. (COURTESY
DAVID YANDO, LANE MOTOR MUSEUM)

1926 TATRA T12. NOTE THE FRONT
TUBULAR SEAT FRAMES, USUALLY FITTED
TO TWO-DOOR FOUR-SEATER SALOONS.
(COURTESY PETER VISSER)

T12 PICK-UP WITH RAISED FRONT
BONNET INDICATING THE EASY ENGINE
ACCESSIBILITY. (COURTESY DAVID YANDO,
LANE MOTOR MUSEUM)

continuous use of this fundamental assembly by Tatra has proved its remarkable characteristics and Ledwinka's technical genius.

The model T12, which followed, differed only by having brakes on all four wheels (although some T11 chassis of later manufacture also had four-wheel brakes) and a more powerful engine with 12-14bhp output. The T12 was supplied to order with 11 different body styles. The T12 saloons had front folding nickel plated tubular front seats fitted from the start of their production in 1926.[5] The T11 stopped being made in 1927, by which time no less than 3767 cars had been produced. The manufacture continued with the T12 model, until 1936 when 7222 units were fabricated.[6]

1925 SPECIAL T15 DRAISINE DERIVED FROM A T11 CHASSIS.

1926 TATRA T12'S REMARKABLE INTERIOR.
TATRA AIMED TO BE AVANT-GARDE IN
ALL ASPECTS OF DESIGN AND USED
CANTILEVERED FOLDING, INITIALLY NICKEL
AND THEN CHROMIUM PLATED, TUBULAR
SEAT FRAMES. AT THE SAME TIME, IF NOT
BEFORE, MART STAM, INSPIRED BY CAR
SEATING, PRODUCED HIS FIRST SKETCH FOR
A CANTILEVERED TUBULAR FRAME CHAIR IN
NOVEMBER 1926. STAM, SEEING A CAR SEAT
IN FRANKFURT IN 1926, SAID: "ONE SHOULD
BUILD A CHAIR LIKE THAT." DESIGN HISTORY
MAY HAVE TO BE REWRITTEN.
(COURTESY KAREL ROSENKRANZ)

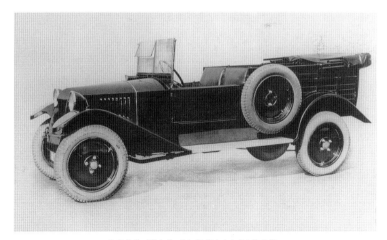

1929 T12 NORMANDIE.

NOTES

1 Miloš Kovařík, *Svět velkých závodů*, Praha: Novinář, 1984, p 14.
2 Karel Rosenkranz, *Tatra Autoalbum*, Brno: MS Press, 2002, p 34.
3 Jerrold Sloniger, 'Hans Ledwinka' in Ronald Barker & Anthony Harding, *Automobile Design: Twelve Great Designers and Their Work*, (first edition 1970), Warrendale: Society of Automotive Engineers, 1992, second edition, p 131.
4 *Český svět*, no. 34, 17.5.1923, p 12-13. Interesting early use of the 'people's car' term (lidový vůz) before it became so well established with the coming of the KdF-Wagen years later.
5 The year 1926 of the archival photo confirmed by Karel Rosenkranz in an email to Ivan Margolius, 10.2.2015.
6 Production numbers differ from publication to publication, as some of the factory order books are incomplete and some were confiscated during WW2 and research continues; the figures in this book are taken from information supplied by Karel Rosenkranz, formerly the Tatra archivist at Tatra Museum, Kopřivnice.

THE RACING TATRAS

The fight to prove that the air-cooled engine had a place in serious automobile construction was going to be a very hard one. It was felt necessary for the new two-cylinder cars to attend and win races, reliability trials and hillclimbs as often as possible. It was generally accepted, then as now, that the most effective automobile advertising was that which highlighted, and was demonstrated by, racing victories. For example, in the latter part of the 20th century the use in advertising campaigns by Lancia of its countless rally victories had immeasurably improved its standing with the general public. Similarly, the continuous first places achieved by Škoda cars in its class in international rallies had strengthened its popularity and rugged image at that time.

Ledwinka, however, unlike his counterpart Porsche, was never a believer in the great benefit of racing or in designing special racing cars, and doubted that the experience of building these cars would add much to his own knowledge of automobile technology. He had no competition record himself, and had still less desire to commit a factory team. But after the victory of a T11 in the Ecce Homo hillclimb at Šternberk in Silesia in 1924, Ledwinka was so overwhelmed he embraced the winner of the 1.1-litre class (time 7:10.8sec), Josef Veřmiřovský (1896-1953), stammering: "Pepek ..." but then his voice failed him.[1]

Ledwinka had feared that the T11s were not up to competition driving, but after the Šternberk wins (Veřmiřovský also won the year before with a time of 8:3.8sec) he changed his mind sufficiently to study lightweight racing car bodies. However, long distance endurance runs were the only form of competitive motoring in which he ever really became interested. Veřmiřovský raced Tatra cars whenever the company would allow him. Eventually, he retired to manage the Tatra Museum at Kopřivnice.

Veřmiřovský was only 16 years old when he decided that his future was in driving cars rather than being an apprentice in the machine shop. Ledwinka sometimes allowed him behind the wheel to bring customers from the railway station to the factory. The local police knew about this practice and quite often there were

STRIPPED T11 RACER DRIVEN BY VEŘMIŘOVSKÝ AT III ECCE HOMO HILLCLIMB, GAINING FIRST PLACE IN 1923.

VEŘMIŘOVSKÝ IN THE T11 RACER AFTER
HIS WIN AT ZIRLERBERG HILLCLIMB ON
OCTOBER 12TH, 1924.

disagreements as Josef had not yet passed a driving test, and anyway he would not be allowed to take one as he was too young.

Finally, after yet another police intervention Ledwinka decided that Josef had to take the driving test. One year was added to his age on the application form and they hoped to negotiate another afterwards. A car was brought out, Ledwinka sat at the back with two other candidates and Josef drove off to Stauding (Studénka) to pick up the examining commissioner Ing Schnabl, who came especially for the test from Brünn (Brno).

Schnabl did not like these driving test examinations. Several times, with would-be drivers at the wheel, the cars had overturned. In those days it took a lot of work to master the skill of driving with all the different hand levers and steering to negotiate, all of which had to be managed at the same time. To this end, Schnabl was justifiably afraid.

At Stauding, when he sat down next to Josef, he ordered the car to be driven out of the town and onto a straight road where the danger of having an accident was less likely. Josef, with great skill, quickly left the town behind

them. When they were five kilometres outside Stauding, Schnabl asked him to stop the car and proclaimed, "Und jetzt kann es losgehen. Der erste Kandidat kann beginnen." (And now we can start. The first candidate can begin now.) Ledwinka promptly replied, "Herr Ing, Sie fahren ja schon die ganze Zeit mit dem ersten Kandidaten!" (You have already been driven all this time by the first candidate, sir!) Schnabl shouted at him, "Mein du lieber Gott, das hätten sie mir aber früher sagen sollen, Herr Ledwinka!" (Good Lord, but you should have told me earlier!)

Soon, though, he remarked, "Das ist dann der erste Prüfling, bei dem ich keine Angst hatte! Wenn Sie schon so ein grosser Künstler und Rennfahrer sind, dann drehen Sie auf dieser schmalen Strasse um, ich aber steige aus!" (This is the first test I've adjudicated during which I have not been afraid. However, if you are such a great artist and driver, please turn the car round in this narrow road, but let me get out first!) Josef performed the prescribed manoeuvre beautifully and passed the test.[2] Schnabl would have been even more satisfied had he known he was signing papers for one of the most successful racing drivers of the future. Incidentally, when Schnabl asked the second candidate a question on his technical knowledge, "Where was the car's differential?" he got a confused reply, "Das ist vorher ausmontiert worden." (It has already been taken out.) Schnabl dismissed him with, "Dann kommen Sie das nächste Mal wieder zur Prüfung, aber mit dem Differenzial!" (When you come for the test next time bring the differential with you!)

In spring 1923, Tatra was preparing the first T11s for the XV Prague Autosalon. Besides the exhibits inside the salon, there were three cars standing outside the hall with a queue of admirers waiting for a test drive. Everybody wanted to try driving a car whose engine was cooled by air. One of these cars' engines performed particularly well and it was decided to enter this automobile for the next Sunday's flying kilometre race at Ledecká Alej (Ledce Track) near Brno. Initially, Ledwinka did not want to allow the T11 to race; he feared failure. In the end he agreed, with one condition that the T11 would enter under the name of a different firm. At the last moment, the firm Edwin Storek from Brno, which supplied the Kopřivnice factory with castings, applied by telephone for a place in the race.

So, on May 13th, 1923, the two-cylinder car with, swing half-axles, and Veřmiřovský behind the wheel, stood at the start of the run-up. This flying kilometre was not the type of race in which the T11 would necessarily have excelled, because of the short length of the run-up to the measured section. To pump up the two cylinders to maximum speed

on a track which went uphill toward Pohořelice took a little time; so Veřmiřovský went through the starting line in third gear. However, in the opposite direction, where the track dipped down, the 100km speedometer could not cope.

The look and sound of the car was not very elegant or pleasing, because the front wheelarches and headlamps were cut off before the race to allow a larger amount of air to enter the engine. The onlookers' remarks reflected the strange state of the car, "Put it out of its misery! Why

THIS VERY RARE TATRA FACTORY 1924 T11 RENNWAGEN ONCE BELONGED TO THE TATRA RACING DRIVER KARL SPONER. IT PARTICIPATED IN SEVERAL RACES, AND WAS RECENTLY FULLY RESTORED IN THE CZECH REPUBLIC AND THE UK. ONLY THE ENGINE, WITH STANDARD CYLINDER HEADS, AND THE FRONT BONNET ARE ORIGINAL. FOUR-WHEEL BRAKES ARE FITTED. (COURTESY SIMON BLAKENEY-EDWARDS)

torture it any further!", "Look at the rear wheels, they have nearly fallen off. How much they slant!" However, the press commented, "The small Tatra driven by Veřmiřovský gave a very good performance. It gained the first prize in the 1.1-litre class with an average speed of 82.09kph."

The small Tatra design concept was amazingly successful on the bad central European roads and resulted in a very safe ride. The T11 achieved victories in many races due to its reliability, ruggedness, construction simplicity and strength.

The Blechdackel (tin dachshund), as the Austrians called the 'kleine' Tatra, (for the Czechs, because of its small size, it was Tatráček), in a special T11 Rennwagen version with higher compression, dual inlet valves, piston rods with roller bearings, a larger carburettor and 27bhp, won the first prize in its class at the Solitude hillclimb near Stuttgart in 1924 (May 9th, 4:47.1sec).

It was Veřmiřovský, with co-driver Jalůvka, who attended the hillclimb. Amongst the large special Mercedes and American Packards the tiny Tatra was lost, and looked a little like a beggar. People could not believe the courage of the drivers to participate in this difficult race in such a flimsy looking automobile. "How do you even dare to come here in such a vehicle?" they asked.

During the races the unbelievers changed their view when the 'kleine' Tatra received the main prize of the city of Stuttgart and a diploma for the best effort in the small car class.

While training for this race, Veřmiřovský had an accident which initially looked bad, but luckily was not too serious. After he had prepared the car for the training run, he went away to steady himself with a quick cup of coffee. While he was away, the apprentices from the German Tatra agency, wanting to please Veřmiřovský, washed the whole engine with petrol. Veřmiřovský, strengthened by the hot drink pushed the car out of the workshop, sat inside and let the car go downhill. He pressed the clutch, selected gear, the engine started – but instantly caught fire! The apprentices came running out with powder extinguishers, tore the bonnet off and dowsed the fire. Veřmiřovský got

VEŘMIŘOVSKÝ AND CO-DRIVER IN THE T11 RACER WITH REAR BRAKES ONLY, AT THE START OF SOLITUDE HILLCLIMB, STUTTGART, MAY 1924.

the engine going again with the starting handle and slowly drove towards the start of the training circuit. There was not much time to spare. In one minute he had to be ready to go. He was flagged off and went away as fast as he could.

In Veřmiřovský's own words, "Suddenly my eyes started to sting. I was young, foolish and light-hearted. I regarded wearing goggles an unessential requirement. My eyes stung more and more every second. Soon I could not see with one eye and only very little with the other. Luckily, by then I had completed the circuit. At the finish I jumped out of the car and ran to the water fountain standing in the centre of the circuit. I dipped my head into the water for a very long time. People thought that I had gone mad and sent a policeman after me. The policeman dragged me away from the fountain while I was trying to explain that I had to wash out my eyes, which were full of powder from the extinguishers, to restore my sight. The policeman could not understand so I told him how my engine caught fire – how the apprentices had cleaned the engine with petrol, some had spilled over the magneto when a spark jumped and the petrol ignited. The powder stopped the fire, but a large amount gathered under the flywheel, which had then fanned the light substance into my eyes ..."[3]

For the difficult Sicilian XVI Targa Florio race, three special two-cylinder T11s,[4] called Targa Florio, were built with two-seater bodies and Rudge-Whitworth wheels, and fitted with four-wheel brakes and swing axles also at the front. Targa Florio was one of the earliest racing cars with an all-independent suspension. These cars, similar to the T11 Rennwagens, differed from the standard serially produced cars in several aspects. The engines had three removable valve heads: one outlet valve and two inlet valves. The engine output was increased from the standard 12bhp to 27bhp and the engine revolutions from 2800 to 5000rpm. The maximum speed went up from 70kph to 120kph. The special two-seater car body made from aluminium sheets for the engine cover and the rest in plywood had an overall weight of only 27kg. The co-driver's seat was set back asymmetrically to allow the driver a better view of the track.

ABOVE AND BELOW: T11 TARGA FLORIO DRIVEN BY SPONER AT THE XVI TARGA FLORIO RACE, SICILY, MAY 3RD, 1925.

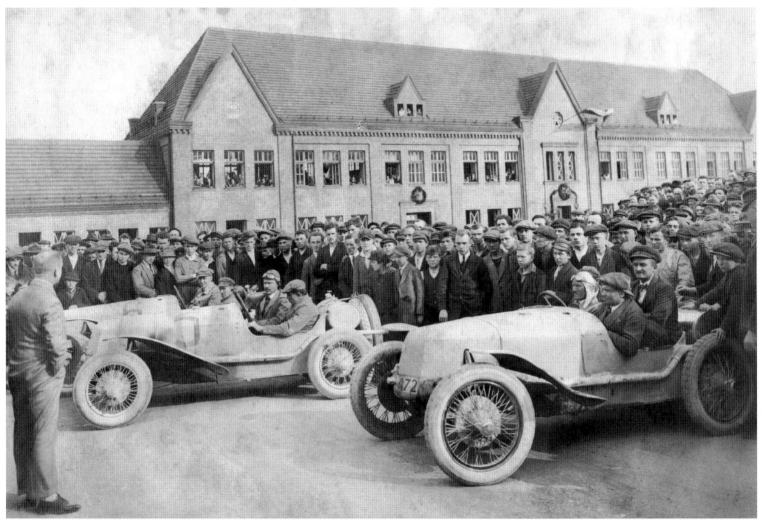

THE TWO WINNING T11 TARGA FLORIOS WITH STARTING NUMBERS 5 (HÜCKEL) AND 6 (SPONER), BACK AT THE MAIN YARD OF THE KOPŘIVNICE FACTORY AFTER THEIR VICTORY IN SICILY IN 1925.

At the back was placed the 60-litre petrol tank and behind it two spare wheels were held with a leather belt. There had to be two spare wheels because the front wheels (710x110) had different tyre dimensions than the rear wheels (710x115).

In April of 1925 two of these cars were driven all the way to Sicily for the race held on a sunny and warm May 3rd, finishing first and second in the 1100cc class and seventh and eighth in the overall placing on the difficult course, which was for that class, 3 laps, 324km long with a large number of bends. The cars were driven by Fritz Hückel and Karl Sponer. Hückel's average speed was 59.5kph and finishing time 05:31:29. Sponer was five minutes slower. The race was won outright by a Bugatti Grand Prix Type 35 driven by Meo Constantini of Italy with average speed of 71.6kph and fastest lap of 01:28:37. Unfortunately none of these Targa Florio racers have survived; however, one restored 1924 T11 Rennwagen is now resident in the UK and participates in local speed hillclimb events.

In August and September 1925, 94 cars[5] took part in the international 24-day, 5300km, 19-stage Leningrad-Moscow-Kursk-Kharkov-Bakhmut-Rostov-Piatigorsk-Vladikavkaz-Tiflis, and back to Moscow via Zugdidi, Novorossiysk, Krasnodar and Rostov, long distance reliability trial, to determine the most suitable cars for the Russian roads.[6] Only 40 per cent of the total journey was on standard roads, the rest consisted of field tracks. Seven cars did not finish the first stage from Leningrad to Moscow. Along the rest of the way a further 29 cars had to give up. The Tatra T11 looked tiny against the other cars, some of which had 100bhp engines. Other drivers looked down on the little car. When the going was on flat and dry land they could well sneer at the Tatra. However, when the rain came, the heavy, large cars sank into the bottomless mud. The Tatra, being small and light, drove easily over the fields and battled through every time. At the control points, barrels with water were placed for the topping up of radiators. The competition cars stood in line behind the barrels in the order of their arrival. The order was supervised by a racing official. The little Tatra did not need to stop for water because its engine was air-cooled. The officials did not always know this and thought that Veřmiřovský wanted to jump the queue, but he simply waved his hand that the water was not needed, and drove off.

When the route took them through the Caucasus Mountains, the water-cooled cars' radiators started to boil, and valuable time was lost in waiting for the water to cool off. Meanwhile, the driver of the small Tatra passed the stranded cars and continued his progress towards an absolute victory, defeating the other entrants in both fuel consumption and reliability. By this achievement Tatra gained very good publicity in the world's media – which was the main reason for its participation.[7]

"In 1924," Veřmiřovský recounted, "I won the main prize with the two-cylinder Tatra for the best performance in the small car class on the Solitude hillclimb near Stuttgart. In 1925, I was again entered for the same race, only in the smaller capacity class, and this time the race was run on a circuit. The new Tatra engine with smaller bore was not that good and in spite of all my efforts its performance was still below par. Ledwinka had worried about discrediting the Tatra image and did not want me to go. In the last minute he conceded and allowed my entry. Both mine and his fears were confirmed during the running-in of the car on the way to Stuttgart. The performance of the engine was not adequate to beat the competition.

"On Saturday evening before the main race the director Eichmann, of our German agency, brought several curious members from the local autoclub to our workshop. They were all interested in an air-cooled engine car. Eichmann, in his eagerness to show them all what the car could do, pushed the engine up to 5300rpm. At that moment there came a loud bang from under the bonnet and that was the end. Quite a mess, on the evening before the race! One valve torn off, a broken piston and a damaged cylinder. The spare parts were available, but there was no time to run the engine in. I had decided to 'run-in' the engine with a file. I could only find a rasp; I tried it anyhow. I drilled several holes round the perimeter into the body of the pistons to ease their oiling and reduce their weight, and I took down one ring from each piston. By sunrise I was already circling the circuit.

"Nevertheless, at the start I was a badly worried man but all went well even this time. After the race the officials spoiled my happy mood; they changed my category from touring to sports car, due to the wire wheels on the Tatra. Their reason was, it seemed, to save at least one trophy for the others! When I returned from Germany, Ledwinka did not believe that the car went so well. Afterwards I let the secret out that the engine had 'aerodynamic' pistons fashioned with an old rasp and a hand drill. And would you believe that the factory production drawings were changed accordingly, to follow my handmade amendments to the pistons!"[8]

Newspaper editor J Kalva raced an express train from Prague to Paris on June 10th, 1926; the small Tatra was in the French capital sooner than the train, covering the 1000km journey in 27 hours and 15 minutes.

Das

Nesselsdorfer (TATRA) Kleinautomobil

4/12PS ○ viersitzig karossiert

der ideale Wagen für den Herrenfahrer

SIEGER in der Alpenfahrt 1924

Schnell=Lastautos für 1000 kg Nutzlast

Nesselsdorfer Wagenbau-Fabriks-A. G.

Repräsentanz: Wien, I. Seilerstätte Nr. 5.
Wiener Verkaufsbureau und Niederlage: I. Kolowratring Nr. 8.
Wiener Werkstätten: XI. Simmeringer Hauptstraße Nr. 98.

Vertretungen für Oberösterreich: Dr. Franz Pisecky, Linz, Schützenstraße 5; für Salzburg: Autohaus Ott, Salzburg Westbahnstraße 11 b; für Tirol und Vorarlberg: Köllensperger Eisen-Industrie und Handels-A.-G., Innsbruck

THE FACTORY DID NOT FAIL TO USE THE ABUNDANT T11 VICTORIES IN ADVERTISING.

The German Tatra agency of Stuttgart received a letter from Mr Alfred Recla dated October 11th, 1927, confirming that his Tatra T11 had covered 338,955km (211,847 miles) from April 2nd, 1924 to the date of his letter; the only overhaul required was the re-boring of cylinders and replacing the pistons in May 1927. Further successes followed. In 1931 a T12 driven by zoologist J Baum and sculptor FV Foit crossed Africa from Alexandria to Cape Town, while another T12 drove over the Australian continent.

The numerous racing successes of the T11 were attributed, apart from other factors like the independent suspension and air-cooled engine, and its general flexibility and ruggedness, to the chassis backbone structure, which allowed the driver to take even the most difficult bends at high speeds.

A list of some of the Tatra T11 achievements from 1923 to 1926 is shown below, but it is evident that despite Ledwinka's reticence toward motor racing, the car scored some notable competition successes that greatly enhanced the company's reputation and standing throughout Europe.

SOME OF THE COMPETITION SUCCESSES OF THE T11

1923

1st prize: Ledecká Alej, Brno, flying kilometre, May 13th, starting number 19, time 43.85sec, 82.09kph, driver J Veřmiřovský.

1st prize: III Ecce Homo hillclimb, Šternberk, September 23rd, starting number 34, time 8:3.8sec, length 7.75km, driver J Veřmiřovský.

1924

1st prize: VIII Zbraslav-Jíloviště international hillclimb trial, April 20th, time 4:24.4sec, driver J Veřmiřovský, T11s also claimed 2nd & 3rd prizes.

1st prize: Awarded for elegance, Stuttgart autosalon.

1st prize: Solitude hillclimb, Stuttgart, May 9th, starting number 9, time 4:47.1sec, driver J Veřmiřovský.

1st prize: Moscow automobile trial.

1st prize: Alpine trial, Austria, 1900km, June 14th-21st, driver J Veřmiřovský.

1st prize: Marienbad international automobile trial.

1st prize: Polish reliability trial, 2500km, July 7th-12th, starting number 26, driver J Veřmiřovský.

2nd prize: Eichwald-Zinnwald (Krkonoše) international Alpine trial.

1st prize: Zirlerberg Alpine trial, October 12th, starting number 1, driver J Veřmiřovský.

1st prize: Württemberg Autoclub reliability trial.

1st prize: IV Ecce Homo hillclimb, Šternberk, September 21st, starting number 70, time 7:10.8sec, driver J Veřmiřovský, T11 also claimed 2nd prize.

1st prize: Tokyo, lowest fuel consumption trial.

1925

1st prize: IX Zbraslav-Jíloviště, international hillclimb trial, April 13th, starting number 70, time 4:20sec, driver J Veřmiřovský.

1st & 2nd prize: 16th Targa Florio, May 3rd, 1100cc class, 108km per lap, 3 laps, times 05:31:29 and 05:36:17, drivers F Hückel and K Sponer in two T11 Targa Florio racers.

1st prize: II Brno-Soběšice hillclimb, May 10th, starting number 54, time 3:14sec, driver J Veřmiřovský.

2nd prize: Solitude circuit, Stuttgart, May 18th, starting number 10, time 7:15.2sec, driver J Veřmiřovský (sports category).

1st prize: Württemberg Autoclub reliability trial, 2 first prizes won.

1st prize: Hungarian jubilee trial.

1st prize: Leningrad-Moscow-Tiflis-Moscow 24-day long distance reliability trial. Awarded for lowest fuel consumption and reliability, 3rd fastest, August-September, starting number 93, driver J Veřmiřovský. (Second Tatra no. 92 finished 3rd, 17th and 5th fastest.)

1st prize: Alpine trial, 2280km, 20th-28th June, starting number 44, J Veřmiřovský.

1st prize: VII Schwabenberg Budapest hillclimb. T11s also won 2nd and 3rd prizes.

1926

1st prize: Mountain trial, Ljubelj Pass, Slovenia, August 8th, starting number 30, driver J Veřmiřovský.

NOTES

1 'Pepek' is a Czech endearment for 'Josef.' For the story see Sloniger, 'Hans Ledwinka' p 134.

2 Kovařík, p 9.

3 Ibid, p 19.

4 Some publications designate these special racers as T11/12 or T12; plus one other was made for spare parts.

5 Various sources quote 75, 78, 96 or 150 cars. Quoted from *Motocykl*, no. 9, 1925, p 336 & no. 11, p 424.

6 *The Straits Times*, 13.4.1925, p 7, announcing the forthcoming trial.

7 Kovařík, p 20.

8 Ibid, p 20.

THE LARGE TATRAS

The great success of the T11 encouraged Ledwinka to design larger automobiles with similar concepts to the T11, and in 1925, the Tatra T17 was launched. The T17 had a water-cooled, six-cylinder engine, and aroused interest similar to that of its smaller predecessor because it combined an original concept with a simple, elegant chassis, together with a highly-efficient modern engine. The most innovative element was the front swing half-axles, constructed on the same principle as the model T11's rear swing half-axles.

The six-cylinder engine had a barrel-type crankcase which formed one unit with the cylinder block, all constructed out of light metal. The cylinder liners made from grey cast iron were exchangeable, and were built into the cylinder block. The camshaft was placed in the removable cylinder head, and was turned by a crown shaft with spiral tooth bevel wheels. The bore was 64mm and the stroke 100mm, giving piston displacement of 1930cc. At 3000rpm, the engine achieved 35bhp, aided by two horizontal Solex or Zenith carburettors.

All the other technical details of the transmission, such as the four-speed gearbox with a ball and socket gearlever, corresponded to the construction of the T11. The model T17 had a wheelbase either 3350, 3500 or 3670mm long, and a wheel track of 1350mm. This car was serially manufactured, equipped with Rudge-Whitworth wire wheels, and reached a maximum speed of 110kph. The T17's body was well designed; its form was harmoniously proportioned, with low, long coachwork and an elegant radiator. In 1926, it was a great sensation at the Prague and Vienna autosalons, and

was received with enthusiasm all over the world. The T17 was also a very practical car with outstanding performance for its time. This car's potential could be fully appreciated by virtue of its good and safe handling characteristics.

In the later model T17/31 the bore was increased to 70mm, giving displacement of 2310cc and a larger power output of 40bhp. The camshaft drive was altered from the expensive main shaft to a duplex chain gearing, and only two carburettors were retained. This six-cylinder touring car was made until 1931.

The successes of the small Tatras had not diminished but, from 1926, the new model T17 appeared on the trial fields with equal abilities to claim racing honours. It received 2nd prize in the X Zbraslav-Jíloviště international hillclimb on May 9th, 1926, with a time of 4:21.5sec and Veřmiřovský as the driver. On June 6th, 1926 the T17 won the city of Brno prize at the III Brno-Soběšice hillclimb with starting number 62 and Veřmiřovský driving. On September 19th, 1926, it gained 1st prize in the VI Ecce Homo hillclimb, Šternberk, time 6:35.5sec, starting number 64, driver Veřmiřovský.

Further air-cooled four-cylinder engine models followed: the Tatra T30, T52 and T54 (T54/30) of which 3847, 1735, and 1414 cars, respectively, were made. One of

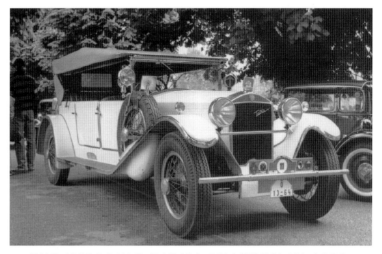

THE IMPOSING T17/31 PHAETON IN 1926. THIS CAR COULD ACHIEVE A MAXIMUM SPEED OF 115KPH.

ŠESTIVÁLCOVÝ OSOBNÍ VŮZ

T17 ARTWORK.

1932 TATRA T54.
(COURTESY DAVID YANDO,
LANE MOTOR MUSEUM)

the T30 models was a six-seater army car with a roll-down canvas roof. Its weight was 1000kg and had a maximum speed of 90kph. There was also a racing version of the T30, of which two were made, which successfully participated in several races at home and abroad. Built on the same principles as the racing model of the T11, the T30 had an air-cooled, 1.9-litre, four-cylinder engine of 35bhp at 3200rpm achieving a maximum speed of 130kph. The T52 was a more luxurious car, and came with several versions

of bodies designed by the Josef Sodomka Coachworks at Vysoké Mýto. The T54 was smaller than the T52, seating a maximum of four passengers, and was powered with an air-cooled, 1.465-litre, four-cylinder engine giving 22bhp and a maximum speed of 90kph.

Among the victories of the T30 racing car was 1st prize at the VIII Schwabenberg, Budapest, international hillclimb on October 25th, 1926, starting number 19, time 3:42.8sec, with Veřmiřovský driving. It also gained first prize in the Zirlerberg Alpine trial near Innsbruck on October 14th, 1928, as well as the Gaisberg (Austria) hillclimb on September 8th, 1929, and three weeks later set a new record for cars up to 2 litres in the Schwabenberg hillclimb. In 1931 in the X Ecce Homo hillclimb Veřmiřovský won in the T30 racer with time 6:6.01sec. Fritz Hückel in the T30 racer and Ing E Krickl-Rheinthal, in a T30 tourer, won the 10,000km trial which ran on a circular route from Prague via Berlin, Lisbon, Rome, Budapest and Vienna back to Prague.

At the Tatra factory, Ledwinka was directing all stages of Tatra production, which meant that he had to deal with

T54 FITTED WITH THE STRONGER T52
1910CC FOUR-CYLINDER ENGINE.
(COURTESY DAVID YANDO,
LANE MOTOR MUSEUM)

THE LONG TRADITION OF TATRA CARS
IN THE MARGOLIUS FAMILY. IVAN'S
GRANDPARENTS VÍTĚZSLAV MARGOLIUS
(1879-1942) AND BERTA (1884-1942),
SITTING INSIDE, WITH THEIR 1931 TATRA
T54. (COURTESY RUDOLF MARGOLIUS)

THE LARGE T52 SPORTS CABRIOLET, 1931.

workers from all divisions of the company. On one notable occasion, a delegation from the rail section came into his office to point out that workers from the automobile division were allowed to borrow company cars and drive them at weekends to the adjacent Beskydy mountains.

TATRA T52 WITH SODOMKA BODYWORK.
(COURTESY JAN TULIS)

They complained that they wanted the same privilege. Ledwinka looked at them for a moment and said, "Sehr geehrte Herren, ich habe keine Einwände. Nehmen Sie einen Eisenbahnwagen und fahren Sie hin wo Sie möchten!" (Gentlemen, I have no objection. Take a railway coach and go wherever you like!).[1]

The success of Tatra cars during the 1920s, both in everyday passenger use and in races, now made the Tatra marque so well known to the general public that in 1924 the directors decided to change the name of Kopřivnická vozovka a s to Závody Tatra akciová společnost pro stavbu automobilů a železničních vozů (Tatra Works Ltd for Construction of Cars and Railway Wagons) and after 1927

VEŘMIŘOVSKÝ WITH CO-DRIVER JALŮVKA IN THE T30 RACER AT THE START OF THE TRAINING
RUN FOR THE SCHWABENBERG HILLCLIMB, BUDAPEST, 1926.

SIX-CYLINDER TATRA
70A IN SODOMKA
COACHWORKS
DESIGNED
BODY, 1934.

the name was more often shortened just to Závody Tatra a s.

Later, at the end of 1935, Baron Hans (Hanuš) Freiherr von Ringhoffer (1885-1946), the proprietor of the Tatra works from 1923, combined his Prague-Smíchov wagon factory with the Kopřivnice complex and the name of the company was changed again to Závody Ringhoffer-Tatra a s. This situation prevailed until 1946 when the factory was nationalised and named Tatra, národní podnik.

Back in 1926, the Kopřivnice factory had employed 3000 workers and 300 administrative staff; annual production varied and was around 500 railway passenger coaches, 3500 railway goods wagons, and about 1200 passenger and commercial vehicles. By 1930 annual vehicle production had risen to around 3550 units.

In 1931 the models T70 and T80 came into production. The T70 had the same 3800mm long-wheelbase and other chassis dimensions as the large T80. Their bodies were also very similar and it was quite difficult to tell one model from the other. The T70 engine was based on the T17/31 unit: a water-cooled, six-cylinder in-line, OHC engine of 3.4-litre capacity, 80mm bore to 113mm stroke giving 65bhp at 3000rpm. The chassis was hung in the front on a cross

THE IMPRESSIVE 5.99-LITRE, TWELVE-CYLINDER TATRA T80 ENGINE.

leaf spring. All four wheels had the Ate-Lockheed hydraulic double circuit brakes.

Four years later this model was modified and became the T70a, which had an engine with a larger 3.845-litre capacity because the bore had been increased to 85mm, and the output changed to 70bhp at 3500rpm. The gearbox had three synchronised gears and free-wheeling. The front swing axles were suspended by two transverse leaf springs placed one above the other with oil dampers attached.

In Germany, these large Tatras, the T70 and T70a, cost RM22,500. Only 51 of the T70 and 66 of the T70a cars were made. Until 1943, they were manufactured to order as touring and representative cars: these automobiles were a

cheaper substitute for the more luxurious – and expensive – twelve-cylinder Tatra T80.

In the early '30s car manufacturers in Czechoslovakia tried to follow general trends by producing large prestigious automobiles. They wanted to prove their ability by illustrating the high level of skills in the Czechoslovak car industry. Unfortunately, it was impossible to sustain the manufacture of so many large, luxurious cars, and sell them successfully, especially at a time of worldwide economic crisis. At home it was not a viable business proposition, and, due to strong competition from other world marques, there was little hope that large cars would make greater headway abroad. This explains why only 26 T80s, including three cars which were kept in reserve for spare parts, were made

THE T80 REAR INDEPENDENT SUSPENSION.

between 1930 and 1938, and Tatra interest was turning to the manufacture of small cars at the same time.

The imposing T80 embodied the end of a long development line of successful Tatra models. With these larger models Ledwinka had proved that his original concept of the central tubular chassis and swing half-axles was suitable for large cars as well as for the small and medium cars he had designed before.

The T80's chassis looked basically the same as the other Tatras; its main departure point was the front water-cooled V12 engine. Contrary to previous Ledwinka engines, which usually had overhead valves, this car had L-head side valves. This construction was possibly chosen to limit, at least partly, the financial outlay. Each of the two blocks of six cylinders were placed at a 65 degree angle on the barrel type crankcase made of silumin. The cylinder blocks were constructed from cast iron. The rolling surfaces of the cylinders extended deep into the crankcase. The engine had removable silumin cylinder heads and horizontally lined valves, which were activated by a central camshaft placed between the cylinder blocks. The camshaft was driven by a chain at the rear, and on its front end there was another chain which drove the six-blade aluminium fan. From the fan spindle extended a

long hollow shaft driving the dynamo at the rear of the engine.

The cylinders had a capacity of 5.99 litres with 75mm bore and 113mm stroke. At 3000rpm the output came to 120bhp with maximum speed of 140kph. By each cylinder block there was one Zenith downdraught carburettor, which had fuel supplied by an electric pump. The electrical equipment consisted of a 12V Bosch or Scintilla battery ignition system. The crankshaft was set in eight friction bearings. The pistons were of the Nelson-Bohnalite type, and the compression ratio was 5.2:1. The clutch was single plate dry.

Accessibility to the engine was remarkably good, the shaft between fan and dynamo could be lifted out instantly, without tools, and, as there was no timing to allow for, it could be replaced with the same rapidity. With the shaft out of the way, access was secured to the space between the two banks of cylinders, and by removing a sheet-metal cover-plate the whole of the valve mechanism was laid bare. The gearbox, which formed the usual monoblock with the engine, was four-speed and synchronised in the two highest gears, and had a fixture for free-wheeling. The construction of the rear swing half-axles was the same as the previous models, but for its suspension two outwardly splayed quarter elliptical springs were used, which allowed the chassis to be positioned lower. The model T80 had slightly different front suspension; the overhead cross spring was fixed over the two steering sliding planes.

The T80 was built to rival the most prestigious cars of that time, such as the Hispano Suiza, Maybach, Rolls-Royce and Isotta Fraschini. A leading British publication, *The Autocar* magazine, after seeing the T80 chassis exhibited at the recent Paris Salon de l'automobile in November 1930 commented that the engine was "astonishingly neat, and compactly arranged."

This car belonged among the largest automobiles and was even bigger than the Maybach Zeppelin. The chassis weight was 1600kg, but with the spacious and comfortable saloon body the weight increased to almost 2400kg.

A variety of further bodies were on offer, a cabriolet or a landaulet. The bodies were made either in the main Tatra works or by Sodomka Coachworks. The T80s were well equipped to order, with wire spoke or disc wheels, Zeiss headlamps and fog lamps. The characteristic radiator grille was well proportioned, which harmonised well with the rest of the body. Among the well-known personalities who owned this Tatra were the first President of the Czechoslovak Republic, T G Masaryk, and the Minister of Foreign Affairs, E Beneš. Masaryk's car, factory number 15588, engine number 112 024, is now exhibited in the Prague National Technical Museum.

The Autocar of November 1931 again highly praised the T80 chassis which could be viewed at the Philip Turner's showroom in St James's Street, London, who had a Tatra concession for the British Empire, which was later taken over by Captain Douglas F H Fitzmaurice of 122A High Street, St John's Wood, London: "... it may safely be said that it is one of the most unorthodox designs of high grade vehicles yet produced, its features being independent springing of all four wheels, the reduction of unsprung weight, a very low centre of gravity, and the disposition of practically all the weight between the axle centres. Coupled with this is a very high power-weight ratio, while the ratio of body space to overall length is also unusually large ..."

1932 V12 TATRA T80 CABRIOLET, RESTORED BY J & D STAUCH, CZECH REPUBLIC. T80S WERE THE LARGEST PASSENGER CARS BUILT BY TATRA. (COURTESY *MOTOR KLASSIK* 09/2011, GERMANY)

In 1931, the Tatra T80 chassis was offered for sale by Turner for £1295. At the 1933 London Olympia Show the chassis price was raised to £1950. In Germany the basic price for the whole car was RM28,500, which was more than the cost of two new Mercedes-Benz 370S Mannheim cabriolets at the time.

NOTES

1 Sloniger, *Hans Ledwinka*, p 138.

THE BRITISH REACTION

From 1931 the dignified successor to the air-cooled four-cylinder T30 was the newly developed Tatra T57. This car represented the peak of the classic Tatra concept of a small capacity people's automobile which was based on the tubular backbone chassis structure, the swing half-axles and the front air-cooled engine. This small car, nicknamed 'Hadimrška' (literally: Slippery Mover), was one of the most popular Tatras. It had a 1.15-litre, four-cylinder engine of 18bhp, and was made in many versions culminating with model T57b. The long history of the production of these cars ceased in 1948.

The British press was impressed by the simple design concept of the tubular backbone chassis and the independently sprung wheels. When describing Ledwinka's 'people's car,' the model T57, *The Motor* magazine wrote: "The technical director of the Tatra concern, Mr Ledwinka, who is entirely responsible for the design, holds the opinion that to spring the wheels independently is not in itself sufficient; the whole chassis must be designed to give the results required. For example, he regards it as being very important to centralize the weights as far as possible, so that the mass-displacement, when any wheel rides over an obstruction, is at a minimum."[1]

The Autocar of November 1932 in its road test of the Tatra T57 drophead coupé, said, "Anyone rash enough to make the generalisation that the design of cars is settling down on more or less accepted lines should find a very fine tonic effect in the Tatra, which has so many unusual points of design as to make it basically different from almost every other car. It is not to be expected that a car so unusual in its essentials would feel like an ordinary car on the road; completely independent suspension in itself is sufficiently unorthodox at the moment to guarantee interest. The way

in which the Tatra rides over really bad surfaces is little short of astounding. It is a form of springing which shows up to its best on the very worst type of potholed byway that can be found, and over this kind of surface the car can be driven at 35 or 40mph, to give an illustration, where, with the vast majority of ordinary cars, almost irrespective of price, one would slow down to 20mph or maintain at most 25mph."

Even *The Tatler*[2] added its comment: "All its wheels are independently sprung. In spite of it having quite a short wheelbase it can be driven fast without the least discomfort

T57 CABRIOLET, 1933. IN BRITAIN
CALLED THE DROPHEAD COUPÉ.
(COURTESY TOM BLIKSLAGER)

over surfaces which bring even the most enormous car, with ordinary springing, down to an absolute crawl. It is very amusing to watch this clever little car negotiating chains of potholes in which you could bury the proverbial dog ... But no, like a big boat negotiating a merely choppy sea, it remains perfectly stable, answers its helm with precise obedience and, what is equally to the point, holds the surface so well that its brakes are always extraordinarily effective. Incidentally, the engine is air-cooled and utterly resists any temptation to get too hot ... Like so many other good things you cannot believe quite how good it is until you try it, and then you wonder why everybody hasn't adopted it."

The Motor magazine of August 1933 again rather enthusiastically comments on what they describe as "the unconventional light car," the T57, by saying, "Tatra, which apart from achieving a considerable sales volume in

T57 SPORTS ROADSTER, 1933.

1935 TATRA T57A
SPORTS ROADSTER
CHASSIS.
(COURTESY
DAVID POUNDER)

Middle Europe, has exerted quite an important influence upon automobile design in Germany and other countries. The chassis is obviously devised to achieve the utmost simplicity in construction, coupled with certain features of performance which are seldom obtainable in a vehicle of light weight ... The 1154cc model when tested ... was found capable of negotiating corners at high speeds, with quite an exceptional degree of stability, could be driven over an atrociously rough surface, such as that of Bishop's Avenue [!], Hampstead, at 35-40mph, without discomfort or steering snatch, and yet, on a main road, afforded quite a high degree of riding comfort. Such results represent a considerable achievement."

At £260 the T57 was, however, fairly expensive for a low performance treasury rated 12bhp car (the manufacturer's rating was 18bhp) and few were sold in Britain.

The series of T75 sports cars was one of the bestselling successes between the world wars. From 1934 until 1940,

T57A SPORTS ROADSTER WITH T2-603 AND T613-3 BEHIND. (COURTESY DAVID POUNDER)

SPORTOVNÍ VŮZ

TATRA 57

T57A ARTWORK.

4054 cars of this type were sold. The sports car body was made to order and was popular. The T75 also came in a six or four-seater saloon version. The engine used was a well tried air-cooled 1.68-litre, four-cylinder giving a maximum speed of 100kph. This type of engine could run for a long time without requiring any overhauls. The car was fitted with Lockheed hydraulic brakes on all four wheels.

The high reputation of the T57 and T75 cars led Neue Röhr-Werke AG of Ober-Ramstadt and Stoewer Werke AG in Stettin to build versions under licence. The Röhr company began by building the T57, but, between 1934 and 1935, cars with T75 engines were offered under the name Junior. Stoewer's model was based on Röhr's type and called the Stoewer Greif Junior, manufactured from 1935 until 1939. This was not the first time that Tatra had been approached regarding licencing its designs. In the 1920s even Daimler-Benz, when it was looking for a small car

1939 TATRA T57B, MANUFACTURED UNTIL 1948. (COURTESY JOSEF KRÜMPELBECK)

T75 SALOON ARTWORK.

ABOVE: 1938 TATRA T75 CABRIOLET.
(COURTESY JIŘÍ M PECHAN AND IVAN HRADIL)

T72 REAR FOUR-WHEEL DRIVE MILITARY CAR
WITH EIGHT FORWARD AND TWO REVERSE
GEARS AND SIX-WHEEL HYDRAULIC
OPERATED BRAKES.

for its production series, considered licence arrangements with Tatra. Between 1928 and 1933 in Hungary, Unitas Automobil in Budapest, built T12s under licence on Tatra chassis, and in 1925 in Frankfurt am Main, Deutsche Licenz Tatra – Automobile Betriebsgesellschaft m.b.H. was set up on Franken-Allee 98-102, which produced and sold T11, T12 and T57 cars. They were also made on chassis supplied directly by Tatra. Initially, the cars were called Delta (acronym of the company's name) and from 1928 Detra (DEutsch and TaTRA) was used. The company was run by Arthur von Mumm and Paul Georg Ehrhardt, one time editor of *Motor-Kritik* and Tatra employee.[3] In Vienna, the Austro-Tatra company built T57a models from 1936 to 1938.

UNITAS AUTOMOBIL BUDAPEST LOGO.

1926 DELTA POSTER.
(COURTESY KLAUS BUSCHBAUM)

Two special Tatra chassis with 1.48-litre engines, and based on the T75 design, were imported to Britain by Captain Douglas F H Fitzmaurice. One chassis, with a 'Fitzmaurice' specially-designed streamlined body made by Thomas Harrington Ltd of Hove, Sussex, was exhibited – together with the other polished chassis and a T72 chassis – at the Olympia Motor Show held between October 12th and 21st, 1933 in London. On the basis of its design Captain Fitzmaurice lodged several patents. The Tatra-Fitzmaurice car was tested and the results published in *The Autocar* of January 12th, 1934. The motor journalists found the car most unusual and intriguing. "It is difficult with a car like this,

so interesting above the ordinary both in the chassis and for the coachwork, to dissociate the two units in the mind, but one feels, on looking at the car and after driving it, that here, somehow, is a glimpse of the future, and that this may

CONTEMPORARY PHOTOPLATE OF
TATRA-FITZMAURICE PROTOTYPE,
1933 WITH HIGHLIGHTED OUTLINE.
(COURTESY LAT PHOTOGRAPHIC)

1927 DELTA 4/12PS WITH FOUR-WHEEL BRAKES.
(COURTESY PHOTO ART
ANDREAS MOOSBRUGGER & CAR OWNER
KLAUS BUSCHBAUM)

TATRA-FITZMAURICE PILLARLESS
BODY ALLOWING EASY ACCESS.
(COURTESY LAT PHOTOGRAPHIC)

well be the kind of car, broadly, we shall be using in a year or two's time."

At a sterling price of £595 the special Tatra was fairly expensive for an average performance car and no further units were made beyond the one full prototype. However, it is worthwhile examining the Tatra-Fitzmaurice car in detail.

Tatra supplied Fitzmaurice with only two of the special chassis of which one still survives today. The engines employed had a reduced cylinder bore from T75's 80mm to 75mm, the stroke was kept the same at 84mm. These were the same bore and stroke dimensions which were applied in the next generation of the Tatra V8 engines used in the models T77 and T87.

TATRA-FITZMAURICE SPECIFICATION

Engine:	1484cc air-cooled, 75mm bore x 84mm stroke, vibrationless, horizontally opposed flat-four-cylinder engine; balanced crankshaft; aluminium crankcase; aluminium detachable cylinder heads; pressure lubrication with electric oil pressure indicator; overhead valves with submerged cam gear; static cooling by high pressure centrifugal air pump.
Electrics:	Bosch automatic advance coil ignition, switchboard, starter, constant voltage dynamo, double filament head lamps, horn.
Fuel:	Downdraught carburettor; electric fuel pump; 7-gallon rear tank; dash petrol gauge, reserve.
Transmission:	Central gear change; 4 forward speeds, third silent constant mesh; clutchless gear change by free-wheel with centre lever control; single dry plate clutch; high efficiency, jointless, double rolling helical bevel transmission; 4-wheel balanced brakes.
Suspension:	Independent shockless steering; 'unwavering travel' distortionless, centralised, underslung tubular chassis with all four hinged half-axles independently sprung; lubricated by twin rotary pumps; high pressure oil gun chassis lubrication; 5 Dunlop well-base disc wheels and Fort extra low pressure tyres, 6.00 x 16"; non-rolling independent transverse quarter-elliptic over-springing, front springs duplicated; 2700mm wheelbase, 1300mm track, 200mm ground clearance. The chassis was fitted with a special one-off coachbuilt 'Fitzmaurice' pillarless saloon body designed by Captain Fitzmaurice.
Bodywork:	Flush-fitting sliding roof; four pillarless doors, any seat with single door entry; winding handle operated frameless windows; separate, adjustable, tubular hammock front seats with folding backs; rear seats adjustable for luggage space increase; built-in luggage trunk and spare wheel container; ventilating back-light; side armrests front and rear seats; rear seat centre folding armrest; private door lock; rear blind operated from driver's seat; stop, tail and reversing lamps; dash petrol gauge; speedometer; clock; tandem electric wiper; interior light; Triplex glass; Latex seat upholstery; bumpers front and rear; flush full-width body sides running into detachable front wings; flush concealed mounting of lamps, horn, traffic indicators, number plates; cellulosed silver grey body, blue wings and bonnet; upholstered in blue leather; grey woodwork; overall length 4115mm.
Price:	£595.

NOTES

1 *The Motor*, 15.8.1933.
2 *The Tatler*, 19.4.1932.
3 For more information on Paul Ehrhardt see Paul Schilperoord, *The Extraordinary Life of Josef Ganz: The Jewish Engineer Behind Hitler's Volkswagen*, New York: RVP Publishers, 2012.

THE VOLKSWAGEN
CONNECTION

T57 – V570 SHOWING THE REAR ENGINE
COMPARTMENT WITH AIR-COOLED
0.854-LITRE TWO-CYLINDER BOXER ENGINE.

Early in 1930, at the time of the worldwide economic crisis, many automobile companies began in earnest to explore the possibilities of a small, low priced, economical, streamlined car design to gain a broader customer base. The difficulties which faced automobile manufacturers were confirmed by Porsche's secretary: "Apart from there being no money, there were no orders."[1] At that time Ledwinka and the Tatra design engineer Erich Übelacker (1899-1977), who started working for Tatra in 1927,[2] together with his team of young engineering graduates that included Hans' second son Erich Ledwinka, who joined Tatra in 1930, came up with their idea of a car with rear air-cooled engine hung on the Tatra's favourite chassis concept – the backbone frame. The first experimental prototype, with rear air-cooled two-cylinder engine placed in the former rear luggage compartment behind the seats, and using the T57 two-seater drophead coupé body, was completed in the Tatra factory late in 1931.[3] One body was built but rejected, and a new one was made using some

1931 T57 – V570, THE
FIRST TATRA REAR
ENGINE PROTOTYPE.

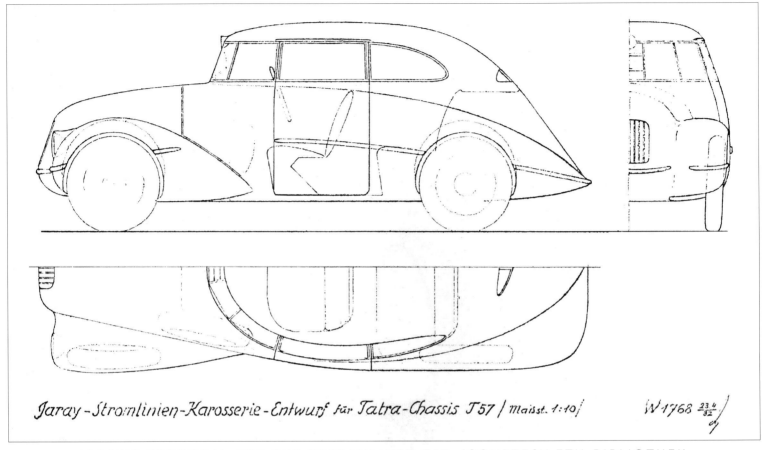

Jaray-Stromlinien-Karosserie-Entwurf für Tatra-Chassis T57 / Maisst. 1:10 / W 1768 23.4 32

JARAY'S PROPOSAL FOR THE STREAMLINED T57. (COURTESY ETH-BIBLIOTHEK, HOCHSCHULARCHIV, HS 1144: 152. PAUL JARAY, STROMLININIEN KAROSSERIE ENTWURF FÜR TATRA CHASSIS T57, APRIL 23RD 1932.)

parts from the first attempt. This new, rear engine position concept reduced the perceptible engine noise in the interior of the car, and made the car lighter because the driveshaft was not needed. The air-cooled engine would weigh less without water jacket, pump, radiator and associated piping and helped to establish the body style according to the streamlining principles as scientifically established by Paul Jaray in the early 1920s.

However, as the engine cooling did not work well, Hans Ledwinka decided to stop the experiment. Übelacker and Erich Ledwinka persuaded him to increase the car size to a 4-seater body to allow more room for the engine and

cooling volume. This proposal was consulted with Jaray who produced his own streamlined design for the T57 dated April 23rd, 1932, leading to the next prototype called V570 which was completed early in 1933.[4] This V570 prototype (V=Versuchswagen, test vehicle, a designation used for prewar Tatra prototypes), which in its way, was as revolutionary as the T11 had been 12 years before. The small Tatra V570 from 1933 had the same rear air-cooled twin horizontally opposed engine of 854cc, a bore of 80mm and a stroke of 85mm as its 1931 predecessor. It had a more pronounced aerodynamically styled four-seater body, and its wooden frame was covered with

1933 TATRA V570, WITH REAR AIR-COOLED 0.854-LITRE TWO-CYLINDER BOXER ENGINE, SHOWING GREAT SIMILARITIES IN DESIGN TO PORSCHE'S AND OTHERS' PROPOSALS AT THAT TIME.

steel sheeting. The front was solid without a bonnet. However, mass production did not follow mainly due to the improvement in economy and continued commercial success of the well-established model T57. Another small Tatra car was not thought necessary in the factory programme at that time.

In 1932, in parallel with the small car experiments, Ledwinka and Übelacker had started designing a large streamlined Tatra car powered by a new rear air-cooled V8 engine later designated as model T77.

Porsche commenced to develop the first Volkswagen designs in 1931-32 with type 12 for Zündapp. There are claims that one or two of his prototypes were made for Porsche by the Czech car manufacturer Wikow (Wichterle & Kovařík) based in Moravian town of Prostějov, using Tatra engines. In fact it was the Wikow factory that produced the first Czechoslovak aerodynamically styled car, Wikow 35 Kapka (Drop) in 1931 which was one of the novel designs with a fin fitted to the rear part of the body without a lid.[5] Between 1933 and 1934 Wikow also produced five prototypes of a small two-seater Wikow Baby car with

F PORSCHE'S TYPE 12 PROTOTYPE WITH REAR WATER-COOLED, FIVE-CYLINDER, RADIAL ENGINE FOR ZÜNDAPP IN 1931-32.

F PORSCHE'S TYPE 32, WITH REAR AIR-COOLED 1.47-LITRE FOUR-CYLINDER BOXER ENGINE, DESIGNED BY JOSEF KALES FOR NSU IN 1933-34.

ŠKODA 932, 1932 PEOPLE'S CAR PROTOTYPE WITH REAR AIR-COOLED ENGINE. THE COOLING COULD NOT HAVE BEEN VERY EFFICIENT, BEING PROVIDED BY AN EXPOSED AXIAL FAN PROTECTED BY A DOMED MESH SCREEN IN THE REAR BONNET. THERE WAS NO DUCTING SHROUD AS USED AND PATENTED BY TATRA.

central tubular chassis, independent suspension using transverse leaf springs and a variety of engines starting with a DKW air-cooled one-cylinder 0.35cc unit placed behind the rear axle.

Also in 1931, Daimler-Benz brought out Hans Nibel's four-seater two-door Mercedes-Benz 120 with rear four-cylinder boxer engine. Then, further rear-engined cars appeared, including the new P-Wagen project in 1933, which was later developed into the Auto-Union racing car, with an engine positioned in front of the rear axle designed by Porsche. This design was followed in 1934-35 by Nibel's concepts; going into production with the rear-engined Mercedes-Benz 130 and mid-engined Mercedes-Benz 150 Sport in the body most closely resembling that of the future Volkswagen, and in 1936 in the Mercedes-Benz 170H. Other manufacturers, such as Opel, DKW, Steyr, Hanomag, and Hansa, were trying out similar small car proposals.

In fact, Ledwinka had been experimenting with rear air-cooled engines since 1924,[6] but the necessary pressure of further developing existing Tatra models had extended this task over a number of years.

It must have been inevitable that when Porsche and Ledwinka met, which happened several times, they discussed and exchanged ideas, especially on air-cooling, engine positions and small car designs – concepts so popular at that time. It is undeniable that Ledwinka's designs, especially the successful production of T11, T12, T57 and the first Tatra rear-engined prototype, had an impact on Porsche's early VW prototypes, which had rear engines, and backbone chassis with all-independent suspension featuring transverse leaf springs at the front and swing half-axles at the rear.[7]

The fact that Tatra designs also partly influenced the subsequent Porsche prototypes, mainly the 1933-34 Type 32 for NSU, 1934 Type 60 and 1935-36 Type V3 for RDA and thus the future Volkswagen, was no secret to Porsche or Ledwinka. The remarkable similarity of their proposals prompted Ledwinka to concede frankly: "Well sometimes Porsche looked over my shoulder and sometimes I looked over his."[8]

Griffith Borgeson stated that: "... the Beetle's chief characteristics – swing axle, central-tube frame, torsion bars, opposed-cylinder air-cooled engine at the rear, and the characteristically streamlined body shape – did not originate with Porsche, nor was the general layout in which he and his many collaborators combined these features new. This is not said in order to deprive Porsche and his team of richly merited credit for having produced the basic design for one of the most notable artefacts of machine civilisation, but to give credit to some of the generally forgotten pioneers whose work served as a point of departure for that achievement."[9]

It is fair to say that, in those days, there were both open discussions and a free exchange of ideas among designers, particularly during racing trials. Consequently, automobile constructors worked simultaneously on parallel concepts and their resulting patent applications covered similar elements. A number of designers were involved in small car design such as Béla Barényi with his 1924-25 theoretical 'people's car' proposals, Karel Hrdlička of Škoda and his little-known but well advanced experimental air-cooled rear-engined Škoda 932 from 1932 and Josef Ganz and his influential 1930 Ardie, 1931 Maikäfer and 1932-33 Standard Superior cars. It is significant that Ganz was well acquainted with Tatra. After unsatisfactory experience with his secondhand Hanomag

2/10 PS Kommissbrot, in 1928 he purchased something more comfortable and reliable of which he was rather proud – a new Delta 4/12PS. At that time, he was designing his Volkswagen concepts, which were inevitably informed by his daily experiences driving the Delta.[10]

Over the last decades many heated discussions had taken place on the origin of Volkswagen, and on the merits of other designers to be included in the development of the 'people's car' proposal. However, it may be stated with confidence that without Ledwinka engaging the ducted cooling, air-cooled engines, backbone frame forked at rear[11] and independent suspension in successful practice in the early twenties and thirties the Volkswagen in its final configuration would have not been conceived.

It is well known that Hitler, who thought up and promoted the idea of the German 'people's car,' greatly admired the air-cooled Tatras. His esteem for the Tatras originated when, during his political campaigns, he was driven around in a T11 covering thousands of kilometres of trouble-free touring.[12]

JOSEF GANZ IN HIS 1928 GREY DELTA 4/12PS, FITTED WITH FOUR-WHEEL BRAKES, TYPICAL HEADLAMP BAR MOUNTING AND TRAFFICATORS, DEMONSTRATING ITS FLEXIBILITY BY REVERSING UP STEPS IN DARMSTADT, 1931. (COURTESY PAUL SCHILPEROORD, JOSEF GANZ ARCHIVES)

When Hitler attended Berlin autosalons (IAMAs) in 1933 and 1934, after visiting the German stands, he always went straight to the Tatra stand to acquaint himself personally with its latest models, asking Ledwinka to explain all the details. The designer would then be asked to return later on at night, to Kaiserhof hotel where Hitler stayed, to explain the features of his cars all over again when Hitler had more time to listen. Hitler greatly respected Ledwinka's abilities and his comment was that any new German popular car should be like the robust air-cooled Tatras.[13] "Das ist der Wagen für meine Strassen!" (This is the car for my roads!), he proclaimed. According to Erich Ledwinka, at one of these late night sessions, the two of them formulated the basic specification for the Volkswagen, which Hitler then passed on to Porsche and asked him to put it into practice. Walter Firgau wrote rather forcefully: "At that time [1921] Ledwinka constructed his 'Volkswagen' [T11] ... and in 1923 started the serial production. This car won many difficult reliability trials in Africa, Russia and Australia and won even in major speed trials. Then, by transferring the air-cooled engine to the rear

THE TANGIBLE TATRA CONNECTION WITH VOLKSWAGEN IS CLEARLY VISIBLE IN THIS 1945 VIEW OF THE SOUTHERN FRONTAGE OF THE VOLKSWAGEN FACTORY IN WOLFSBURG, SHOWING A PARKED T87 WHICH WAS OWNED BY MAJOR IVAN HIRST, WHO INITIATED POSTWAR VW PRODUCTION. (COURTESY VOLKSWAGEN AG CORPORATE HISTORY DEPARTMENT)

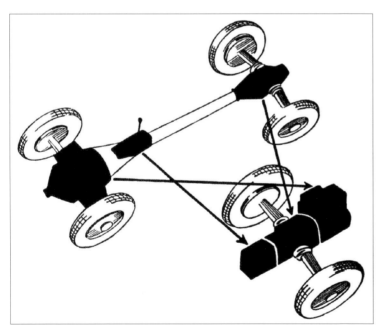

THE PRINCIPLE OF THE REAR ENGINE ASSEMBLY.

FERDINAND PORSCHE IN CONVERSATION
WITH THE FAMOUS CZECH BUGATTI RACING
DRIVER ELIŠKA JUNKOVÁ AND HANS
LEDWINKA AT MASARYK RACE CIRCUIT, BRNO,
AUGUST 25TH, 1935.

and by developing the aerodynamic body, came into being the forerunner of today's VW [T97] which Ferdinand Porsche on Hitler's orders copied for the Wolfsburg production."[14] Firgau's opinion stretched too far, but it is sure that there was mutual cross-pollination between the two designers and their staff, and that Ledwinka's ideas formed a large piece in the final Volkswagen mosaic.

In light of this, it is not surprising to learn that Tatra had several claims for patent infringements against the KdF-Wagen company (later renamed Volkswagenwerk GmbH). These included ducted forced air-cooling, engine position and gearbox layout. When Porsche was asked about these unlawful imitations he explained to Ledwinka that he acted under Hitler's orders and was told to go ahead and build cars, using whatever sources he chose – the patent problems would be determined later. By this time it was 1938, the time of the Munich Agreement of Sudetenland

takeover. The Germans were in charge at Tatra, and these infringements became academic.[15]

However, after the end of the war, Ringhoffer's heirs, through the western branch of Ringhoffer-Tatra (München-Wien) were assigned a settlement decided by the judgement of the Düsseldorf Regional Court on October 12th, 1961, although the court sustained only one of the ten claims.[16] One of the people who helped to support the Tatra case was obviously Ledwinka himself; another was an Austrian garage owner. In his garage one of the early VW prototypes had needed a wing exchanged, and while the work was being carried out he watched so closely that he could later confirm the similarity of the VW prototype's basic design, and thus support the patent suit brought by Tatra.[17]

Later VW company spokesmen Wiersch and Nickel stated that, "Many of the ideas which Ledwinka realised in the Tatra were used in similar fashion on the Volkswagen."[18]

In the end, in 1965, the large sum of money[19] that changed hands was agreed upon out of court, and by doing so VW admitted infringement.[20] Ledwinka attempted to obtain a share of this money, but could not afford an attorney, and seemed to be unable to find one to take the case on speculation. Finally, his friend Felix Wankel learned of the situation and volunteered the services of his own legal counsel. However, Ledwinka died before any results could

HANS AND ERICH LEDWINKA WITH FELIX
WANKEL. (COURTESY WERNER LEDWINKA)

be had.[21] In some sources, Oskar Pitsch, who had worked with Erich Ledwinka, is quoted confirming that Ringhoffer's heirs, after threats of further legal action by Erich, passed on to Hans Ledwinka the sum of DM80-100,000.[22]

Erich Ledwinka confirmed that the settlement was not only intended to compensate Ringhoffer-Tatra for the loss of patent licences but, despite not ending up all in Ledwinka's own pocket, was also aimed to ensure that no publicity or public acknowledgement was given to Ledwinka's great contribution to the Volkswagen legend. Porsche himself, and later on after his death, his family, were directly in contact with Ledwinka in attempts to assure themselves that the settlement money had indeed

quenched Ledwinka's desire for fame. However, Hans was a modest designer through and through, and not a greedy businessman. He kept his word. Only recently when the Volkswagen's history was being pieced together were the facts of the case slowly emerging.

After the end of the Second World War, large numbers of German speaking Tatra employees left Czechoslovakia and moved to Germany. Many of them found employment in the new Volkswagen producing factory, obviously being fully maximised for their knowledge obtained in Moravia. It was also in this roundabout way that both Ledwinka's and the Tatra factory contribution to the Volkswagen legend was further enhanced – but again hardly ever openly admitted.

NOTES

1 Jonathan Wood, 'Project Porsche: The Early Years,' *Thoroughbred & Classic Cars*, June 1983, p 87.
2 Wolfgang Schmarbeck, *Hans Ledwinka: Seine Autos – Sein Leben*, Graz: H. Weishaupt Verlag, 1997, p 119.
3 The 1931 date was confirmed by Karel Rosenkranz in an email correspondence with Ivan Margolius, April 13th, 2012, the date was originally consulted by Rosenkranz with Erich Ledwinka and Josef Veřmiřovský. The archive photograph numbers partly confirm the date, however Rosenkranz believed that the photograph evidence was not reliable as photos were not taken directly on the date every time a prototype was completed. Many archive documents were lost and removed at the Third Reich takeover of Tatra factory in 1938. This 1931 date is also confirmed by Schmarbeck, p 117 and all the other available publications on Tatra.
4 Hubert Procházka, Jan Martof, *Automobily Tatra*, Brno: CPress, 2011, p 81.
5 Very little information is available due to factory fire when documents got lost; about three prototypes were made each with different front headlamp arrangement.
6 Jonathan Wood, *VW Beetle: A Collector's Guide*, Croydon: Motor Racing Publications, 1997, p 13.
7 Ibid, p 13.
8 Schmarbeck, p 121 and Wolfgang Schmarbeck, *Tatra: Die Geschichte der Tatra Automobile*, Lübbecke: Verlag Uhle & Kleimann, 1989, p 42. See also Jonathan Wood, p 13 where it is Porsche who says: "Well, sometimes I looked over his shoulder and sometimes he looked over mine." (As used in the first edition of this book.)
9 Griffith Borgeson, 'In the Name of the People: Origins of the VW Beetle,' *Automobile Quarterly*, Fourth Quarter 1980, Volume XVIII, number 4, p 340.
10 Paul Schilperoord, *The Extraordinary Life of Josef Ganz: The Jewish Engineer Behind Hitler's Volkswagen*, New York: RVP Publishers, 2012, p 29. The Darmstadt photo is dated 1931 and is of Delta 4/12PS, contrary to the 1929 date and information published elsewhere, as confirmed to the authors by Paul Schilperoord. Also confirmed in emails from Klaus Buschbaum, Delta/Detra historian, to Ivan Margolius, 27.1. & 3.2.2015 & on 3.2.2015 by Tatra Museum archives: Ganz's car chassis no. 7277 was part of T11 chassis consignments of nos. 7078 – 7377 despatched to Delta Frankfurt between 28.2.1927 and 28.2.1928. 7277 was received in Frankfurt on 5.1.1928.
11 Tatra S A, French patent 762.657, deposited October 20th, 1933. (In Germany DE 636 633, filed on December 18th, 1932, interestingly it cannot be invoked in West Germany from July 1962). Schilperoord claims on p 248 that the forked engine mounting was described in *Motor-Kritik* in October 1932.
12 Sloniger, 'Hans Ledwinka,' p 137; Brian Palmer, 'Forgotten Genius,' *Thoroughbred & Classic Cars*, June 1983, p 14 picture caption; Jonathan Wood, p 18.
13 Sloniger, 'Hans Ledwinka,' p 137.
14 Walter Firgau, *Die Süddeutsche Zeitung*, 29.4.1965.
15 Sloniger, 'Hans Ledwinka,' p 137.
16 The only sustained claim was regarding the Tatra patent for rear engine mounting. Schilperoord, p 248.
17 Jerry Sloniger, *The VW Story*, Cambridge: Patrick Stephens, 1985, p 24.
18 Borgeson, p 361.
19 Schmarbeck, p 174 quotes DM1mil. B.P.B. De Dubé, 'The Constant Czech,' *Automobile Quarterly*, Winter 1969, Volume VII, number 3, p 315 quotes DM3mil.
20 Schmarbeck, p 174.
21 Borgeson, p 361 and De Dubé, p 315 (De Dubé's biography shows that he was Ledwinka's friend and that he had interviewed him.)
22 Marián Šuman-Hreblay, *Aerodynamické automobily*, Brno: CPress, 2013, p 62.

THE STREAMLINING ERA

The rear engine prototypes T57 and V570 served the Tatra designers as study models while they were searching for new directions in automobile construction and styling. They aimed at keeping on a level with the contemporary progress in the fields of new technology, architecture, design and the visual arts.

Paul Jaray (1889-1974), born in Vienna, of Hungarian descent, who worked for Zeppelin in Friedrichshafen, Germany, had published scientific papers since the early 1920s setting down the basic design parameters in aerodynamics. He tested streamlined automobile models in the Zeppelin wind-tunnel, and the forms which he had evolved profoundly influenced contemporary car, industrial and aircraft designers. Jaray provided scientific justification for streamlining in terms of advantages of increased speed and stability, which directly improved fuel consumption, leading to the use of smaller capacity engines, and safety. Jaray designed special streamlined bodywork for a number of manufacturers, such as Apollo, Dixi, Ley, Mercedes-Benz, Audi, Fiat and others. Tatra negotiated with Jaray to licence his patents and Jaray provided several proposals starting with his improved T57 body design from 1932.

When Ledwinka and his design team established the principle of a streamlined rear-engined car, they claimed that their intention was not to seek originality at all cost. Their ideas were based on sound engineering judgement and that the form of the automobile had to follow its function with the best possible results.

These new developments also responded to changing road conditions and the requirements of a growing

DRAWINGS FROM THE 1933 TATRA WORKS T77 PROMOTIONAL LITERATURE, ILLUSTRATING THE ADVANTAGES OF STREAMLINING, AND SHOWING THE INCREASED COMFORT WHEN PASSENGERS ARE SEATED BETWEEN AXLES.

Autobahn network. In addition, it was necessary to produce something spectacular and different which would appeal to the extensive foreign markets, most of which were within easy reach of the Central European, Moravian factory. The car required would have to be fast, silent, stable,

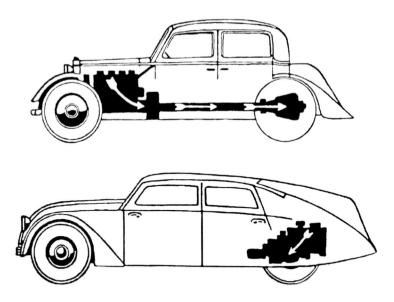

REAR-WHEEL DRIVE IS SIMPLIFIED WHEN THE
ENGINE IS POSITIONED AT THE BACK.

comfortable, hold its value, be economical and built to the most rigorous engineering standards, and also reflect modern aerodynamic research. This attitude brought a new model of Tatra car into being, and taking into account about a hundred Rumpler's Tropfen-Autos, 12 Burney-Streamlines and later 25 Crossley Burneys, it was one of the first rear-engined automobiles with a truly aerodynamic body to be serially produced in the world.

Ledwinka had continued to argue consistently in favour of rear-mounted engines and air-cooling. He claimed that the method of mounting the engine in the rear, and thus doing away with the driveshaft, would bring about a number of advantages. Firstly, there would be no efficiency loss in the universal joints of the driveshaft. Also, there would be no noise or vibrations (often caused by the driveshaft being off balance or otherwise damaged). This would eliminate the need for the floor tunnel running through the centre of the car, and inconvenience for the passengers. The rear engine position would allow the seating of the passengers to be fairly low, and well forward of the rear axle which is the steadiest and the most comfortable part of the

car. Mounting the engine in the rear would necessitate lengthening the car's tail and shortening the front end, which would automatically provide the opportunity for adopting functional streamlining. By shortening the front of the car the driver's visibility would be greatly improved. Having placed the seats low and forward, a very favourable inter-axle weight distribution would be achieved, and the stability improved. Also, the centre of gravity would be lowered, and the driving safety, especially on bends, would be greatly increased.

The rear air-cooled engine would be supplied by air led down from the roof top or high sides of the car where it would not be dust-laden, so that it could not cause quick choking of air filters and result in reduced performance, increased fuel consumption, and premature cylinder wear. The power unit would be readily accessible, easily removable and would be flexibly mounted on large silentblocs, so that neither noise nor exhaust fumes could bother passengers, while there would be no possibility of vibrations being transmitted to the bodywork. At a speed of 50kph the engine would be hardly heard inside the car. And after all, rear-mounted power units were as old as the motor car itself – both the Benz and Daimler automobiles of the 1880s, as well as the early Nesselsdorfers, possessed that layout.

The advantages of air-cooling were obvious, Ledwinka argued. Every driver knew the troubles involved in trying to prevent freezing of water which might cause the engine block or the radiator to crack, a fact even more probable in the harder winters of Central Europe. Whereas, in summer or in the tropics, especially on a long swift run, hot weather often caused the coolant to boil. Under more unfavourable conditions, all water could evaporate causing the engine to seize up or the bearings to melt. Long climbs to high altitudes could also be treacherous, as in a thin atmosphere water boils at less than 90°C and prolonged climbing at wide throttle openings could bring about considerable overheating of the engine.

These troubles would be eliminated with air-cooled engines. The high efficiency cooling fans forced an equal amount of air through the cowlings to the finned surfaces at each row of cylinders simultaneously, thus ensuring uniform and adequate cooling of the engine. Whether climbing hills in low gear or running at top speed on the flat, the cooling efficiency would increase in conformity with the engine's needs – the revolutions of the cooling fans increasing in equal ratio to the increase in engine revolutions.

In the tropics, where air temperatures often exceed 50°C, the difference between air temperature and boiling point of the coolant in a water-cooled engine is only 50°C. Whereas, air-cooled engines achieve a temperature difference of 130°C under the same conditions, ie the difference between air temperature of 50°C and the running temperature of a combustion engine, which is about 180°C. An additional advantage is that the air-cooled

engine is simpler to produce, as water channels do not have to be integrated in the engine block, and the whole unit is lighter than the water-cooled unit. (No hoses, radiator or pumps are required.)

Further points, which Ledwinka stressed as important considerations, concerned body streamlining. At high speeds, air drag increases at a rate of the square of the speed, and easily consumes the greatest part of the engine power. If the designer wanted to avoid continually increasing engine power, and thus fuel consumption, and

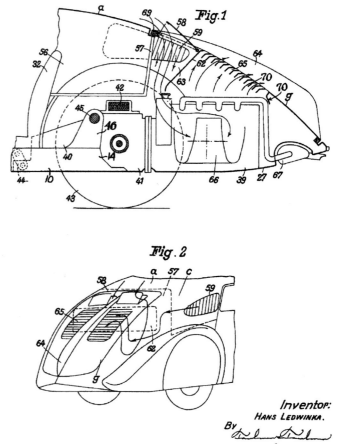

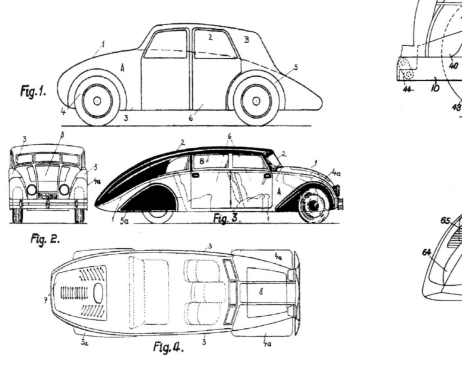

TATRA FILED FOR PATENTS IN GERMANY FOR 'IMPROVEMENTS IN OR RELATING TO AUTOMOBILES' AND FOR 'POWER VEHICLE' ON JANUARY 16TH, IN 1933, INDICATING THAT THE T77 DESIGN HAD ALREADY BEGUN IN THE LATTER PART OF 1932.

the total weight of the car, there was nothing else for it but to adopt the functionally streamlined form, which offered the least resistance within the car's speed range. The laws of aerodynamics require the front part of the car before the windscreen to be shortened, and the tail end to be lengthened, thus making it natural for the engine to be located there, and with the underside to be smooth without protrusions as the only way in which the characteristics of streamlining may be used to full advantage.[1]

It is significant that Tatra-Werke Automobil-und Waggenbau filed for a patent for 'Improvements in or relating to Automobiles' already on January 16th, 1933 in Germany (the same patent, under no. 430,353, was accepted in Great Britain on June 13th, 1935). This indicated Tatra's first streamlined car proposal with the driver in the central position and provided "an automobile body which presents a small resistance to air without unduly restricting the space inside the vehicle" with the lower portion of the wide body as seen in side elevation having substantially the shape of the cross section of an aircraft supporting plane.

This proposal overcame Jaray's tight overall drop body designs which limited the car interior size. Another patent submitted by Ledwinka for 'Connections of the Driving

Two views of the new streamlined car soon to make its bow on the American market. Note how widely it departs in appearance from the conventional present-day automobile.

JOHN TJAARDA'S "STREAMLINED REAR-ENGINE CAR DESIGNED FOR AMERICAN MARKET," 1931. (COURTESY *MODERN MECHANICS AND INNOVATIONS*, 1931)

WIKOW 35 KAPKA, 1931, DESIGNED WITHOUT JARAY PATENTS, THE CAR CAUSED A SENSATION AT THE PRAGUE AUTUMN AUTOSALON IN 1931. THE STREAMLINING WAS NOT PERFECT, WITH AN EXPOSED UNDERSIDE AND A BODY THAT WAS TOO HEAVY. THE THREE PROTOTYPES HAD VARIED HEADLAMP FENDER ARRANGEMENTS: SET FLUSH, ATTACHED INDIVIDUALLY AND IN HEADLAMP HOUSINGS FLARED FROM THE FENDERS.

Unit to the Frame of a Motor Vehicle' filed on December 17th, 1932, showed the future T77 V8 engine proposal fitted to a backbone box frame split into a fork, and a patent for 'Power Vehicle' also filed on January 16th, 1933, indicated detail design for the T77 air intakes into the rear engine compartment. This means that Ledwinka and Übelacker must have started to design the first large Tatra streamlined car and its engine already in the latter part of 1932,[2] and concurrently with the small V570 prototype. They might have been inspired and spurred on by John Tjaarda's streamlined rear engine car designs published in *Modern Mechanics and Innovations* magazine in July 1931,[3] the local appearance of the Wikow Kapka in the autumn of 1931, and by the large streamlined V12 Maybach DS8 by Spohn, shown at the 1932 Berlin autosalon. Later, the Tatra patent for its 'Internal Combustion Engine' filed on September 13th,

1933, indicated the ducted air cooling arrangement by one fan for each row of cylinders in a V8 engine.

However, it took nearly a year and a half to complete the T77 design, construction and tests for the first public display. On March 5th, 1934, in the Prague branch of Tatra Works, a press presentation was staged for one of the world's first aerodynamically styled automobiles with a rear air-cooled engine to follow into serial production. The demonstration continued on the road leading to Carlsbad, with the prototype driven by factory test driver František Chovanec. It was the T77 prototype with the shaped split-openable windscreen and registration M46.913. This car was one of the six or seven prototypes with a number of variations tried: body with protruding or flush headlamps; small or large rear fins (these helped to divide the air pressure on both sides of the car, a technique used in aircraft

TATRA T77
PROTOTYPE
DRAWING.

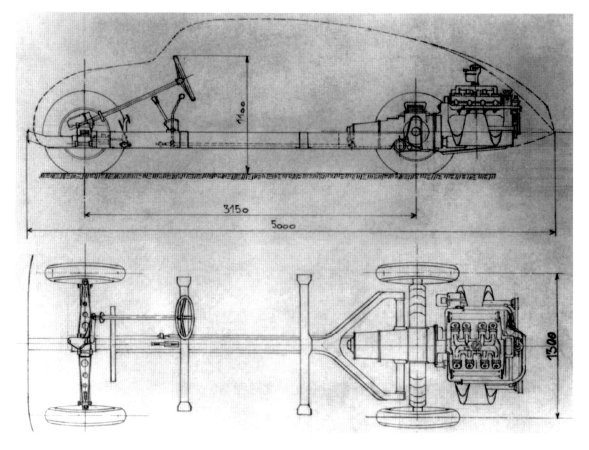

THE FIRST STREAMLINED 1933 TATRA T77 PROTOTYPE WITH POINTED SPLIT OPENABLE
WINDSCREEN, WAS DEMONSTRATED TO JOURNALISTS ON MARCH 5TH, 1934.

design); one, two or three piece windscreens; varied forms of front and rear fenders, or with a ponton body without the expressed front or rear fenders (like the postwar Tatraplan); individual roof scoops (some even glazed); and side scoops or grille air intakes. Three days later, another T77 prototype, this time with the three-piece windscreen, centre steering and registration M46.941, was introduced for the first time to the general public in Berlin. The press noted: "At the Berlin Internationale Automobil-und Motorrad-Ausstellung which opened on March 8th, 1934 ... [the] Tatra stand was constantly besieged, engineer Ledwinka gave information tirelessly and regretted only that he had no demonstration models. The Tatra T77 was the only large automobile with a rear engine, the only such in almost ideal streamlined form, and a similarly built but smaller Mercedes [130] cannot be at all compared with the Tatra."[4] A month later, in April, two T77 prototypes were displayed at the Prague autosalon,[5] and in October 1934, at the Salon de l'Automobile de Paris,

T77 2.9-LITRE V8 ENGINE/GEARBOX
MONOBLOCK PROTOTYPE.

T77 PROTOTYPE WITH CENTRAL
STEERING, THREE PART WINDSCREEN,
AND PRESENTATION V8 2.9-LITRE ENGINE
MONOBLOCK, AT THE 1934 BERLIN
IAMA, MARCH 8-18TH. (COURTESY PAUL
SCHILPEROORD, JOSEF GANZ ARCHIVES)

the more definitive pre-production T77 model with the three-piece windscreen with curved splayed side panels, LHD, wide-body roof air intake scoops, large rear fin and registration M47.318 was exhibited.[6]

This car with its overall futuristic concept overtook the general contemporary state of the world motor car industry by several decades. It is true there were one off exceptions such as: Rumpler's Tropfen-Auto with Siemens & Halske 2580cc W6 engine, which appeared in 1921; Burney Streamline using Beverley Barnes 2956cc straight-eight engine in 1930; the previously mentioned very advanced and influential John Tjaarda's 1931 mid-rear-engined Sterkenburg proposal for GM, as well as the later 1933 Briggs/Tjaarda 'Dream Car;' the 1932 Scarab with rear Ford V8 engine designed by William B Stout; the front-engined Chrysler Airflow, styled by Carl Breer and James Zeder, and built between 1934 and 1937. The T77 was aerodynamically more efficient by meticulously following, with truly scientific precision, all the Jaray principles. The streamlined Tatras became a long-term commercial success unlike the Rumpler and Burney which failed to sell in large numbers. Thus, most significantly, as opposed to the other mainly singular experiments, Tatra towers above all by establishing a continued string of successful streamlined models produced for 40 years right up to 1975 with over 30,000 units made.

In July 1934 Paul Jaray submitted his own design for a streamlined Tatra with his typical curved windscreen, which might have also been intended as a proposal for the next generation of Tatra models, and which Übelacker and his team used to confirm their own Tatra design, as the T77 construction had started already a year before on May 19th, 1933, under the prototype number V578.[7]

The new four to six-seater Tatra T77 was hailed by the press as the outstanding exhibit of the 1934 Berlin IAMA Motor Show. The T77 was a new technical achievement typical of the Tatra factory. As the T11 had done before it, this car also broke all the accepted conventions. It introduced several innovative ideas apart from its original exterior body shape. Ledwinka and Übelacker had replaced

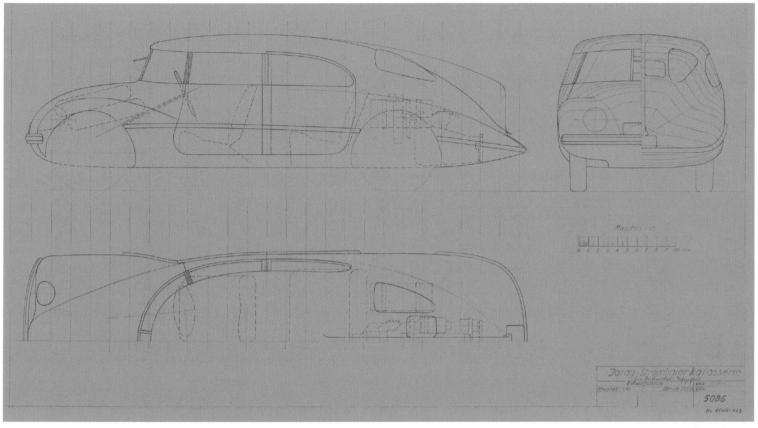

PAUL JARAY'S PROPOSAL FOR THE TATRA STREAMLINED BODY WITH THE ENGINE ON TOP
OF THE REAR AXLE, AND WITHOUT THE REAR BULKHEAD LUGGAGE COMPARTMENT, DATED
JULY 27ᵀᴴ 1934. (COURTESY ETH-BIBLIOTHEK, HOCHSCHULARCHIV, HS 1144: 173. PAUL JARAY,
STROMLINIENKAROSSERIE FÜR HECKMOTOR-FAHRGESTELL, JULY 27ᵀᴴ 1934.)

WOODEN MODEL OF A TATRA BASED ON
JARAY'S DRAWING.

the usual central tubular chassis with a welded box-type frame, forked at the back to enclose the engine. The whole unit was a large monoblock bolted together: the engine with the gearbox and the axle drive. This monoblock could be easily removed from the chassis for repair and changing parts. Gear change rods, cables and fuel lines ran down the central box frame, while the battery, 18-gallon petrol tank and two spare wheels, as well as hand luggage, were carried in the nose. The main boot space was found above the rear suspension behind the rear seats; all passengers and the driver sat between the axles, in the most comfortable position. In some units the driver was positioned centrally

in the front seat with passengers sitting on each side. Passengers riding in the front enjoyed a divided seat with an armrest in the middle for the LHD or RHD options. Each half of the front seat was equipped with a separate reclining mechanism. In the rear, a larger armrest could be pulled down to divide the seat.

The aerodynamic shell was, in fact, one of the world's first all-enveloping streamlined bodies, based on a concept of self-supporting, part-steel, semi-monocoque structure on timber frame. The T77's body was among the first designs whereby the rear fenders became an integral part of the body, though in some of the prototypes they were still bolted to the rest of the coachwork.

The detailing of the bodywork was meticulous. The front windscreen was angled at 45 degrees to achieve the least air resistance; some prototypes and units had one-, two- or three-piece windscreens, and even rounded corner panes. Running boards were dispensed with for the first time. Importantly, the underbody was sheathed to create a smooth plane without protrusions, and the large stabilising fin at the rear, which became a Tatra trademark, incorporated a rear stop light and number plate illumination. T77s usually had only two

ABOVE AND OPPOSITE: ARTWORK FROM ONE
OF THE FIRST T77 BROCHURES.

THE COVER OF VERY RARE T77 BROCHURE
PUBLISHED FOR THE 1934 BERLIN IAMA,
THE TEXT IS CREDITED TO PAUL EHRHARDT.
(COURTESY JAN TULIS)

headlamps inserted into the frontal compartment, and all door hinges and handles were flared or set into the body. The T77's wheelbase was 3150 or 3250mm long, and because of its aerodynamic form the fuel consumption was low, 14-16 litres per 100km. It reached a maximum speed of 150kph.

The air-cooled 2.9-litre, OHC, V8 engine, 75mm x 84mm stroke, located behind the rear axles, was remarkably compact, and had a 60bhp output at 3500rpm. Two banks of four finned cylinders were set at an angle of 90 degrees. Each row of four cylinders had a separate air blower which was powered by a V-belt directly from the crankshaft. The crankshaft was placed in three friction bearings, and was made of silumin. The cylinders were surrounded as a whole by a jacket, which was open on one side to the entry of cooling air delivered under pressure from sirocco fans, and at the other to permit the exit of the heated air after it had done its work.

In the cowling which covered the engine unit, in effect the rear car bonnet, there were top air intakes facing forward into the airstream through which cool air was admitted to the pump and fan casing. The fuel mixture was prepared by the Zenith dual downdraught carburettor. In conjunction with the carburettor, there was a hinged metal hood or slide which had three positions that could be regulated so as to control the admission of the air to the intake. It was possible to arrange that either fresh cold air entered the carburettor after coming into the engine compartment, or that the carburettor be shut off entirely as regards the external atmosphere, and receive only heated air rising from the cylinders.

The engine monoblock, connected to the axle drive by way of a single plate clutch, powered a special steel spring shaft. Helically toothed pinions in constant mesh were employed in the four-speed gearbox for second, third and direct top gear, the transmission had third and fourth synchronised gears. Lubrication of the engine was provided by a dry sump system; oil was held in a reservoir on the offside of the crankcase, and passed in its circuit under pressure through the engine into radiators exposed to the cool airstream. The construction of the rear swing half-axles, with the transverse cross leaf spring over them, typically followed Ledwinka's established concept. The welded box type frame had side brackets which carried the body. At the front there was an independent suspension which consisted of one cross leaf spring with two trapezoidal slide bearings placed below, and hydraulic shock absorbers. Bosch electrical equipment was used. A clever 'one-shot' lubricating system was built into the T77, it was foot-operated from the driver's seat and, by a single

TATRA DESIGN OFFICE WITH SEVERAL T77 MODELS INDICATING THE SEARCH FOR THE PERFECT STREAMLINED BODY FORM, ALL OF WHICH WHICH SEEM TO HAVE BEEN TESTED AS ACTUAL T77 PROTOTYPES.

TATRA T77 WOODEN FRAME BODY STRUCTURE.

ANOTHER 1934 T77 PROTOTYPE WITH FLUSH HEADLAMPS AND ONE-PART WINDSCREEN.

1934 TATRA T77 PROTOTYPE WITH ROOF AND SIDE AIR SCOOPS, WEBASTO ROOF, AND FRONT HEADLAMPS SET INTO THE BONNET.

SPACIOUS AND LUXURIOUS INTERIOR OF THE SAME PROTOTYPE.

ARMY OFFICERS FROM AUTOZBROJOVKA, PŘELOUČ, JULY 3RD, 1934, TAKING DELIVERY OF A REMARKABLE T77 PONTON BODY PROTOTYPE WITHOUT THE USUALLY EXPRESSED FRONT OR REAR FENDERS, WITH CENTRAL STEERING, ONE PART WINDSCREEN, PROTRUDING HEADLAMPS, LARGER REAR FIN, SIDE AND ROOF AIR SCOOPS.
(COURTESY GARY CULLEN)

TATRA T77 PROTOTYPE AND THE SPECTACULAR SPECIAL 1934 PRAGA SUPER PICCOLO (THREE OF THESE WERE BUILT FOR THIS RACE) AT THE START OF THE 1000 MILES RACE IN FRONT OF THE PRAGUE AUTOKLUB.
(COURTESY *MOTOR REVUE*, JULY 5TH, 1934)

ANOTHER T77 PROTOTYPE BEING TESTED ON THE FAMOUS GROSSGLOCKNER ALPINE ROAD IN THE AUSTRIAN ALPS.

TATRA T77 PROTOTYPE PARTICIPATING IN THE CZECHOSLOVAK 1000 MILES RACE, 1934 DRIVEN BY FRANTIŠEK CHOVANEC AND J HOLUB. IT SUSTAINED DAMAGE BY HITTING SEVERAL BOLLARDS, GAINED FOURTH PLACE IN THE OVER 2000CC CLASS WITH 16:29:28 TIME, AVERAGE SPEED OF 96.6KM, AND RECEIVED A SECOND PLACE IN THE SALOON BODIED CARS CLASS (THE WINNING CAR WAS AN OPEN-BODIED WALTER WITH THE TIME OF 15:22:37.)

ABOVE AND LEFT: RECENTLY RENOVATED 1936 TATRA T77 WITH 3.4-LITRE V8 ENGINE. THIS CAR WON THE 2014 PEBBLE BEACH CONCOURS D'ELEGANCE STREAMLINED TATRA CLASS. (COURTESY DALIBOR LUPÍK)

THE T77 ENGINE UNIT WAS ACCESSIBLE AND EASILY DISMOUNTABLE FROM THE CAR BODY FOR MAINTENANCE, ALWAYS A DESIGN PRIORITY INSISTED ON BY LEDWINKA.

DETAILS OF THE FRONT WINDSCREEN OF THE T77 PRE-PRODUCTION UNIT WITH A SMALL ADJUSTABLE OPENING PANE TO CREATE DRAUGHT-FREE INTERIOR VENTILATION, AND WIPERS SET INTO THE GLASS AS SHOWN AT THE 1934 PARIS AUTOSALON.

TWO-TONE VERSION OF THE T77.

compression of the pedal, all major points were reliably lubricated. This eased the servicing and reduced the wear of the parts.

106 units of the T77 were made. In 1936 an improved version of the T77 appeared and was named the model T77a. There were several main changes to the previous model: the air-cooled V8 engine size was increased to 3.4 litres by enlarging the cylinder bore diameter to 80mm; the output now reached 70bhp with a maximum speed of 150kph; there were three headlamps at the front, and some models had the central lamp geared to the steering, which enabled the lamp to turn together with the front wheels.

The Tatra T77a achieved excellent performances thanks to its good driving characteristics; 167 of the cars were manufactured up to 1939. In each series of the T77 and T77a, individual cars differed in small body details such as the position or mounting arrangements of the front headlamps and the position of the roof and side air scoops. These modifications were done in search of the best solution to the overall concept, and for the car to attain perfect aerodynamic qualities. Canvas Webasto

manufacturing label inside the engine compartment stated the type as T77a. Drag coefficient of the T77 1:5 model was tested in the Military and Aircraft Research Institute Letňany tunnel, obtaining an average reading of 0.245.[8] The T77a has not been tested to date.[9] In 1935 the T77 with the 2.9-litre engine was offered for 98,000Kč, and 101,000Kč for the same model supplied with the 3.4-litre engine.[10]

The firm Stoewer negotiated with Tatra to manufacture the T77a under licence after thorough and successful testing. Only its eventual unfavourable financial situation prevented the realisation of this plan.

Ing Übelacker, who was mainly responsible for the T77 concept, had previously been toiling with a project involving a new engine development for the future series of the model T57. This work did not progress well and he was threatened with dismissal. Then suddenly, he surprised everybody by suggesting a design for a new car with aerodynamic bodywork.[11] Übelacker believed that his lucky number was seven, so all the models he worked on had a seven as the last digit of the type number (T57, T77, T77a, T87, T97).

ABOVE: 1934 ORIGINAL PHOTOGRAPH OF T77 COMPARED WITH A 2014 T77 IMAGE, HRADČANSKÉ NÁMĚSTÍ, PRAGUE. (COURTESY PAVEL KASÍK, KAREL THÉR, DALIBOR LUPÍK)

1937 TATRA T77A AT TATRA REGISTER UK STAND AT 2010 NEC CLASSIC MOTOR SHOW WHERE IT GAINED THE 'CAR OF THE SHOW' AWARD.

roofs were installed to order both in the T77 and T77a. Some later production T77s had the larger 3.4-litre engine installed, still retaining the two headlamps only, but their

FRONT COVER OF THE T77A BROCHURE.

T77A ARTWORK.

When the T77 arrived in 1934, it embodied the first practical production of this unusual and seemingly promising construction concept. Tatra's realisation of the aerodynamic car body pointed towards a technological breakthrough, and generally helped to prepare the ground for a totally new direction in automobile construction. This concept carried on up to the early 1960s when many manufacturers had at least one type of rear-engined model,

Tucker 48 (inspired by Tatra[12]), Renault 4CV, 8, 10, Dauphine, Alpine A110 with central tubular chassis, Fiat 500, 600, Simca 1000, Rootes' Hillman Imp, NSU Prinz, Chevrolet's Corvair, Porsche 356, 911, etc. Subsequently, this hopeful design concept was to become unpopular, and has later only been used occasionally in passenger car construction (Renault GTA, Škoda 110, etc).

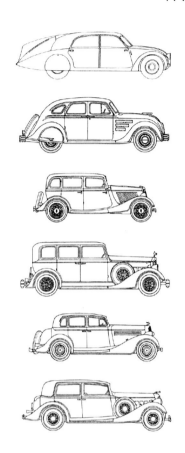

who studied aerodynamic phenomena and published his conclusions in *Horizons* in 1932, together with some relevant designs. His deductions were based on the belief that "speed is the cry of our era, and greater speed is the goal of tomorrow." Other important designers who were involved in the development of this dynamic style were Henry Dreyfuss, Walter Dorwin Teague and Raymond Loewy.

The development of an aerodynamic shape actually brought car design onto the same level of modernity as the other arts and manufacturing fields of the epoch, such as graphics, applied art, design and architecture. To this end, it was no coincidence that several famous architects and designers became involved in automobile design.[13] They mostly supported the trend based on streamlining principles. The Swiss architect Le Corbusier co-operated with Citroën on its car body proposals and designed an interesting small car, the Voiture Minimum (1935-36). In his well-known book, *Vers une architecture*, published in 1923, which included previously printed articles in *L'Esprit Nouveau* magazine, Le Corbusier even devoted one chapter to automobile design. The German architect Walter Gropius, founder and first director of the Bauhaus movement, extensively designed for Adler in the early thirties. He created, for example, the elegant eagle emblem fixed on the Adler radiators. The American architect, Buckminster Fuller, proudly displayed his innovative three-wheel Dymaxion car prototype 3 at Chicago World's Fair in 1934, and Frank Lloyd Wright suggested a number of new ideas and improvements to existing automobile designs such as the Lincoln Continental. The Czech architect Lubomír Šlapeta designed a body version for the Tatra T57. The streamlined body and interiors for the Slovak Arrow railcar were proposed by architect Vladimír Grégr. It was this inter-relationship between design disciplines, epitomised by the architects' involvement, that succeeded in establishing principles of car design which, from then on, truly sought to reflect contemporary tastes and fashion.

Ledwinka and the Tatra engineers succeeded where Rumpler had failed 13 years earlier with his Tropfen-Auto. Rumpler could not achieve his aims fully because the time had not been right; car design and construction had not progressed far enough to market unusually constructed vehicles to the general public. When Tatra came up with the T77 in the early thirties, the idea of a rear-engine aerodynamic car was new, but no longer shockingly grotesque.

The awakening of the streamlining fashion in the early thirties did not only appear due to practical and functional considerations. It also became the embodiment of contemporary cultural and artistic trends. Streamlining was not only synonymous with dynamism and modernism, but it also gave rise to a 'style.' This trend was popularised by the visionary American designer Norman Bel Geddes,

Even manufacturers of everyday objects, such as staplers, pencil sharpeners, smoking pipes, telephones,

PRIMROSE 6877.

122A, HIGH STREET,
ST JOHN'S WOOD, N.W.

29th October, 1935.

Messrs Tatra Works, Ltd,
Kartouzska 3,
Prague-Smichov,
CZECHO-SLOVAKIA.

Dear Sirs,

Re Tatra 77.

When this car was "run in" and had covered about 10,000 kilometres, I had a good opportunity of trying it for maximum speed and on the main Coventry road, with driver and two passengers, the speed of 95 m.p.h. was obtained. The gradient of the road was slightly favourable.

Points that strike me and my friends about the car are:-

First class road-holding without anxiety.

Excellent suspension and wonderfully light and untiring steering control at all speeds.

PRIMROSE 6877.

122A, HIGH STREET,
ST JOHN'S WOOD, N.W.

-2-

The wide field of vision makes fast driving safer.

The excellent braking.

The petrol consumption, considering the performance, is abnormally light.

The increased loading space is a great advantage.

There is no doubt that you have provided a solution of the owner driver's Reisewagen de luxe for general world use that is years ahead of any similar product.

Yours faithfully,

Douglas Fitzmaurice

CAPTAIN DOUGLAS FITZMAURICE'S T77 APPRECIATION LETTER OF OCTOBER 1935. HE OWNED A T77, UK REGISTRATION BUC 319.

electric irons, vacuum cleaners, electric heaters, wireless cabinets and clocks, commissioned designers to apply streamlining principles to the design of their products. Rail locomotives, motorcycles, scooters, coaches and steamships were also aerodynamically formed. A E Palmer designed streamlined car bodies for Sir Charles Dennistoun Burney, and more and more car and motorcycle producers and coachworks began to explore the new forms: Zündapp, NSU, Mercedes-Benz, BMW, Maybach, Peugeot, Voisin, Sodomka, Erdmann & Rossi, and many others.

From 1931 onwards, other manufacturers in Czechoslovakia experimented with aerodynamic bodies and very advanced designs followed from the likes of Wikow, Škoda, Praga, Zbrojovka and Jawa, including special sports cars for the 1933, 1934 and 1935 1000 mile races held between Prague, Brno and Bratislava. It was now obvious that aerodynamic forms were not only starting to affect automobile and industrial design but, most importantly, were beginning to be exploited in aircraft design as well, starting with the Boeing 247 and Douglas DC1 in 1933.

Ledwinka was aware of the great importance of keeping the external look of his products on the same advanced level as their technical elements. It was always

Bez kouře a bez komínu,
na půl auto, na půl vlak,
jako střela krajem letí
tmavorudý motorák

přes sedm řek, sedm vrchů,
od Vltavy k Dunaji.
Kola tlukou na bubínek,
kolejnice zpívají.

TATRA M290 SLOVAK ARROW RAILCAR
ILLUSTRATION USED IN A 1946 CHILDREN'S
BOOK: JOSEF HONS & ZDENKA VALENTOVÁ,
SVEZTE SE S NÁMI, OSTRAVA-PRAHA:
JOSEF LUKASÍK.

BOTH ABOVE: ONE OF SLOVAK ARROW'S
POWERED FOUR WHEEL AXLE BOGIES AND
THE LUXURIOUS INTERIOR.

Ledwinka's goal to achieve in his designs a perfect synthesis of contemporary aesthetics with up-to-date technology. Therefore, the public was offered Tatra automobiles with clean, functional, rational lines, which were pleasing to the eye and fully complemented modern houses, as well as all the other modern objects being designed and manufactured at that time. Ledwinka and Tatra management consciously employed the best commercial designers of the day to produce their advertising materials, posters and brochures. Most of the 1930s designs were crafted by the avant-garde graphic artist and architect Petr Flenyko (1900-61) of AUR Studio, and by KBZ.[14] Later the

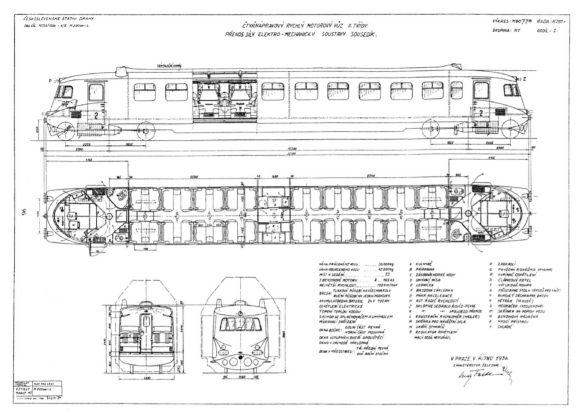

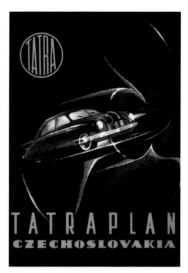

FRANTIŠEK KARDAUS'
ARTWORK FOR THE
T600 TATRAPLAN.

1936 DRAWING OF SLOVAK ARROW SHOWING THE OVERALL LAYOUT
AND THE DRIVERS' CABINS, SEATING AND CENTRAL KITCHEN.

renowned designer František Kardaus (1908-86) of graphic design Studio BaR (Josef Burjanek a Remo) was involved, including proposals for actual car body designs. Recently it came to light that the world-famous photographer Josef Sudek (1896-1976) took photographs for one of the early T77 brochures.[15]

In the UK, the T77, called by the British press "a design of great interest embodying in principle the ideals of many designers,"[16] was offered by Captain Fitzmaurice as model Tatra 20/60, and priced at £990 (£1250 in 1948). The car was distributed in London and the Home Counties by Airstream Ltd of Davies Street, London W1. Fitzmaurice campaigned his own T77, registration BUC 319, in the 1935 Brighton Councours d'Elegance. However, the

cost of the Tatra car and its advanced futuristic look was, unfortunately, too much for the conservative British public and very few were seen on the roads in the UK. It is known that, in 1936, Morris Commercial of Birmingham bought a T77a (registration COE 858) that remained in the UK until the 1970s, and which is now restored and on display in Southward Car Museum in New Zealand.[17] Nevertheless, the Tatra T77 was perceived to be so forward-looking that it was chosen to star in a 1935, British-made, science-fiction film, *Transatlantic Tunnel,* about the building of a tunnel between England and America.

In the 1980s, an amusing story appeared in the British press concerning a T77. Two English friends obtained a crumpled 1934 model from a diplomat, who had brought

1936 TATRA T77A AT SOUTHWARD CAR MUSEUM, NEW ZEALAND. ORIGINALLY REGISTERED IN THE UK BY MORRIS COMMERCIAL OF BIRMINGHAM. (COURTESY GARY CULLEN)

the car from Prague to London in the late thirties. They decided to shorten the car because of the damaged back, and impressed by the air-cooled V8 motor, they went about the job of transforming the car into a centrally-engined sportster. They turned the engine around, positioning it in the space where the rear seat used to be, rerouted the gear linkage and reconnected the electrics. A special new engine cover was made and the whole 'new Tatra' repainted flaming red. Finally, the day came for the car to be taken out and tested. To great cheers, the noisy beast was brought to life, first gear was selected and the clutch popped. The 'Tatra' hurtled backwards crushing everything in its path and totally demolishing the car in the process. In turning the engine around, the two enthusiastic car builders had constructed a 'Tatra' which had four reverse gears and one forward one!

NOTES

1   Julian Edgar, 'Modifying Under-Car Airflow, part 1', 9.3.2005, quoting Dr Simone Sebben of Volvo (SAE paper 2004-01-1307) http://www.autospeed.com/cms/article.html?&A=2455: air drag created: by the front/radiator of the car: 32%, rest of the body: 33%, car underside: 35%.
2   1932 date is also confirmed in *Tatra, podnikový zpravodaj*, no. 10, 1947, p 1.
3   Fawcett's *Modern Mechanics and Inventions*, July 1931, pp 180-181.
4   *Československý Motorista*, 24.3.1934, p 76.
5   Email from Pavel Kasík to Ivan Margolius, 25.4.2015.
6   Tatra used factory registration plates, the same ones being reused on a number of different cars, therefore caution has to be exercised ascertaining individual models by registration plates only.
7   Rosenkranz, p 81.
8   Bohumír Mimra, 'Vývojové směry moderního automobilismu', SIA 1936, Technická práce na Ostravsku 1926-1936, Moravská Ostrava 1936, p 593.
9   The figure of drag coefficient 0.212 circulating in the media for the T77a, in fact relates to the T87 and possibly refers to a 1:5 or 1:10 model test, not of the real car, see Jerrold Sloniger, 'Hans Ledwinka' in Ronald Barker & Anthony Harding, *Automobile Design: Twelve Great Designers and Their Work*, (first edition 1970), Warrendale: Society of Automotive Engineers, 1992, second edition, p 136, and 'Leben und Werk des Automobilpioniers Dr. tech. h.c. Hans Ledwinka', as spoken by Erich Ledwinka at Akademischen Feier der Technischen Universität Wien on May 19th, 1978, published in *Blätter für Technikgeschichte* 39./40. Heft, Springer Verlag, Wien 1980, p 151. The best Tatra car drag coefficient figure of 0.32 belongs to the Tatraplan measured on a real car.
10 'XXV. Jubilejní autovýstava,' *Auto*, no. 13, volume XVII, 1.11.1935, p 290.
11 Rosenkranz, p 84.
12 Phil Egan, who worked for Tucker, confirmed that Preston Tucker had been heavily influenced by seeing a Tatra in Europe during the war. Email from Gary Cullen to Ivan Margolius, 31.12.2014.
13 Ivan Margolius, *Automobiles by Architects*, Chichester: Wiley-Academy, 2000.
14 Despite extensive research no details about KBZ were possible to obtain.
15 *Novojičínský deník*, 26.10.2014
16 *The Autocar*, 15.2.1935.
17 T77 Register, www.tatraworld.nl, according to the present register there are only 19 known T77 and T77a left in the world, most of them in the Czech Republic.

THE ULTIMATE TATRA
ACHIEVEMENT

TATRA T87'S STREAMLINED SLIPPERY BODY FORM ALSO EMPHASISING THE IMPORTANCE OF A SMOOTH UNDERSIDE.

In 1936 the most famous of all Tatra's models, and Ledwinka's favourite creation, the T87 (prototype number V717), left the Kopřivnice factory. Again, fairly fundamental changes were made, to make this car quite different. It was to be an improvement on the T77 and T77a's rather heavy rear which did not give altogether satisfactory handling when combined with the high roll centre induced by the swing axle's arrangement.

The shortened aerodynamic body was now totally self-supporting, and fully integral with the welded box frame. The body formed a large steel girder, enveloping the interior compartment and all essential units of the car, increasing the safety of passengers. This monocoque body had a greater resistance to distortion than the conventional design, and was fairly light in weight. In the door construction tension cables were used to stretch the door skins. The chassis backbone was again formed by an all-steel rectangular girder which was forked in the rear and welded to the bodywork to form one unit. The engine, with the gearbox and the rear axle centre housing, was mounted in the rear fork on three silentblocs which isolated the power unit from the bodywork. This arrangement eliminated the transmission of noise and any possible vibration, and also made the engine removal simple.

The overall form of the bodywork, in contrast to the rather stiff appearance of the T77, was very graceful. The air scoops appeared on either side of the car body behind the rear doors. As adopted from the previous model series, the windscreen consisted of one large

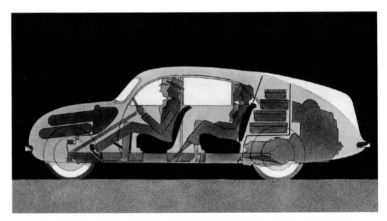

TATRA T87 INTERIOR VIEW INDICATING SPACE USAGE.

flat glass sheet with one small glass panel on each side, giving good outward vision – shaped safety glass was not available in those days. However, the rear view through the ventilation louvres tilted horizontally in the back lid, which remained, was very restricted. The overall image of the T87 appeared imposing, with its smooth flowing horizontal lines along the length of the body, and surfaces ending at the rear in the beautifully formed back with the usual large stabilising vertical fin, which in some early units included the stop light and number plate illumination.

Despite the reduction of the wheelbase, the interior of the car was spacious and comfortable and was thoughtfully designed. The front seats could recline to form two couchettes. The back seat rest could be hinged down for access to the rear boot space behind. The wide doors, which were hung on the set-in central pillar, made entry and exit easy, however, the doors had protruding hinges and rather spoiled the smooth body skin. The interior of the car was well soundproofed by the rear luggage compartment bulkhead, and engine noise was hardly noticeable; the noise of the wind and air currents caused by the moving car was louder.

Ledwinka's aim was to make this model less heavy; therefore the T87 had a magnesium alloy, air-cooled 2.97-litre, V8, OHC engine, which resulted in an overall 24 per cent saving in weight (430kg) over the model T77a. Both camshafts, each one over four-cylinder heads, were driven by duplex-chains, with each row of four, individually cast, finned cylinders cooled by one fan. The engine had a built-in oil cooler and oil filter, the transmission had third and fourth synchronised gears, and the fuel was mixed by means of the Zenith Stromberg or Solex dual downdraught carburettor. The engine had a compression ratio of 5.6:1,

THE REAR ENGINE ASSEMBLY OF THE T87, 1936.

each cylinder size was 75 x 84mm and the output 75bhp at 3500rpm. Again the 'one-shot' lubricating system was built into the T87.

The car gave a very smooth ride and good road holding, at least at medium speeds, which was achieved

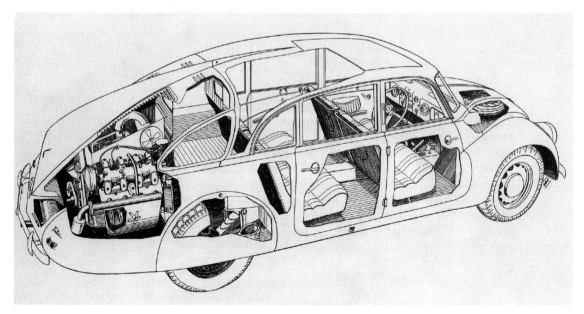

SCHEMATIC CUTAWAY DRAWING OF THE T87.

T87 BACKBONE BOX-FRAME CHASSIS.

by the sensible weight distribution between the front and rear axles. However, the front was still on the light side, even with the two spare wheels and battery stored there. Approximately 37 per cent of the car's overall weight, which was 1370kg, was on the front axle and about 63 per cent on the rear axle.[1] This state of balance was hardly affected by the additional weight of two, four or six occupants.

This Tatra, with its maximum speed of 160kph, was one of the fastest serially manufactured cars of that time with excellent acceleration – the third gear could reach 120kph – light, easily handled steering and low fuel consumption of 12.5 litres per 100km. All these factors, married with the car's appearance made the Tatra substantially different from other contemporary cars, and for that this car was greatly valued. The T87 sold in Germany for RM8450 and at this price it belonged to the luxury end of the market. 3102 units were made by 1950. Subsequently between 1950 and 1953 about 14 units of T87 were made with T603 2.5-litre engines with smaller fins, enlarged rear lids and glass rear view panes.

The owner of such a car had to get used to its rear-engine driving characteristics which were rather different from that of a front-engined car. However, once the drivers became familiar with the Tatra, they were rewarded with

the wonderful excitement and satisfaction of overtaking most other cars on the roads of Europe.

In all aspects this was a highly original automobile of a new construction, and, as such, deeply impressed the public as well as the engineering world, in particular the Germans. Even after 80 years since its conception, people are still astonished at the beauty of the car, having seen it displayed at exhibitions, design museums or even art galleries as in the 2006 Victoria & Albert Museum show on 'Modernism,' and on permanent display at Minneapolis Institute of Arts, as well as having read about it in many recent articles in the world media.

The smaller T97 (prototype number V777), built concurrently with the T87 using many same body components, had a magnesium alloy, air-cooled 1.75-litre, horizontally opposed, four-cylinder engine with 40bhp output and a maximum speed of 130kph. Again the wheelbase was shortened to 2600mm to decrease weight and make the car cheaper and more compact. The windscreen glass was in one flat piece. This model, similar

T87 WITH THE FRONT BONNET OPEN.

to the T77, had only two headlamps, using the T87 parts, placed on the wheel fenders, as opposed to the T77a's and T87's standard three lamps, and in some units as well as in some T87s, these were attached rather than being seamless. Two prototypes were made without the vertical rear fin, one with a triangular split rear window and one with a square split window, which was exhibited at the Geneva XV Salon international de l'automobile, February 11th to 20th, 1938; however, the serial production of the following 509 units had the fins incorporated. One or two units also had three headlamps installed using the T87 bonnet, which were interchangeable.

Later, in 1939, Übelacker left Tatra for Steyr, subsequently for Daimler-Benz and Borgward, after disagreements with the director of the Tatra research and design car engineering division, Ing Alfred Nitsch. Following his departure, Erich Ledwinka replaced Übelacker in the role of the chief Tatra car designer in 1940.

The T87 achieved further distinction, albeit under unfortunate circumstances, among the world's automobiles during the Second World War. After the Munich agreement, signed on September 30th, 1938, the Germans took over the Tatra company on October 10th, 1938. Kopřivnice was

ATTRACTIVE BIRD'S EYE VIEW OF THE T87.

T87S HARMONISED WITH 1930S MODERN ART, ARCHITECTURE AND DESIGN. EVEN IN 2006, A 1938 T87 WAS DISPLAYED AS THE SYMBOL OF MODERN MOVEMENT DESIGN AT THE 'MODERNISM' EXHIBITION AT VICTORIA & ALBERT MUSEUM IN LONDON, AND A 1948 T87 IS ON PERMANENT DISPLAY AT THE MINNEAPOLIS INSTITUTE OF ARTS.

THE FIRST T97 PROTOTYPE WITHOUT THE REAR FIN IN 1936.

T97 CHASSIS.

THE SECOND T97 FINLESS PROTOTYPE ON THE TATRA STAND AT THE 1938 GENEVA AUTOSALON. AFTER THE 1939 IAMA IN BERLIN THE POSSIBLE LARGE MASS PRODUCTION OF THIS MODEL WAS PREVENTED BY THE GERMANS BECAUSE OF ITS CHALLENGE TO OTHER GERMAN MADE CARS; BY THEN THE FACTORY WAS OCCUPIED.

included in the Sudetenland more by design than chance; the new border ran along the fence of the Tatra factory. According to the evidence of Oskar Pitsch, within ten hours of factory occupation, a group of Third Reich Ministry of Industry officials had arrived and confiscated many important Tatra production documents and drawings, later some ending in the archives of Dr Ing h.c. F Porsche KG, Stuttgart.[2] At that time the factory had over 5200 employees, a quarter of them still residing in the area that remained of the curtailed Czechoslovak Republic. Tatra was ordered

1938 TATRA T97 WITH A STOP LAMP IN THE FIN. (COURTESY IAN TISDALE)

FRONT COVER OF A T97 BROCHURE.

by Hermann Göring to stop all production of vehicles, all its patents were confiscated, and the company was only allowed to manufacture spare parts. Ledwinka believed this order had been prompted by pressure from the main German motoring manufacturers, who feared the great success of the Tatra products, particularly the T87. However, later when the rest of the Czech lands became totally occupied and renamed Protektorat Böhmen und Mähren (Slovakia became an independent fascist state), Tatra, now under full German dictatorship, was permitted to continue

E ÜBELACKER IN 1935, TESTING THE SPECIAL T77A COUPÉ FITTED WITH A T87 ENGINE.

E ÜBELACKER WITH FRITZ HATTESOHL DRIVING THE 1955 TRAUMWAGEN WHICH ÜBELACKER DESIGNED FOR BORGWARD.

SPECIAL T87 CABRIOLET WITH NOTEK LAMP. TWO WERE ORDERED BY THE WEHRMACHT AND MANUFACTURED IN 1940. THE COACHWORK WAS PROBABLY MADE AT BOHEMIA COACHWORKS, WHICH WAS OWNED BY RINGHOFFER-TATRA IN ČESKÁ LÍPA.

production of vehicles, such as the T27b trucks and military model T57K light passenger cars for the Wehrmacht.

Subsequently Dr Fritz Todt, the German general inspector of the Autobahn network, who particularly favoured the big Tatra T87 cars and owned one himself, proclaimed that the T87 was the Autobahn car.[3] As a result Tatra was allowed to go on building passenger cars for civilian use. Tatra became the only company in Europe, and possibly in the world, to produce passenger cars throughout the entire war, but not the T97, which competed too closely with German made cars. The ban was not due to the T97's look, or its high price of RM5600, but because of its small size, construction details and engine, possibly challenging the KdF-Wagen project. Ironically, despite Ledwinka's great contribution to the KdF concept, the Tatra models T57 and T97 were ordered to be removed from the Tatra stand 35 in hall one at the 1939 Berlin IAMA held between February 17th and March 5th. Oskar Pitsch confirmed: "Hitler and Porsche came to see the exhibits. They looked at the T97 and compared the design. Porsche came to me and said that it was so similar that he saw a Volkswagen."[4] At that

MILITARY TATRA T57K MADE BETWEEN 1941 AND 1948.

time Tatra also had the following models on its production programme: T70a, T75, T77a, T87 and T24, T27 and T85a, T92, T93 trucks.[5]

During the Second World War, the T87s were particularly liked by the German Army officers. They often drove them hard and enthusiastically, sometimes too enthusiastically,

TATRA T87 BROCHURE COVERS.

JAY LENO'S TATRA T87 IN FRONT OF ARTWORK BASED ON THE 1948 TATRA BROCHURE COVER. THE TATRA T87 IS NOW THE MOST DESIRABLE TATRA MODEL, MUCH SOUGHT-AFTER BY SERIOUS AUTOMOBILE COLLECTORS, CAR MUSEUMS, AND EVEN ART INSTITUTIONS. (COURTESY GARY CULLEN)

ending up in ditches rather frequently. In the end, they were forbidden to drive the T87s as the Wehrmacht Command decided that they did not want to lose their best officers before they even got to the front.[6] This fact, often considered apocryphal, was however confirmed by Ing Albert K Richter. He had used to work for Tatra from 1924 for four years and then serviced the cars. Due to his knowledge Richter was called up to the Wehrmacht Berlin Command headquarters during the war to be questioned on the safety of T87 cars.

He tried to convince the Germans of the good driving characteristics of the Tatras. "At modest speeds the Tatra is perfectly safe, indeed superior in many respects, to most vehicles on the road," he argued. Nevertheless, the order was imposed.[7]

The T87 driver's manual provided sound advice to its users immediately on its first page: "The Tatra Works, by creating the Model 87, present to you a car capable of a top speed of 150 to 160 kilometres per hour (94 to 100mph). Not so many years ago this was the record speed of automobiles and for anybody but a professional driver it is, under normal road traffic conditions, a highly commendable performance for a touring car. A ride in a streamlined rear-engined Tatra car gives you the unusual sensation of safety floating along. Thanks to the drop shape the ride is so smooth and steady, that you have to look at the speedometer to realise you are travelling at a speed far in excess of your estimate. Please therefore do not forget, whenever you are driving, though you may be travelling on an excellent road and your brakes are perfect, that you are driving a very fast car the stopping distance of which at 160kph is two-and-one half times as long as at 100kph. *Please therefore drive carefully and always with the greatest possible vigilance!*"[8]

It is interesting to note that similarly to Great Britain, Sweden, Portugal, Austria (except Tyrol), Hungary, Luxembourg, and Italy (in most of the large towns only!) motor cars also had to keep to the left side of the road in Czechoslovakia, although the Czechoslovak government had been considering a change to the right side for some time. In those countries that the Germans came to occupy

OPPOSITE, THIS PAGE, AND OVERLEAF: VAUXHALL MOTORS' PHOTOGRAPHS OF THE T87 USED BY THE GERMAN MILITARY POLICE, WHICH WAS BROUGHT TO BRITAIN FOR TESTING FROM LIBERATED EUROPE IN 1946.

1:5 T87 MODEL WITH MODIFICATIONS TO THE WINDSCREEN, FRONT FENDERS AND REAR SIDE SCOOPS AS TESTED AT THE DVL WIND TUNNEL AT ADLERSHOF, GERMANY.

at the beginning of the Second World War, the rule of the road was changed to the right within days. This right-hand rule was retained after the end of the war. Hence, the prewar-made Tatras for the Czechoslovak market were RHD.

In 1946, following arrangements with the British Intelligence, Vauxhall Motors in Luton evaluated a T87, which had been brought over from Germany, but in poor engine, brake and tyre condition, which would have had an effect on some of the comments regarding its handling. The car was thoroughly tested in Vauxhall's passenger vehicle experimental workshop, and a long report prepared by the company's experimental engineer, H A Dean. The report commented that, "The designers of this unorthodox car have produced a vehicle that is full of interest, having several good features. Although the body is of striking design, this has not been accomplished at the expense of passenger accommodation: on the contrary, the front seats are of generous proportions, and the rear will accommodate three persons in real comfort."

The report continued, "The rear engine location gives the considerable advantage of maintaining an approximately constant ratio of front to rear wheel loading, irrespective of the number of passengers carried ... the forward driving position combined with the windscreen side glasses results in excellent forward vision ... there is a noticeable absence of roll due to the low body and the high roll centre at rear ... by far the worst fault of the car, and one which can be dangerous, is the vicious oversteer, which may cause the driver to lose control on a fast bend or corner ... under less extreme conditions the handling of the car gives quite a good impression and is free from vices ... the effortless motoring at medium speeds in top gear, good ride over rough roads, and silence at normal road speeds are worthy features, but it must be remembered that the car is high-priced coming well into the luxury class."

Much later, in 1979, R Buchheim tested a T87 in the Volkswagen Klima wind tunnel. The car he had borrowed for the test was from the Deutsches Museum, Munich, originally donated to Volkswagon by Ledwinka. The test proved that the T87 had a very low drag coefficient reading. The resultant Cd coefficient of a real 1:1 car was recorded as 0.36. (Rumpler's 1924 Tropfen-Auto, measured at the same time, achieved a reading of 0.28.[9]) Already in 1941, at Technical University of Stuttgart tests were carried out of 1:5 models of Tatra cars with the T87 achieving 0.251[10] and a T97 0.259.[11] Another figure for a 1:5 T87 car model test was 0.244 tested at Deutsche Versuchsanstalt für Luftfahrt at Adlershof.[12] From these varied readings it is clear that test readings carried out on small car models cannot be applied to actual real size cars.[13] In comparison the VW Beetle drag coefficient is 0.45 due to the flat windscreen, broken fender lines and short roofline.[14] In the trials on the Padua autostrada in the late 1937, a T87 achieved 151.2kph and did 7.2km to the litre. A T97 tested at the same time returned 118.2kph and 8.5kpl.

There is no doubt that the T87 was one of the most interesting and innovative cars produced in the thirties. It was this car, perhaps above all, that proved Ledwinka's forced air-cooled rear engine streamlined cars were a pioneering achievement of the highest order.

NOTES

1 Julius Mackerle, *Automobily s motorem vzadu*, Praha: SNTL, p 111.
2 Rosenkranz, p 99.
3 Sloniger, 'Hans Ledwinka,' p 136.
4 Jan Ražnok & Radim Zátopek, *Hans Ledwinka: Od Präsidenta do síně slávy*, Kopřivnice: Tatra Muzeum, 2009, p 38, quoting from O Pitsch's memoirs.
5 *Ringhoffer-Tatra-Werke* AG Presse-Informationen, Internationale Automobil – und Motorrad – Ausstellung, Berlin 1939.
6 De Dubé, p 312, Ray Thursby, '1939 Tatra 87,' *Road & Track*, April 1987.
7 Palmer, p 15. Palmer interviewed A.K. Richter for his article.
8 Quoted directly from the *Manual for the Streamlined Automobile Tatra Model 87*, Tatra National Corporation, Kopřivnice, 1948, p 1.
9 Ralf J F Kieselbach, *Stromlinienautos in Deutschland*, Stuttgart: Verlag W Kohlhammer, 1982, p 141.
10 See also the previous chapter, the source of the figure 0.212, mentioned by Sloniger and Erich Ledwinka, could not be ascertained.
11 Karel Rosenkranz, *Tatra Passenger Cars: 100 Years*, Praha: GT Club – Motormedia, 1998, p 300.
12 Reinhard Koenig-Fahsenfeld, *Aerodynamik des Kraftfahrzeugs, Band III and IV*, Heubach: Kurt Maier Verlag, 1984, p 63 and Mackerle, p 41.
13 Josef Svoboda & Zdeněk Kleinhampl, 'Aerodynamikou k rychlosti,' *Svět Motorů*, Volume V, number 102, p 1009.
14 Jan P Norbye, *Streamlining & Car Aerodynamics*, Blue Ridge Summit: Tab Books, 1977, pp 51 & 55. VW30 prototype tested in 1937 had a Cd of 0.49, see Wood, p 25.

TRUCKS AND
AEROPLANES

vehicles. The central tubular frame protects the driveshaft from dirt and damage, and is a solid base for heavy load and long service life.

The first commercial vehicle based on this concept was the T13 in 1924. It had an air-cooled one-litre, twin-cylinder engine of 12bhp, and was manufactured with various body versions: platform vans, box vans, ambulances and coaches. Between 1924 and 1932, 716 T13 commercial vehicles were sold. This model was based directly on the T11/12.

In 1925 Tatra designed a special armoured draisine designated model T18, with a four-wheel chassis powered by a T11 engine positioned crosswise between two axles. Seven were made, as well as nine chassis. These were supplied to the Polish and Czechoslovak armies. In 1939 one unit was taken over by the Wehrmacht.

Exceptionally good driving characteristics over rough terrain were achieved by the first six-wheel lorries T26/30 and T26/52. The Czechoslovak Army was supplied with these vehicles to be used as staff and reconnaissance cars, trucks, ambulances or machine gun carrying transport. The engines employed were either the air-cooled, four-cylinder

Τhe central tubular frame and the independent suspension by jointless swing half-axle concept were also used successfully by Ledwinka in the Tatra trucks. Tatra was the first, and still is, the only commercial vehicle manufacturer which applies this principle to goods vehicles. This concept and its advantages are more marked the tougher the operational conditions. The independent swing half-axles, combined with extraordinary long suspension travel, ensure a faultless performance by absorbing and preventing unevenness being transmitted into structure, load and driver – as is the case in other

1925 TATRA T13
TRUCK.

1928 TATRA T23, 20-24 PERSON OMNIBUS, WHICH HAD A WATER-COOLED FOUR-CYLINDER, 7.5-LITRE, 65BHP ENGINE.

1926 T26/30 TRUCK CHASSIS WITH TWO REAR POWERED AXLES.

1925 T18 ARMOURED DRAISINE.

T30 of 1.68-litre or T52 1.9-litre units. By using reduction it was possible to set eight gear ratios forward and two in reverse. In civilian life these vehicles were used as coaches, platform lorries, tourist and postal buses, ambulances and fire fighting vehicles.

In 1927, Tatra began manufacturing a model T23 truck with a water-cooled four-cylinder petrol engine, with the later addition of a 6-8 tonne, three-axle T24. Again both types provided a large amount of body variations.

Between 1930 and 1939, 206 goods-carrying three-wheelers were made in order to bring to the market place as cheap a vehicle as possible. These one- to two seater model T49s were constructed very simply to allow easy servicing, and had a vertical air-cooled 0.5-litre one-cylinder

1929 T49 THREE-WHEELER.

7bhp engine. The rear wheel was powered by a driveshaft. The engine was attached to a central carrier tube supporting the front axle. The suspension was provided by cross leaf springs, while the platform for goods was positioned above the front wheels. The maximum speed was 50kph.

In 1931, the production of a 3 tonne commercial vehicle T27 with swing half-axles and newly developed hydraulic brakes began. This vehicle was greatly respected and had been well tried and tested. In all terrains this type had shown excellent road holding and driving characteristics and was manufactured until 1943 as T27a, T27b and T27H versions.

In the thirties Ledwinka concentrated on the modernisation of the commercial Tatra T26/30 and subsequently many variations of the new six-wheel model T72 were manufactured for civilian and army use. Traditionally, it was equipped with an air-cooled, horizontally opposed, flat-four-cylinder 1.9-litre engine. The engine had 8 forward and 2 reverse gears. The design of the four-wheel drive undercarriage enabled the vehicle

TESTING OF T72 POLICE BRAKE IN 1935.

to achieve excellent performance in difficult terrain due to the distortionless central tubular frame and having all four wheels hinged on independently sprung half-axles. This vehicle was also manufactured under licence by the French company Lorraine-Dietrich. In Britain, the T72 chassis was offered at a price of £695 in 1933.

This model was followed by additional six-wheel vehicles: T82, T92, T93 and from 1936 on, the T85, a five tonne platform truck; all these were in production until the beginning of the Second World War.

An interesting construction can be seen in the traction towing winch vehicle T84, which boasted six-wheel drive, arranged on three pairs of swing half-axles. The water-cooled, four-cylinder engine was placed behind the cabin, regardless of the convention of that time.

In 1940, a ten-wheel, two-axle driven vehicle model T81 with locking differentials, two-speed range selector and a carrying capacity of 6.5 tonnes was produced. This truck had a water-cooled V8 engine of 160bhp output, with a choice of petrol or diesel versions. This truck was the forerunner of the famous Tatra T111 truck which was already being designed.

Ledwinka was one of the first in the world to introduce air-cooled diesel engines in the late thirties, ranging from four up to 12 cylinders, and, as a prototype, even 18-cylinder engines using the early Nesselsdorfer technique of adding pairs of cylinders to increase power output, which moved from 70bhp to 210bhp. The eight and 12 cylinders were V engines, the 18 had cylinders arranged in three rows in a

1938 TATRA T86 TROLLEYBUS PROTOTYPE.

THE WORLD-RENOWNED T111 HEAVY TRUCK, WITH UP TO 8.5-TONNE CARRYING CAPACITY, MANUFACTURED FROM 1942 TO 1962.

1940s TATRA BROCHURE SHOWING THE T27B, T87 AND T57B PRODUCTION MODELS THAT CONTINUED THROUGHOUT THE SECOND WORLD WAR.

W formation. All engines had axial blowers on the front of each row with direct injection and swirl pattern pistons.

A competition was held among manufacturers: Mercedes-Benz, MAN and Tatra. The engine test results were: 1. Tatra, 2. MAN, 3. Mercedes-Benz, after the Benz engine failed immediately at the start of the test. The same air-cooled diesel engines are still in use today and are fitted

in the trucks that so successfully compete in the Dakar Rallies.

In 1942, a derivative of the T81 model gave impetus to the creation of a very popular six, eight and later ten tonne truck T111. The power unit used was an air-cooled 14.8-litre twelve-cylinder diesel engine of 210bhp output. The T111, a truck capable of overcoming 50 per cent gradients, was manufactured with many variations until 1962. The eight-cylinder engine in smaller capacity variation was used in the model T128 cross-country vehicle, built after the war. Good performance was also achieved by model T141 which was a heavy tow truck based on the T111.

Starting in 1934, to broaden the production, a short, but not insignificant, episode in the history of Tatra was the manufacture of aircraft and inverted four-cylinder engines which were constructed in the Tatra branch factory at Studénka. This branch was founded as Moravskoslezská vagónka, a new wagon works, by the Schustala brothers after they had sold the Nesselsdorfer plant to Hugo Fischer von Röslerstamm in 1895. As Tatra had no experience in aircraft production they hired staff from other aircraft manufacturers and bought licences both for engine and plane designs. In 1935 the T-100 95bhp engines, using Hirth HM-504 A-2 engine licence, were placed into Tatra T-131

TATRA T-131 BIPLANE.

TATRA T-101 MONOPLANE.

biplanes built under licence, based on the commercially successful model Bücker BÜ-131 Jungmann. The next model was the T-126 biplane based on the British Avro 626, and using the Avia RH-17 nine-cylinder radial engine. Later Tatra produced its own monoplane design, developed into models T-001, T-101 and T-201 using the T-100 engine. The next planned models – T-301 and T-401 – were not realised.

On March 16th, 1938, at Brno airport the T-101-1 under registration OK-TAO attempted to break the FAI record in the category III (2-4 litre capacity, one or more seats). The pilots, Majors Brázda and Valda, achieved an extraordinary height of 7113 metres, and thus established a new record. Later on the same day Major Brázda exceeded this height, and set a new record for single-seater planes. One hour and 12 minutes after taking off he reached the height of 7470 metres. On May 17th, 1938, pilots Matěna and Ambruš, in the T-101-1, achieved a world distance record by flying a non-stop 4340km from Prague to Khartoum.

LEDWINKA'S GREAT CONTRIBUTION

JOSEPH LEDWINKA (1870-1949).

Ledwinka, who at the age of 27, had become technical director and, subsequently, chief design director of the Tatra factory, was fully committed to the improvement and design innovation of passenger cars, commercial vehicles and railway rolling stock throughout his tenure in Moravia. He achieved many triumphs with designs that others pronounced unworkable; he was always willing to stake his reputation on any idea, once convinced it would work. On the other hand, he always knew when to throw away ideas that he eventually found fruitless; this might have been his most useful talent. Such an example was the fate which later befell the six-seater passenger saloon car T90. This project was stopped after only two prototypes had been manufactured in 1935.

Hans Ledwinka was by no means the only automobile innovator in his family. An engineer, Joseph Ledwinka (1870-1949), a distant relative of Hans, had been born in Vienna and emigrated to the United States, arriving on SS Lahn from Bremen via Southampton on July 30th, 1896. Together with another engineer, E G Budd, they were employed by the Hale & Kilburn Co, where they pioneered the pressed steel car body panel manufacturing process in 1909. Later, in 1912, they established their own factory, the Edward G Budd Manufacturing Co in Philadelphia, where they formed panels by drop pressing and power hammering. Further sophistication followed with the two-stage operation of drawing and stretching panels to achieve more rounded modern forms. From 1922, Budd Co had a monopoly on all-steel car bodywork construction. It supplied panels to Dodge, and in 1923,

André Citroën took up the Budd licence for his B12 saloons and tourers with all-steel bodies. Hans Ledwinka had direct contact with the Budd Manufacturing Co, when he obtained its licence to manufacture the new streamlined steel bodywork for models T77 and future models in the early thirties.

In April 1934, Citroën introduced the famous 7CV Traction Avant saloon which, as well as having novel front-wheel drive concept, had a new and extremely rigid chassis-less construction relying, for its strength, on box sections rather than stressed panels. The idea for this particular front-wheel drive arrangement, as well as the vehicle structure,

J LEDWINKA AND THE ADVANCED FRONT-WHEEL DRIVE RUXTON WHICH HE DESIGNED IN 1929.

was first developed in an experimental Ruxton prototype of a four-door saloon version by the Budd Manufacturing Co This pioneering concept was the result of a design study carried out under the direction of Joseph Ledwinka in 1929. At that time, André Citroën visited the Budd factory and acquired drawings of this advanced vehicle, having had a long-standing relationship with Budd, and took them back to France.

The front-wheel drive was not a new notion, Gräf brothers started to construct one model in 1897, but a front-wheel drive concept for a mass produced vehicle was not developed until the early thirties. Joseph Ledwinka, who applied during his long career for over 100 patents, and is the holder of the 2,000,000 US patent for 'Vehicle Wheel Construction' filed in 1932, was also involved in the body design of the Chrysler Airflow, and in 1936 with Porsche, in the design of steel body panelling for the final KdF-Wagen prototypes. So, yet other famous automobile proposals, owe their creation to the Ledwinka family's genius.

Similarly, both Hans Ledwinka's sons, Fritz and Erich, followed in their father's footsteps and became engineers. Initially, Fritz was employed at Tatra but eventually became

a sales director of Steyr-Daimler-Puch's head office in Vienna. Erich, who took over from Übelacker in 1940 at Tatra, was involved in the rear-engined prototypes, T87 and T97, engine design. Then he worked on his own, designing diesel engines after the war. In 1950, he joined Steyr-Daimler-Puch as its chief constructor. There he developed several radical designs starting with Steyr 2000 Grand Vue. His small Puchs 700C and 500D had platform chassis and air-cooled engines with 4 and 5-speed gearboxes. Later Erich was responsible for the design of four-wheel drive in the Puch-Haflinger and the Puch-Pinzgauer 6x6K, and ultimately for the concept of the Puch G 280GE, which was also used in the Mercedes-Benz G Wagen, and more recently in the Nissan MID-4.

Hans Ledwinka's entire pioneering output, apart from his brief involvement with steam power, can be summarised as follows. He began with hemispherical combustion chambers, overhead camshafts, engine-gearbox monoblocks, six-cylinder engines, and heavy trucks with bevel-wheel drive and hub transmissions. The next stage included the Steyr cars, the use of the rear swing half-axles, and the famous Tatra concept of central tubular chassis frame and the forced ducted air-cooled engines at front. Then came the all independent suspension with jointless half-axles, rear air-cooled engines, aerodynamic body streamlining and the progress from two-cylinder petrol motor to 12 or even, experimentally, 18 cylinder diesels, as well as his interest in commercial transport design.

Ledwinka had been credited as the inventor of the jointless swing half-axles, but a similar system was patented by the German firm Adler in 1903 to the design of Edmund Rumpler, and also tried by La Buire of Lyon, in 1909. The first production car fitted with swing half-axles was introduced in the USA in 1913. It was the all-independent suspension Cornelian built by the Blood Brothers Manufacturing Co of Kalamazoo. Also, the central tubular chassis was used before in the French 1910 car Simplicia, and an American, Edward Salusbury, had patented the central tubular chassis cycle car with swing half-axles filed in 1916 and granted in 1918 as the US patent 1,273,412. Air-cooling too, was

H LEDWINKA WITH HIS BELOVED T87 GIVEN TO HIM BY FELIX WANKEL, AND THEN DONATED TO THE DEUTSCHES MUSEUM, MUNICH, IN APRIL 1965. (COURTESY DEUTSCHES MUSEUM ARCHIVES)

THE IMPOSING 1946 TATRA T87. (COURTESY BINKY NIXON)

known well enough but usually considered to be inefficient; F W Lanchester, for example, produced prototypes of air-cooled cars as early as 1896, and the H H Franklin Manufacturing Co successfully made air-cooled vehicles from 1902 until 1934.

Ledwinka's main contribution was the forced ducted airflow, and his perception that, in replacing a perimeter frame with the central tubular structure, the chassis would gain torsional stiffness and make lighter bodywork possible. This would then result in the vehicle being easier to handle at high speeds and on bends, as well as cheaper to make. Another clever innovation was the use of a double bevel drive coupled to a differential. Ledwinka himself never

claimed to have invented any of these features, but he did make them work well together; sometimes all in one automobile.

For example, for the Type S, Ledwinka designed a completely new gearbox, using known experimental features but turning them into a workable production assembly. Apart from the engine plus gearbox monoblock innovation, he had refined the actual elements. The common gearbox of that time needed skilful handling. To improve its operation, Ledwinka substituted radial engagement of an entire toothed flank for the sliding axial mesh. This so-called 'bell' or 'Glockengetriebe' gearbox was connected to an oil-bathed, cast iron cone clutch, an

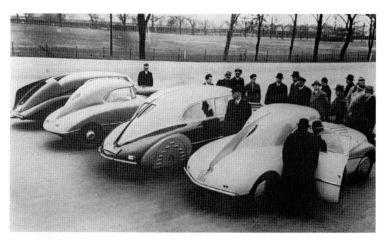

PAUL JARAY'S FAVOURITE CARS WHICH WERE DESIGNED USING HIS STREAMLINING PATENTS. FROM LEFT: T77, FIAT BALILLA, MAYBACH, AND AUDI FRONT, ASSEMBLED ON THE OCCASION OF THE 1935 IAMA BERLIN AT AVUS RACE TRACK.

idea taken from American machine tools. Only the top gear was engaged by sliding the gear wheel axially to meet its pinion. The clutch pedal simultaneously released the lock of the gear wheel so that without pressing the pedal, the gear could be selected.

After firstly examining the whole car, trying out the seating and testing the controls, Ledwinka made a habit of driving the first few hundred metres in each brand new prototype. If he came back smiling all was well, but all hell could break loose if he found a real fault in the assembly. Ledwinka seldom got excited if there was a basic design problem. He would sit in his office, which was a simply furnished glass box in the middle of the shop floor, and for hours on end he would work out corrections.

He insisted on meeting all the important deadlines regardless of how busy the factory was and how much overtime might be involved. While closely following the work in progress, he would sign letters, even dictate them during his work on the shop floor; and when he returned from a trip, even if it was after midnight, Ledwinka was quite likely to drop in at the factory to check what progress had

been made in his absence. However, he always looked after his staff well, often ordering food and drinks for them during overtime work. At more leisurely times Ledwinka never felt tied to the time-clock; he would go home for a mid-afternoon rest if he felt like it, and generally did as he pleased. It was very much his own company so far as design and production was concerned.

The situation prevailed due to the proprietor, Baron Hans Ringhoffer's trusting attitude. He left his designers strictly alone and was interested only in final results. This autonomy which was afforded to Ledwinka, it is believed, was the main reason why he never took the decision to set up his own design office or build cars with a 'Ledwinka' marque, though it is probably true to say that his unassuming demeanour must also have played a contributory part in this decision.

Ledwinka, who used to sketch out his ideas quickly and clearly, also liked to talk to himself while he worked. Always conscious of the great importance of every detail and of allowing access to all serviceable engine parts, Ledwinka was once designing a crankcase access panel using his own unusually small hands as scale. Suddenly he tore his drawing in half and started shouting at himself: "Du, Hansi, das ist verkehrt, denn alle haben ja nicht so kleine Hände!" (Hansi, you have messed it up, surely not everybody has such small hands!)[1]

Ledwinka's ideas were so precise and clear there was no need to amend his first sketches or dimensions. When something did not please him in the factory, he never blamed the workers but simply started from a completely different viewpoint. Sometimes he would suggest they might try another approach and always supplied a quick drawing to show what he had in mind. With this attitude and personal supervision of the workshop, he assembled his own team of men who were to remain loyal to him, following him to Steyr and back to Tatra and through successive changes of the company proprietors, not to mention differing national political situations.

Hans Ledwinka retained his use of the German language even after he became chief design director of the Czech Tatra. Throughout all the Central European frontier changes after the end of the First World War, Ledwinka considered

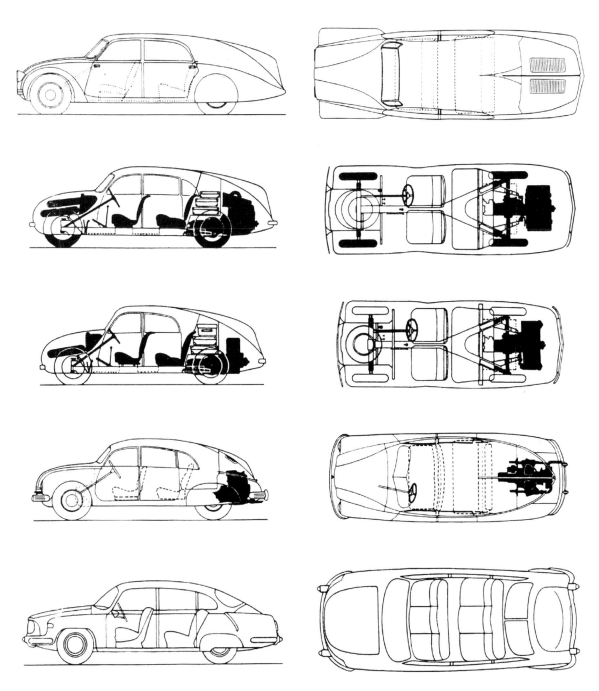

COMPARISON DIAGRAMS OF THE TATRA STREAMLINED MODELS IN PRODUCTION FROM 1934 UNTIL 1975. FROM TOP: T77, T87, T97, T600, T603. OVER 30,000 UNITS WERE MADE.

himself to be an Austrian, and kept turning down offers of both Czechoslovak and German citizenships.

However, on June 3rd, 1945, at the end of the Second World War, he was taken into custody and accused by the Czechoslovak authorities, instructed by the Soviet liberators, of collaboration with the Nazis. At his postponed trial, in September 1948, despite local opposition, Ledwinka was sentenced to a six year term of imprisonment on the charge of his 'zealous support' of the Third Reich war effort during the time of the country's occupation and dealing with the Nazi regime's principals in economic and military spheres. For a time he was kept in jail in Nový Jičín. Later, because of his advanced years, he was allowed to finish his sentence working in nearby gardens and fields. During his captivity he continued to work on car designs. When the Communist Czechoslovak government finally released Ledwinka on September 26th, 1951,[2] after having spent three months recuperating in a Prague hospital, it was suggested that he should remain and run the Tatra factory again. Ledwinka refused and was driven to Gmünd in Austria by Oskar Florian's son Kurt where his son Erich was waiting for him.[3] *Automobil-Revue* of December 1951 saluted his return to freedom: "After his imprisonment in Czechoslovakia Dr Ledwinka has not given in to the brutal methods of the Communists any more than he had in the past bowed down to the Nazi rulers." Ledwinka was fully rehabilitated posthumously by the Czech Republic's High Court on February 14th, 1992.

It is interesting and ironic that Ledwinka's contemporary, Ferdinand Porsche, was similarly treated after the war, but in his case, by the Allies. The Americans arrested him on the charge of furthering the German war effort and moved him to France. His captivity, though, was shorter than Ledwinka's, barely two years, from October 1945 until August 1947.

TATRA T87 ADVERTISEMENT. "TATRA FORGES THE WAY FORWARD FOR THE CARS OF TOMORROW!"

NOTES

1   See testimony of Antonín Klička, Sloniger, 'Hans Ledwinka', p 124.
2   Confirmed in a letter to Patrick Granger dated 13.6.2006 from Zemský archív, Opava, and in Zpráva o výkonu trestu, Lst 78/48, Čís. 485 dated 29.9.1951. Schmarbeck, *Hans Ledwinka*, p 163 has an incorrect date of September 16th.
3   Email from Nick Florian to Ivan Margolius, 24.11. 2014.

TATRA WITHOUT LEDWINKA

In 1946, decisions were being made at the Tatra factory about a new type of a passenger car which would supersede the successful T57b, and at the same time, with its characteristics, emulate and continue the tradition of the streamlined Tatras and achieve greater improvement of aerodynamics and comfort. The goals were to lower the overall weight, distribute it evenly over the chassis, increase the interior space, design a body with smallest drag coefficient, improve operational economy and introduce an all-metal monocoque body. The new model, initially named T107, was to be based on the prewar Tatra T97. At this time it was also necessary, with the general rationalisation in the postwar Czechoslovak economy, for the Tatra factory to prove its effective ability to compete successfully in home and export markets.

With Hans Ledwinka in prison, the factory was left without a strong designer. The Tatra directors, Jaroslav Růžička and Josef Heske, appointed engineer Milan Cvetnič to take on the role. Initially Cvetnič proposed a modernisation of the T97 model, but this was not accepted. Then came Professor Vladimír Souček, from Brno Technical University, under whose leadership a new car began to emerge. Josef Chalupa, director of the body design department, proposed the concept of a self-supporting steel monocoque streamlined ponton body, years ahead of the world development, with a flat punt-type frame with perforated welded box side members and a central rib that forked into a Y-form at the rear to accept a new air-cooled horizontally opposed four-cylinder engine monoblock mounted on three silentblocs. The first prototype, called 'Ambrož,' was completed in December 1946.

However, the tests which followed found bad stability, inadequate power, poor engine cooling and interior heating. The second prototype, 'Josef,' made in spring 1947, did not solve any of these problems and, Souček departed. Engineer Vladimír Korbel, assisted by designer Vladimír Popelář, was asked to build five prototypes for the 1947 Prague autumn autosalon. To find the best way forward, Popelář and Chalupa, through Ledwinka's former chauffeur Alois Kopečný, arranged a meeting with Ledwinka to obtain his advice. In May 1947, at midnight, the visitors came to see Ledwinka in his Nový Jičín prison cell, bringing all the drawings of the new car with them. Delighted, Ledwinka welcomed them with open arms, saying: "Kinder, ich bin so froh, euch zu sehen." (Children, I am so pleased to see you.)[1] After a two and half hour consultation he gave his views. He liked the form of the car but suggested redesigning the gearlever arrangement, engine support, location of the handbrake and bevelled gearing of the cooling fan. On their return the designers enlarged the engine capacity, redesigned the engine fan-cooling arrangement and rear axle assembly, introduced roof air intakes and kept the traditional Tatra rear fin, which was missing on the first prototypes.

1947 DESIGN SKETCH PROPOSAL FOR THE NEW TATRA T107 BY JOSEF SODOMKA. TATRA CONSIDERED THIS INTERESTING IDEA TOO FUTURISTIC AT THE TIME. (COURTESY JAN TULIS)

THE NEW T600 TATRAPLAN, AS ITS NAME IMPLIED, WAS COMPARED TO AN AEROPLANE IN TATRA SALES BROCHURES.

T600 BROCHURE COVERS.

The T77, T87 and T97 production models were a step back from a full streamlined ponton form as they expressed the front wings separately from the main body. This is where the new postwar model succeeded. It had the best Tatra streamlined body design, a true teardrop form, fully enclosing the wheels, wide at the front, with a sloping two part split-windscreen, concealed door hinges and the back dissected by a small, almost symbolic, fin sweeping to the pointed rear lid.

The previous models' horizontal side line under the windows now sloped down towards the rear giving the car form a more dynamic look expressing the main body shape in a true aircraft wing profile. Tatraplan's independent all-round suspension consisted of two superimposed leaf springs forming a parallelogram in front, and torsion bars and swing half-axles

1949 TATRAPLAN AND DE HAVILLAND 89A DRAGON RAPIDE BIPLANE.

in the rear. The weight of a fully loaded car was almost equally distributed with 44 per cent on the front wheels and 56 on the rear ones.[2] The 'one-shot' lubrication system similar to the one used in the T77, T77a and T87 was also fitted.

The five prototypes, now named T2-107, were delivered to the Prague autosalon with only hours to spare, and to a widely acclaimed success. It is interesting to note that the front of the body, up to the post between the front and rear doors, was designed by František Kardaus, the first industrial designer involved with Tatra car bodies proposals. In the winter of 1947, this car type number designation was changed from 107 to 600. Initially the T600 had a rear air-cooled, single carburettor 1.75-litre OHV, flat-four-cylinder engine of 48bhp, air-cooled by a fan with vertical shaft. After the first series, early in 1949, a larger, 1.95-litre OHV, flat-four-cylinder engine of 52bhp was fitted, with a horizontal axis fan and two Zenith or Solex carburettors.

1949 TATRAPLAN 1952CC FLAT-FOUR ENGINE.

BIRD'S EYE VIEW OF TATRAPLAN, EMPHASISING THE FULLY ENVELOPING DROP BODY.

When tested in a wind tunnel the T600 had an impressive 0.32 drag coefficient,[3] the best of all Tatra models. The car was also named Tatraplan, implying its connection to a contemporary two-year economic 'plans' as well as its streamlining inspired by aeroplanes (colloq. Czech: éroplan'), from the originally designated name Tatra Autoplan; Kardaus is credited for suggesting the name Tatraplan in some sources.

The Tatraplans were triumphant in a number of domestic and international rallies, especially in the 1949 Österreichische Alpenfahrt where they claimed the first four places. These Tatraplans, painted yellow or grey, had specially-prepared lighter, stiffened bodywork, which, for example, had sealed rear doors.

From the T600 model several further variations were derived; a 1949 T601 Tatraplan Monte Carlo, a two-door

INTERESTING COMPARISON OF T87 AND T600 PROFILES AT WREST PARK, BEDFORDSHIRE, WHICH ILLUSTRATES THE T87'S HORIZONTAL AIRCRAFT WING PROFILE AS OPPOSED TO THE T600'S MORE DYNAMIC WING PROFILE WITH DOWNWARD-SLOPING REAR.

TATRA T600 TATRAPLAN DRIVEN BY JOSEF CHOVANEC AND JAROSLAV PAVELKA AT THE START OF THE 1949 INTERNATIONAL ÖSTERREICHISCHE ALPENFAHRT. NOTE THE SEALED REAR DOORS WITHOUT HANDLES TO LIGHTEN AND STIFFEN THE CAR BODY.

1949 TATRA T601 MONTE CARLO COUPÉ, FIRST VERSION. NOTE THE AIR INTAKES BEHIND THE REAR WINDOWS.

coupé with aluminium body into which, over time, different engines were installed; three prototypes of diesel Tatraplan whose 1.95-litre engine was adapted directly from the petrol version, one with a single fan and another two with two-fan 42bhp engines; and the front-engined T201 ambulance bodied by Sodomka Coachworks. Other T201 variations were a pick-up body model which accompanied the factory Tatraplans to rallies and races, and two delivery vans, one of which was used as a police vehicle in the 1962 film, *Šťastnou cestu*, celebrating the next Tatra model, the T603. The string of prototypes was concluded with a luxury one-off cabriolet, whose special body was also made by Sodomka in 1949. At the same time as the Tatraplan manufacture, Tatra continued the production of the T87 model, with the redesigned front part of the body now having three headlamps set flush with the metalwork. Several were made with only two headlamps and the very last models had T603 engines. The production of this model stopped in 1950, with 1745 of the total of 3102 units made after the war.

1949 TATRA T201 AMBULANCE WITH THE BODY DESIGN BY JOSEF SODOMKA COACHWORKS, CENTRAL TUBULAR CHASSIS AND THE STANDARD T600 REAR ENGINE REVERSED AND POSITIONED AT THE FRONT.

In 1951, on the orders of the Minister of Industry, Gustav Kliment, to rationalise the Czechoslovak economy, and under the auspices of the nationalised Československé závody automobilové a letecké, which managed production of passenger cars and aircraft in the republic, the manufacture of the Tatraplan, including all the documentation, parts and materials, was transferred to Škoda (AZNP). Škoda, in Mladá Boleslav, Bohemia, was the other major Czechoslovak automobile manufacturer, and where T600 production started in August of that year. Tatra was, from now on, allowed to produce commercial vehicles only, to the staff's great regret. At the time, a mock Tatraplan funeral procession was conducted with a Tatraplan model being carried through the factory led by one of Tatra designers dressed as priest waving a thurible, followed by Julius Mackerle, Popelář and the factory workforce. Popelář, who was the funeral organiser, was disciplined at the regional State Security offices in Ostrava afterward.[4] At Škoda, Tatraplans, now carried a manufacturing label instead of 'made at Tatra, národní podnik závod Kopřivnice,' stating: 'Automobilové závody, národní podnik, závod Mladá Boleslav ČSR,' and were fitted with rounded rear lids although this design change had already been carried out in Kopřivnice with the production there of the last several hundred units.[5]

By the beginning of 1953, overall 6342 units (including seven prototypes) of the T600 had been produced both in Tatra and Škoda, of which over a third were exported to 22 countries (Austria, China, East and West Germany, Sweden, Canada, Belgium, Portugal, Switzerland, Hungary, USSR, Poland, Finland, Yugoslavia, The Netherlands, Egypt, Morocco, Albania, Romania, Australia, Argentina, Sudan) but not into the UK.

At the end of 1947, at Tatra, the type (T) numbering of products was reorganised. The old system, dating from 1919 when the original alphabetical system ceased, no longer suited the large variety of products now being made there. Three figure numbers were established, with the first number indicating the use of that particular product. 100 was reserved for light trucks, 200 for delivery vans, 300 for rail vehicles, 400 for trolleybuses, 500 for coaches, 600 for passenger cars, 700 was used for machinery, 800 for heavy trucks and special technology, and 900 was for engines.

The good characteristics of air-cooled engines and construction elements of Tatra cars showed themselves to be effective in ordinary use, as well as in the trials of racing and rally cars. The first air-cooled T603 1.9-litre OHV, V8 engine was designed by Mackerle, and constructed by Jiří Klos in 1948-49.[6] In 1950, two Tatra T607 Monopost racing cars were produced. One used the 1.9-litre engine and the other had the higher 2.35-litre capacity engine, placed just in front of the rear axles. The compression ratios were 11.5:1 and 13.5:1, with the output increasing from 96bhp in the first car to 163bhp in the second. In 1953, three more Monoposts were made, designated T607-2, this time with T603 2.54-litre engines with outputs ranging between 183 and 200bhp. These racing cars followed in the footsteps of two two-seater Tatra T602 Sport racers built in 1949. The T602 Sport had a standard Tatraplan air-cooled 1.95-litre flat-four engine placed ahead of the rear half-axles. With various improvements including the use of four Solex carburettors, the engine output was raised to 84bhp.

1949 TATRA T602 SPORT WITH BRUNO SOJKA.

1953 TATRA T607-2
MONOPOST WITH
A COLLECTION OF
VINTAGE TATRAS IN
THE BACKGROUND.
(COURTESY
KAREL ROSENKRANZ)

At that time, in its category, the T607 Monopost was the fastest car made in Czechoslovakia and the holder of the national speed record of 207.972kph, achieved in 1953 by the driver Adolf Veřmiřovský, son of Josef Veřmiřovský.

In 1957, after the improved T607-2 Monopost, a new racing training car T605 with an air-cooled 0.6-litre, two-cylinder in line engine placed ahead of rear half axles was developed using the cylinders from the T603 engine. With two Weber Carburettors of 40mm diameter 54bhp was obtained. The engine and gearbox sat on three silentblocs to allow their fast removal. The two-seater aerodynamic body consisted of two removable parts. The front part covered the front half-axles and the seat area; the back section was placed over the rear axles and engine. The weight of the car without fuel was 320kg which enabled it to achieve good acceleration and a maximum speed of 168kph.

1957 TATRA T605 TRAINING RACER.

The series of victories these cars accumulated proved the high quality of the Tatra engines. The Tatra Monoposts became test cars for many types of engine which were later used in special prototype automobiles, such as the military T802 and T803. Then followed the T805 light van, which went into production, as well as the T603 passenger cars, using the same engine.

Late in 1953, a government decision was made, within the nationalised motor car manufacturing industries, for the Tatra company to concentrate on the production of large luxury cars, leaving the Škoda company in Mladá Boleslav, to cope with the market requirements for small to medium passenger cars. However, even before this official decision, the Prague Tatra design office had started in secret to propose a new Tatra passenger car in 1952. Under Mackerle's leadership, first designs were produced for the next generation of Tatra passenger cars. The shape and form of the body began to be developed by testing models in a wind tunnel of the Military and Aircraft Research Institute at Letňany. Kardaus was engaged again to offer proposals, working together with Tatra designers Popelář and Chalupa. Additional refinements came from Zdeněk Kovář (1917-2004), another well-known Czech industrial designer. The proposal was completed by the end of 1954 for the new car with the type designation 603. In March 1956, in an article in the internal Tatra factory magazine, it was suggested the new car be called 'Diplomat,' however this had not been adopted.[7] Similarly, the same name was previously unofficially used for the postwar series of the T87. The T603 base design and its derivatives would become the only passenger car model made by Tatra in the following years.

The T603 full-size maquette still had the traditional large rear fin, which was dropped on the first prototype made in Kopřivnice in 1955, leaving just a small ridge between the rear split window; a year later a further nine cars were made. These units had windscreens in two parts, joined with a rubber gasket, and the three close-grouped centre headlamps were covered with one piece of glass. Initially the T603s had an air-cooled, 2.54-litre, V8, 95bhp

1957 TATRA T603 WITH MIG 15 EMPHASISING TATRA STREAMLINING COMPARABLE TO AIRCRAFT DESIGN.

1961 TATRA T603, AT SLAVÍN, BRATISLAVA. (COURTESY STUDIO OLGOJ CHORCHOJ)

engine with two Jikov 30 SSOP carburettors, which was designated T603F. The first serially produced T603 left the factory in December 1956, now with one full size windscreen and the close headlamps covered in three-piece glass. Later T603G 100bhp engines of 2.472-litres were being installed. During the long production of the T603 there were many body changes introduced, with four closely placed headlamps, first in 1963 with the model T2-603 and later, with further modification to the front, wider four-headlamp spacing. Lastly, 105bhp T603H engines were used. In the early 1960s, special design studies led to a modernised prototype T603A but no production followed. Similarly, in the Tatra branch in Bratislava, another prototype T603X was developed as well as a 13-seater front-wheel-drive T603MB minibus. By June 1975, when manufacture of the T603 ended, 20,422 units had been made.

In 1959, in Wiesbaden, West Germany, a white Tatra T603 was awarded a Golden Ribbon for its looks and elegance. Between 1957 and 1967, T603s participated in 79 domestic and international competitions, rallies and races and during these they had gained 60 first, 56 second and 49 third places. The biggest success these cars achieved was in 1966, when three special rally T2-603s of the B5 category with 150bhp output took part in the 84-hour Marathon de la Route. In competition with 37 cars of major world marques, the T2-603s were awarded the first, second, and the third

T603 BROCHURE.

T603 PARTICIPATING IN THE 1959 ALPINE TRIAL.

THE MODERNISED T2-603 MODEL WITH CLOSELY-SPACED HEADLAMPS MADE BETWEEN 1963 AND 1967. (COURTESY SIMON REDRUP)

TATRA RALLY T2-603 B5.
(COURTESY SIMON REDRUP)

TATRA T2-603 REAR ENGINE COMPARTMENT
WITH T603H V8 ENGINE.

1970 TATRA T2-603.

place in the 2500cc and below class, and the third to fifth place in the overall placing behind Ford-Lotus and BMW.

Then, production began of a new type of luxury passenger car with an air-cooled 3.495-litre, V8, 165bhp engine placed above the rear axle based on three prototypes,

one of which had a coupé body made in 1969. It was named the T613 and was called unofficially 'Chromka.' Its body was styled by Vignale of Italy and it had a maximum speed of 190kph. Its manufacture was transferred to the Tatra branch in nearby Příbor, where Tatra parts as well as engine part assemblies were made from 1951, and the full production of T613 started there in 1975.

Further development continued with variations of the T613 such as the models T613-2, T613 S and T613-3, these being manufactured in small numbers. In 1991 the production continued with the improved model T613-4. At the 1991 Prague autosalon, the firm Metalex introduced a special MTX Tatra V8 sports car designed by Václav Král, with 3.9-litre capacity engine producing 217.5bhp. Another version followed, which achieved a higher maximum speed of 265kph. Further special variations of T613-4 model continued with the T613-4 KATi-Electronic, T613-4 Mobicom, T613-4 Mi Long and four RHD units of T613-5 intended for the British market. The last Tatra passenger car was the model T700, which started to be developed from February 1995 and was

1978 TATRA T613 'CHROMKA' WITH VIGNALE BODY. (COURTESY PETER VISSER)

1980 TATRA T613 SPECIÁL. (COURTESY PETER FROST)

TATRA T613-3S MANUFACTURED FROM 1986. (COURTESY SIMON REDRUP)

COLLECTION OF BRITISH-REGISTERED
TATRAS: 1990 T613-3, 1970 T2-603 (AT
TIMES, UNOFFICIALLY, THIS MODEL IS ALSO
DESIGNATED AS T3-603), 1949 T600 AND 1995
T613-4MI LONG M95.

TATRA T700 3495CC V8 ENGINE.
(COURTESY DAVID YANDO,
LANE MOTOR MUSEUM)

TATRA T700, THE LAST TATRA MADE
PASSENGER CAR MODEL.
(COURTESY DAVID YANDO,
LANE MOTOR MUSEUM)

introduced in Prague in April 1996. The British designer Geoff Wardle and Jiří Španihel, sculptor and designer, were involved in its design. In 1997 the manufacture of passenger cars moved from Příbor back to the mother factory in Kopřivnice, where it was planned to produce the model T700 to special orders. However, the last two T700s were made in 1999 and Tatra passenger car production ceased for good that year.

Building on the tradition of the well-known T111 truck, in 1959 Tatra came up with a new line of heavy lorries of the T138 series, which again introduced several constructional innovations. Tatra was the first company to incorporate a new type of suspension in utility vehicles using sprung suspension rods, and continued with the use of swing half-axles, making these vehicles very flexible in all terrains. The equipment of these trucks and the driver's comfort considerations came very near to the level of those of the passenger cars. Again Kovář was engaged to propose the truck cabin and front mask, including studies for a tanker truck. The most effective of the heavy terrain trucks were the two- to four-axle driven vehicles T813 with engines of 250 to 274bhp. The first prototype T813 was tried in 1960, and production started in 1967. In 1970, Tatra commenced the serial manufacture of the T148 truck with V8 212bhp engines, which superseded the T138. The number of T148s produced exceeded 110,000 units.

FROM THE LATEST TATRA TRUCK RANGE: TATRA T815 TERRNO1. THESE TRUCKS STILL RETAIN THE CENTRAL TUBULAR CHASSIS AND INDEPENDENT ALL-ROUND SUSPENSION MAKING THEM IDEAL VEHICLES FOR USE IN HEAVY ROUGH TERRAIN.

TATRA T138 S3 DUMP TRUCK AT 1965 TATRA TOUR OF AUSTRIA.

TATRA T813 8X8 KOLOS TRUCK. (COURTESY SIMON REDRUP)

In the 1960s the largest Tatra commercial vehicle, T813 8x8, which had an air-cooled V12 diesel engine with 20 forward and four reversed gears, was produced both for civilian and military use. In 1982 Tatra introduced the serial production of a new truck, type T815, in many variations with a range of engine sizes. This model combined the best characteristics of the previous T148 and T805. The technical parameters were increased and, as a result, the utilitarian value of the new vehicle was raised. Special attention was given to the reduction of noise levels and exhaust emissions, to active and passive safety, and to an increased workspace environment and comfort for the driver. Through several recent changes of Tatra company ownership and management, these T815 commercial vehicles and their successful introduction and continuation to date of serial production, represent the culmination of Tatra's development policies and the benefit of a long history of the manufacture of motor vehicles in Kopřivnice.

NOTES

1 Karel Rosenkranz, 'První poválečný aerodynamický automobil pokrokové koncepce – Tatraplan,' *100. Výročí zahájení automobilové výroby v Tatře Kopřivnice*, Praha: NTM, 1997, p 98.
2 Mackerle, p 111. For comparison: a fully laden T603: 44% at the front, 56% at the rear; VW Beetle: 41% at the front, 59% at the rear.
3 Karel Rosenkranz, *Tatra Passenger Cars: 100 Years*, Praha: GT Club – Motormedia, 1998, p 300, and in *Tatra Autoalbum*, Brno: MS Press, 2002, p 107.
4 Karel Rosenkranz, 'První poválečný aerodynamický automobil pokrokové koncepce – Tatraplan' in Pauly a Kožíšek, p 98.
5 Tatra, *Dílenská příručka pro osobní vůz Tatraplan*, Kopřivnice: Tatra n.p. 1950, p 263; the last unit made with pointed rear lid was body number 75.732. The last known highest number T600 made at Kopřivnice was 76.867, but there appear to be gaps and some units were made after 76.867 but with a lower number. The last T600 made there was 76.408 on 22.10.1951.
6 Jan Tuček, *Tatra 603*, Praha: Grada Publishing, 2005, p 27.
7 Ibid, p 48.

LEDWINKA'S LEGACY

Ledwinka continued to be a protagonist of swing half-axle trucks and, even after his retirement in Munich, he tried to persuade British and German manufacturers to include this basic design concept in their new truck design. He advised Perkins, Klöckner-Humboldt-Deutz and Magirus on truck engines and suspension design, sometimes suggesting the use of water cooling, even though his past dedication leaned towards cooling by air. His prime concern remained with driver and passenger comfort, which took precedence over pure, traditional engineering theory. He got so carried away sometimes that he would almost shout at his audience: "Wie vor hundert Jahren sind auch die heutigen Lastkraftwagen eigentlich nichts anderes als Bauernwagen, in die man einen Motor eingebaut hat!" (Similarly as 100 years ago, our trucks today are made like peasant carts, except they have an engine installed!)[1] In the mid-1950s, for Harald Friedrich of Alzmetall, Ledwinka reconfigured a little three-wheel Spatz sports car with four-wheel backbone chassis and air-cooled one-cylinder two-stroke 191cc 10bhp Fichtel & Sachs engine placed in front of the rear axle. Over 850 units were built by Bayerische Autowerke GmbH and later 729 units by Victoria-Werke with a larger 250cc 14bhp engine.

Ledwinka was one of the most original and logical thinkers to work in the motor industry. He believed the automobile was destined to become an object of everyday use to modern man. However, he developed his innovative ideas in all aspects of transport design. There was the streamlined prototype V855 from 1942 of the propeller-driven snow sledge powered by a T87 engine, now renovated and exhibited at the Tatra Museum in Kopřivnice, the design for the stageless electro-mechanical rail carriage transmission, and a pneumatic suspension for trucks. The list of some of the many patents which he applied for in the Tatra name speaks for itself: engine arrangement in

HANS LEDWINKA, AGED 80, IN 1958.

combination with the central tubular chassis; air-cooling turbine fan for the horizontally opposed engine; three point engine fixing on silentblocs on a backbone chassis car; a backbone chassis structure made of hollow box frame forked at one end; a rear-engine car with a rear opening engine compartment; car suspension with swing half-

HANS LEDWINKA SPEAKING AT THE
DEUTSCHES MUSEUM, FEBRUARY 12TH, 1967.
(COURTESY WERNER LEDWINKA)

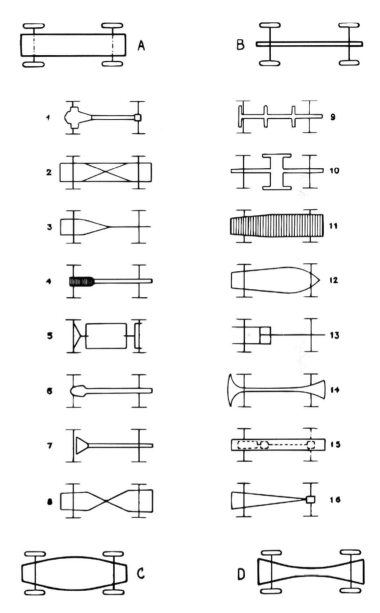

JUNE 1941 *MOTOR-KRITIK* SURVEY OF
CHASSIS CONCEPTS. TATRA SHARED
PATENTS FOR 1, 3, 7, 9, 10, 13; BÉLA
BARÉNYI CLAIMED B, D, 1, 4, 7, 12,
14; FERDINAND PORSCHE: B, 2, 4, 9
CHASSIS FORMS.

axles fixed to an engine monoblock; four-wheel drive for a petrol-electric railcar; improvements in streamlined bodies; particularly for motor vehicles; improvements in cooling air guiding means for air-cooled rear-engine motor vehicles having aerodynamic bodies, and so on.

Hans Ledwinka, one of the early pioneers and innovators of motor car design, died in Munich on March 2nd, 1967 at the age of 89. He had consistently refused all rewards and honours offered him during his long life, accepting only an honorary doctorate in 1944 from the Vienna University of Technology, an honorary decoration from the Institute of German Engineers in 1952, the Austrian Medal for Science and Arts (1st class), and a Gold Rudolf Diesel-Medal of the German Inventors Association, both in 1961.

As a man, Ledwinka always avoided unnecessary personal publicity, preferring to concentrate on his passion for automobile construction, which, at all times, reflected the current state of technology and design. So great was his ability and technical perception that he almost always correctly predicted future developments and trends in automobile technology.

TATRA V855 PROPELLER-DRIVEN SNOW SLEDGE, 1942. TWO WERE ORDERED BUT ONE WAS MADE FOR THE WEHRMACHT TO HELP FIGHTING ON THE RUSSIAN FRONT. THE PROPELLER WAS DESIGNED TO MOVE THE VEHICLE ONCE IT GOT UP TO A CERTAIN SPEED. THE REAR DRIVE DRUM HELPED TO GET THE VEHICLE MOVING AND CLIMBING HILLS. WHEN THE BRAKE PEDAL WAS PUSHED, THE FRONT SKIS SKEWED INWARD TO A SNOW PLOUGH POSITION. THERE WERE PINS THAT PUSHED DOWN THROUGH EACH REAR SKI AND A SMALL BRAKE DRUM ON THE REAR DRIVE DRUM TO ASSIST IN THE BRAKING. THE DRUM HAD THREE SPEEDS AT WHICH IT TURNED, AND THE PROPELLER WAS COUPLED DIRECTLY TO THE ENGINE. THE REVERSE MOVEMENTS WERE ACCOMPLISHED BY THE REAR DRUM.

HANZELKA'S AND ZIKMUND'S SPECIAL
T805 EXPEDITION TRUCK AND A T57.
(COURTESY PETER VISSER)

At the instigation of Ledwinka, the Tatra company has continued to manufacture air-cooled engines from 1923 onwards, providing many years of experience in their construction and production. Thanks to these engines and to the backbone chassis concept with swing half-axles, Tatra cars find their full application in especially hard working conditions such as tropical, Alpine, or polar regions, as well as in ordinary day-to-day use.

From 1947 to 1950, Jiří Hanzelka and Miroslav Zikmund, two Czech journalists, took a silver T87 across the whole of the African and South American continents with great success, overcoming many obstacles put in their way by nature and the local population. Having been first refused by Škoda, the Tatra factory sponsored the trip and supplied the T87. However, after a five-week journey from Prague, the travellers had a serious accident, smashing the T87 into a concrete border post between former Libyan colonies Tripolitania and Cyrenaica, when all brakes – including the handbrake – suddenly failed; later confirmed as due to possibly deliberately cut cables and hydraulic lines. A new Tatra had to be sought as a replacement. Luckily,

THE 9TH PARIS-DAKAR RALLY, 1987, WHERE
A TATRA T815 4X4 FINISHED SECOND.
TATRA WAS MORE SUCCESSFUL IN
FOLLOWING YEARS.

three T87s were being delivered in Alexandria for intended customers in Africa, but had black paint livery, so one had to be resprayed to silver to be more suited for the tropics.[2] This T87 behaved admirably along the rest of the journey. The pair travelled overall through 44 countries, covering over 110,000km on a journey that lasted 1290 days, again proving the T87 to be a first class machine, and reaffirming

T815 4X4 AT 2003
DAKAR RALLY DRIVEN
BY KAREL LOPRAIS
AND HIS TEAM.

its excellent reputation. Between 1959 and 1964 they went on another long trip through the Eastern Europe, Asia and Pacific Islands, this time in two T805 prototype box body expedition vehicles.

In the commercial field, the new Tatra T815 4x4 trucks gained many successes in long distance international rallies such as the Dakar. In 1987, 1996, 2000 and 2002 the Czech drivers came second. However, in 1988, 1994, 1995, 1998, 1999 and 2001, Tatra, in the hands of the most consistently successful driver Karel Loprais, achieved well deserved victories in the truck class.

In 70 years of active involvement, of which 40 were spent in heading the design at the Tatra factory, Ledwinka, the individualist was frequently regarded as a car construction genius. According to Josef Ganz, one of the pioneers of small car design and an outstanding engineer in his own right, Ledwinka was the greatest master of

European automobile design. Others hailed him as, "one of the great – truly great – designers of the early days."[3] Even Porsche called him, "the artist of engine design."[4] Certainly, it remains undeniable that the Volkswagen era would never have come about, and carried on so successfully for such a long time, without Ledwinka's influence. His foresight for a need of a 'people's car' at the beginning of the 20th century, his experience and advice, helped in establishing this triumphant concept, which was based directly on his practice with the development of his own cars – the Nesselsdorfers/Tatras.

Ledwinka helped to lay foundations of modern car design and manufacture by producing a number of the most impressive achievements of his era. Almost all his vehicle designs represent visionary, innovative notions and theories, boldly turned into practical realisation and standard serial factory production. He constantly pushed the established

THE FRONT COVER OF THE 1936 T87
SALES BROCHURE.

principles to higher and previously unforeseen levels. To this end, Ledwinka rightly belongs to a select pioneering group of some of the great constructors of all time, together with Karl Benz, Gottlieb Daimler, Willhelm Maybach and Ferdinand Porsche. This was confirmed when in 2007 Ledwinka was inducted in the European Automotive Hall of Fame. In 1968 Steyr honoured Ledwinka by naming one of the town's streets after him. Kopřivnice followed similarly in 1999.

The car historian Hans-Heinrich Fersen correctly stated that the present state of automobile technology is indebted to Ledwinka's genius, which can be only fully appreciated by those who have a comprehensive knowledge of the car's history and development through the ages.[5]

In assessing that development, particularly in an automobile industry that has become increasingly motivated toward economy, utility, uniformity and standardisation, Ledwinka's and his contemporaries' endeavours stand as models of design excellence, reflecting a period of great advance in automobile engineering. The fact that Ledwinka's name is not as synonymous with this era of innovation as that of Benz, Daimler or Porsche, can be attributed to a number of complex factors, not least of which was Ledwinka's modest temperament. However, what is certain is that Czechoslovakia's increasingly secluded location after the Second World War has raised barriers to the Western world's perception of some of Central and Eastern European culture, not to mention technical prowess, to the point of being forgotten. Now, in the 21st century, these barriers have come down, and it is the right time to emphasise some of the past constructors' achievements. Within these achievements, a fresh reappraisal of Ledwinka's influence and genius, which manifested itself in the revolutionary designs of his Tatra cars, is now well justified.

1947 ARTWORK FOR TATRA.

NOTES

1 For similar quote see: Sloniger, 'Hans Ledwinka,' p 138.
2 Jiří Hanzelka & Miroslav Zikmund, *Afrika snů a skutečnosti*, Praha: Naše vojsko, 1957, pp 82-85, 163-164, 'Národní poklady na čtyřech kolech,' *Hospodářské noviny víkend*, 9/2006, pp 13-14.
3 E R Bonner, *Motoring Life*, October 1957.
4 Schmarbeck, *Hans Ledwinka*, p 121 and Schmarbeck, *Tatra*, p 42.
5 H-H von Fersen, p 207.

APPENDICES

TATRA T77 BROCHURE WITH LINE-DRAWN IMAGES. FIRST PUBLISHED IN GERMAN IN 1933, THIS IS THE ENGLISH VERSION FROM 1936. (COURTESY GARY CULLEN)

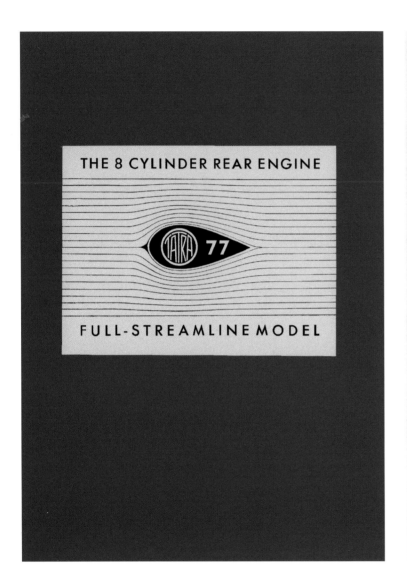

THE 8 CYLINDER REAR ENGINE FULL-STREAMLINE MODEL

When now 15 years ago, the Tatra works brought out their aircooled, two-cylinder, kneeaction equipped car, its reception by the automotive industry at large was anything but enthusiastic.

Most of the prominent designers had no more than a passing interest for such revolutionary ideas of construction not at all fitting into a scheme of mass production as practiced in the USA taking its quick profits from the general prosperity which was never thought to end.

Standardization and massproduction of types whose engineering was dictated by cheap production and development of high pressure sales policies were the cry of the day.

But 15 years have changed much. The public dissatisfied with buying the same model car year in year out began to demand definite improvements. And so the little Tatra 2 cylinder, so misunderstood when first built came into its own.

Engineers looking for new constructive ideas began to take that car apart studying it and now there is hardly a modern car built, not embodying some of its features.

The Tatra Works, rather insignificant measured by American standards, all of a sudden became famous.

The success, which came to Tatra with this car and the new ideas it stood for, was a result to build a pioneer of the roads for roads that were not as yet developed and for countries where the routine care for a car is indeed very difficult.

This is in short the history of the small Tatra 12, the car with the small, economical but under all conditions efficient engine, the car you could drive over any road, the car that did not need water, the car with the mimimum dead weight.

In short the car ideally fitted for European conditions.

When now, considering the above, learn, that Mr. Ledwinka, the father of the above described car, has left all the ideas of

1

construction underlying the small Tatra and embarked upon the manufacture of a vehicle totally different from anything existing, it would be interesting to trace the reflections prompting him to build the revolutionary 77.

Let us see whether we cannot take these considerations step by step as they must have occurred to him.

WHY PUT THE ENGINE IN THE BACK

This is really already the cardinal question, the key question of the whole problem.

The old orthodox grouping of engine transmission and driving apparatus in one long line stretching from radiator to gas tank has so long been considered a dogma that all other constructive ideas had to be subdued not to disturb it. It is therefore understandable that somebody wanted to make himself free from this forceful arrangement forbidding real improvements.

The evident thing to try was to bring the power plant as near as possible to the actually driven parts, the back wheels. It is clear that if such a move was practically possible the weight of all moving parts would be reduced to a minimum and the loss of energy between power plant and wheel would be eliminated.

The so developed powerplant only takes a small fraction of the room totally available and dictated by the overall dimensions of the vehicle to be built. The power plant, separated by itself into a comparatively small room, has lost its hold and its importance for the total shape and construction of the whole vehicle, which for the first time in automotive construction becomes independent.

Now, that it was decided to have the powerplant where the power was needed, the next consideration and dilemma must have been:

Shall we drive the front wheels with an engine sitting in front or the back wheels with one sitting in back?

Tatra chose to place the engine in back, prompted by the following reasons:

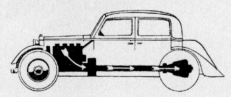

A front drive car necessitates the building in of joints. They must be rugged to stand all that is asked of them and therefore increase the mass of unsprung weight. But if we want an easy riding car we would have to add big shockabsorbers again increasing the unsprung weight.

As you know the application of every joint means loss of power, again to be avoided if possible.

The frontdriven vehicle, because of combination of powerplant and steering apparatus in front is a hard one to steer, another fact no desirable.

When negotiating mountains, a front driven car is hard to keep in balance.

Even if it were possible to eliminate all these apparent disadvantages, the placing of the engine into the back appears simpler and therefore more desirable. But such an arrangement has also some positive advantages. It becomes possible to move the rear axle right to the center of gravity of the entire power aggregation, therefore achieving a balance hitherto unknown.

The motor in the back, is easily accessible from all sides. It transmits the generated power, without universal joints and loss of power. Direct connection between rear axle and engine, proves to be most efficient.

And herein we have explored the first secret of the wonderful Tatra 77 performance, propelling itself, 5 grown-up people and plenty of luggage, over all roads, plains and mountains at a comfortable cruising speed of 80 miles per hour with only 70 hoursepowers available.

And now the constructor has a free hand to do with all the room left as he pleases, knowing to have a more than an efficient power plant ideally located.

Tatra pioneered the famous backbone tube construction on the small Tatra. It was a frame and a home for the power transmission at the same time. With the rear engine it has outlined its usefulness and strength and rigidity is all we ask of the new center frame construction.

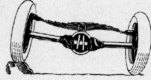

2

3

THE SELF-SUPPORTING BODY
HOW THE FRAME BECAME A BODY

The Tatra 77 has no frame in the usual sense of the word. The frame is in reality replaced by the entire body construction, which solves all the problems of balance and motion in itself.

The basic constructive idea underlying it is the following: As we already stated the engine in the back in a separate isolated room, supported and attached with rubber isolation at three points taking care of its own problems of vibration and noise, both of which never reach the passenger, makes reflection how to prevent vibration, noise, smell etc. within the car unnecessary.

The passengers enjoy their ride, without being bothered by all these disagreeable phenomena, not disagreeably conscious of the propelling force.

WHY INDEPENDENTLY SPRUNG WHEELS
AND A STEERING ROD
FOR EACH INDIVIDUAL WHEEL

The answer to this question is really given in the general construction of Tatra 77.

We shall therefore try to answer it only with reference to the uncanny roadability and balance of this car.

In the closed self-sufficient organism, which the type 77 is, the position of the front axle can be chosen independently so that perfect roadability and springing can be attained by the very favorable position of the center of gravity.

The bottom of the whole vehicle is firmly connected with a center frame which acts so to say as the backbone of the entire vehicle, the connection being of course much less rigid than it would have to be with a conventional frame.

To this central backbone, the front-wheels are attached by means of the tried and proven construction of parallelly individually sprung wheels, the whole construction forming a distinct unit.

In considering the height of the car and with this the probable position of the gravity center, there is only one factor deciding: The road clearance of the vehicle.

In our case same is 8.8 inches, sufficient to clear even the most uneven terrain.

A further advantage is the fact of an absolutely even car bottom which protects the car and makes obstruction by obstacles on the road hanging on protruding parts impossible.

Into this even and roomy bed it is easy to put comfortable reclining seats which allow of a natural and comfortable position. In spite of the extremely small height of the entire car there is plenty of headroom and the car can be entered easily, naturally and without contortions of the body.

The formula which every experienced engineer tries to follow: Lowest center of gravity plus independent wheel suspension equals good roadability and finest performance. This formula is satisfied by the construction of this car to the fullest possible extent..

As the center of gravity lies directly under the backseats the passenger riding there is subject to no motions, vibrations and rides comfortably even over the most uneven roadbed.

It is important to mention that the accumulation of weight in the back of the car makes the use of a strong and stiff spring possible, without the use of shock absorbers in the back, giving a knockless and easy riding over uneven road beds.

The frontwheels, however, are independently sprung by means of softer springs, feeling their way so to say along the road, seemingly gliding away over every obstacle.

Thanks to this arrangement and the correct position of the gravity center the front seat passengers also feel no more than a mild soft swinging. The car lies absolutely safely in the hand of the driver, which is especially evident over bad roads and while negotiating sharp turns.

It has recently been discovered that for a safe negotiation of curves the adhesion to the road of the back wheels only is important. This new

4

5

Tatra works with the utmost application of this principle. The back wheels remain firmly pressed to the ground and present a very decided counterforce to the centrifugal forces trying to press the car out of its way, in a turn, commonly known as side sliding.

WHY REAL STREAMLINING?

It is to be regretted that the current advertising of streamline and airflow designs for bodies which have nothing whatsoever in common with real streamlining have left such a bad impression with the automobile buying public that many manufacturers have returned to a somewhat conventional design.

It is evident that the average layman is in no way aware of the fact that by far the greatest percentage of power produced in the engine of his car is being used up to overcome the resistance of the air.

This percentage becomes larger with increased speeds and at 35 miles per hour there is more power used to overcome air resistance than to move the car itself.

At all speeds above 20 miles per hour 80 per cent of all energy developed is used to combat air resistance.

What would be more logical for the engineer than to try to outsmart this consumer of power developed, this resistance of the air taking as high as 80% of your transportation dollar, with the means already tried and proven practicable by the automobiles brother, the airship and the airplane. The science dealing with this problem is called aerodynamic. The solutions for the automobile have been known for some time, but they all fizzled out because there is no compromise between a scientifical aerodynamically

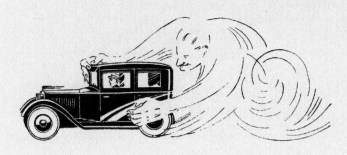

constructed body and an old fashioned chassis. The cars of mostly American manufacture claiming, streamlined, etc. bodies on frame chassis with engine in front are all appearances notwithstanding no more streamlined than your good old car of yesterday.

The new Tatra, however, in no way hampered by an already existing chassis, absolutely free from all antiquated prescriptions as to the shape of the entire vehicle, could well afford to build the first really streamlined car. Its shape is by calculation and experience the shape offering the least air resistance at any given speed for a body of its dimensions.

Its form very much like a fish in shape, blunt in front, pointed in back, is surrounded and helped along by the hurricanes we cause in the air by fast driving. Its form, alike the fish, surrounds all its organs, to the smallest, like wheels, handles, hardware etc. The whole car is like a bullet shooting through the air unhindered and hampered by old enemy air resistance.

The inside of this new fish is very comfortable. It contains five wide seats plenty of leg and headroom, a large compartment for luggage. It is appointed with the utmost of luxury. The seats are of a fine grade leather or a fine plushy velvet as you please.

The hardware is of the finest quality obtainable all in all a fine luxurious piece of machinery even the most particular judge of fine cars would not mind owning.

We have talked of lowered air resistance. This would mean that we can travel faster with the same expenditure of energy or just as fast as before spending less energy or less money.

It pays to be thrifty and it is becoming smart to be thrifty and thrift indeed is the purchaser of a Tatra 77 travelling faster, cheaper and with much less wear to his car.

But there are more comforts yet to be enjoyed in a really streamlined car. All the noises we know so well appearing when we run through a self-created hurricane of 60 miles per hour velocity are totally eliminated. The air surrounding the entire car like a cushion sucks constantly the air from the car replacing same with fresh air creating perfect ventilation. There is no dust or bugs to cling to your windshield no evil smells, no impossibility to smoke a cigarette in comfort and no disagreeable drafts. The car remains

6

7

cleaner of dust and dirt than any other and even the washing of the bottom is just the cleaning of one even steel plate.

The beauty of real streamlining cannot be denied. Simplicity is always beautiful and while some of us find the cars of Grandfather's time good-looking very few of us would like to be seen driving one.

Another advantage is the aircooled engine. This system of cooling has been successfully tried by others and it is a well known fact that not only are the most efficient airplane engines aircooled, but once the owner of an aircooled vehicle, without freezing in the winter or boiling in the summer always ready to go, always an air cool enthusiast.

Now the aircooling is fine on conventional cars but really comes to its greatest development in a streamlined rear engined car the cooling absolutely being independent of the speed.

The purpose of this little book has been achieved if you will take all the advantages here related with a grain of salt, with the idea perhaps that we see this car we are all so proud of through rose coloured glasses. If you will then decide to let us prove our claims, if you but will allow your Tatra dealer or ourselves, to drive you in a Tatra over the worst road, the most treacherous curves over the sharpest incline you know, we shall be fully repaid.

We don't say other cars are bad but we do say that if the purpose of a car be to do certain things Tatra 77 does these things better and cheaper.

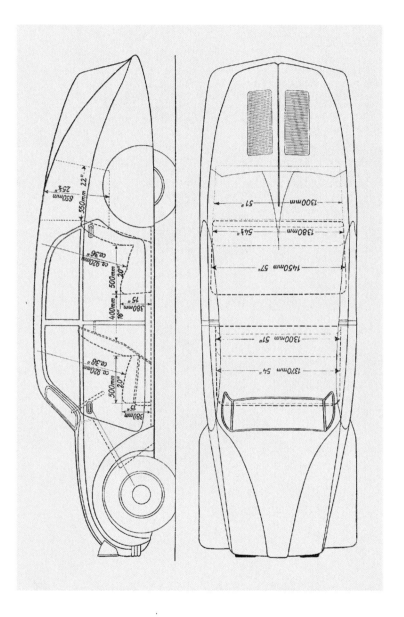

1934 TATRA T 77 FOLD-OUT BROCHURE WITH DRAWN IMAGES AND THE CLASSIC TATRA COVER. THE ILLUSTRATIONS MAY HAVE BEEN INSPIRED BY SIMILAR STREAMLINING DIAGRAMS BY NORMAN BEL GEDDES AND BUCKMINSTER FULLER. (COURTESY IVAN MARGOLIUS)

TATRA ANTISTANDARD SEIT 1921!

Prosperity! Massenproduktion! Standardisierung! — Drei Schlagworte, die Jahre hindurch als letzter Schluß wirtschaftlicher Weisheit galten. Der Taumel großer Zahlen hatte die Welt ergriffen, die Stückzahl ist entscheidend — steigende Masse = sinkende Preise — Jedem sein Auto! • Was bei alledem vergessen wurde, was hinter der Armee von Maschinenkolossen, die seiner Erzeugung dienten, völlig verschwand, war das Erzeugnis selbst. Nichts ändern, nichts verbessern — jede Aenderung des Produktes bedeutete ungeheuerliche Kosten im Etat der Maschinenarmee. • 30 Jahre hindurch beherrschte der Standardwagen den Kraftfahrzeugmarkt der Welt. 30 Jahre hindurch wurde das Kraftfahrzeug ängstlich vor jeder grundlegenden Neuerung behütet. • Vor nunmehr 12 Jahren erschien der kleine Zweizylinder **Tatra** mit Luftkühlung, Zentralrohrrahmen und Schwingachse. In den Kreisen der Fachwelt lächelte man mitleidig über diese ausgefallenen Ideen. Man schwieg sich geflissentlich darüber aus, als der kleine Sonderling in schwierigen Prüfungsfahrten ungeahnte Fähigkeiten und Leistungen bewies. Nur Wenige erkannten, daß hier zum ersten Mal das Fahrgestell des Kraftfahrzeuges als konstrukti...inheit, als rollender Organismus vor uns stand, ein Gebilde höchster Zweckmäßigkeit, dessen Triebwerk zugleich das tragende Rückgrat der federnden, schwingenden, rollenden Extremitäten von größter

Anpassungsfähigkeit an die Fahrbahn bildete. • Was Tatra vor 12 Jahren erstmalig geschaffen, gilt heute als Kennzeichen moderner Bauart. Was Tatra seit 12 Jahren seinen Kunden geboten hat, wird heute von einst glühenden Vertretern des Standardbauprinzips als letzte Errungenschaft der Technik ihrer Neukonstruktionen gepriesen. • 10 Jahre technischer Vorsprung, 12 Jahre konstruktive und produktionstechnische Erfahrung in Bauprinzipien, die den meisten Andern völlig neu waren oder von ihnen vor nicht allzu langer Zeit übernommen wurden, liegen **hinter** Tatra. • Den Vorsprung der Tatra-Werke, den Andere einzuholen bemüht waren und eingeholt haben — den gleichen Vorsprung holt Tatra mit der neuen Type 77 wieder ein. • Wenn Tatra vor 12 Jahren das Fahrgestell als rollenden Organismus schuf und den Fahraufbau als selbständiges Gebilde in der überlieferten Karossenform damit kombinierte — die Type 77 des Jahres 1934 gestaltet zum ersten Mal das Fahrzeug als in sich geschlossene Einheit, als organisch aus den Grundbedingungen des „Fahrens" heraus gewachsenen Körper • Dem Tempo der Zeit entspricht der Schnellverkehr. Automobil ist neben dem Flugzeug das typischste aller Schnellverkehrsmittel. Schnelligkeit bedeutet Kampf gegen den Luftwiderstand, Luftwiderstand bedeutet Kraftvergeudung. Kampf dem Luftwiderstand war daher die grundlegende Forderung, die den Bau des neuen Tatra bestimmte. Die Gestaltung der Außenform mußte den Gesetzen der Aerodynamik gehorchen, ein Körper kleinsten Luftwiderstandes sein. Zugleich aber war sie an das Viereck der vier Räder des Fahrzeugs gebunden und — im Gegensatz zum

Flugzeug und Luftschiffkörper — an die Bodennähe. Diesen formbestimmenden Bedingungen war gleichgeordnet die Forderung nach größtmöglicher Ausnutzung des von der Außenform eingeschlossenen Raumes für die Zwecke der Personenbeförderung, außerdem Schaffung bestmöglicher Sichtverhältnisse für die Insassen dieses geschlossenen Körpers. ● Ein derart zu hoher Geschwindigkeitsentwicklung befähigtes Fahrzeug stellte nun gleichzeitig noch wesentlich erhöhte Forderungen an seine Fahrsicherheit und setzte eine Beherrschung der dynamischen Kräfte voraus, die nur der zu erzielen imstande ist, der dieser Dynamik des Fahrvorgangs die maßgebende Bedeutung beigemessen hat, die einst den kleinen Tatra Type 12 und seinen Nachfolger entstehen ließ. ● **Unabhängige Einzel-**

radfederung und **Einzelradlenkung** waren das erste Kennzeichen dieser fortschrittlichen Bauart. Größtmögliche Konzentration von Totgewichten und Nutzlast ist ebenso bedeutsames Merkmal wie richtige Lage des Schwerpunktes unter gleichzeitiger Annäherung an die Fahrbahn. ● Von den bewegten Massen ausgehende Kräfte sind bestimmend für die Dynamik des Fahrvorgangs. Geringste ungefederte Massen ergab die **achslose Aufhängung** der Vorderräder und die **schwingende Halbachse** der Hinterräder. Anordnung des Nutzraumes **zwischen** den vier Rädern bedeutete den ersten Schritt in der Konzentration der veränderlichen Massen; Schaffung des Triebwerkblockes, der nicht nur Motor, Kupplung und Getriebe möglichst nahe an die getriebene Achse

heranrückt, sondern die getriebene Achse in die Mitte dieses Aggregates verlegt, die endgültige Maßnahme zur Konzentration der Massen des Fahrzeuges. ● Die lange, die Längsmitte des Wagens durchsetzende Reihe der Triebwerksteile, die in Verbindung mit dem die Triebwelle umschließenden Tragrohr das Rückgrat des Tatra-Wagen bildete, war verschwunden. Der Triebwerksblock, der alle Triebwerkorgane vom Motor bis zur Achse in eine kurz bauende Einheit zusammenfügt, war nicht mehr bestimmend für die Gestalt des Fahrgestells, machte den Begriff „Fahrgestell" überhaupt hinfällig. Das Triebwerk wurde dorthin verlegt, wo seine den Schwerpunkt bestimmende Masse erforderlich war: in das **Heck,** den rückwärtigen Teil des Fahrzeugs. ● Der Fußboden, die Unterkante des Fahrzeugkörpers, konnte nunmehr an den tiefsten, überhaupt zulässigen Punkt verlegt werden, das heißt die gesamte Bauhöhe wird durch den

notwendigen Bodenabstand bestimmt. Die Vorderachse wird so angeordnet, daß der Schwerpunkt des Wagens im Bereich der veränderlichen Masse, also der vor den hinteren Kotflügelmulden liegenden Hintersitze liegt und für Vordersitze ausreichend Raum zur Verfügung steht. Wie naheliegend wäre es nun für Tatra gewesen, die bewährte Zentral-Rohranordnung zwischen Vorder- und Hinterachse auch hier anzuwenden. Man überließ dieses blinde, an Tatrabauprinzipien Hängenbleiben Andern und wählte die den neuen völlig geänderten Gesichtspunkten allein entsprechende **organische** Lösung: Die Verbindung zwischen Hinter- und Vorderachse

bildet der Fahrzeugkörper selbst, der als räumliches Fachwerk gestaltet ist und alle Tragfunktionen erfüllt sowie alle beim Fahren auftretenden Kräfte mit höchster Widerstandsfähigkeit aufnimmt. Zugleich aber kommt diese Gesamtbauanordnung den aerodynamischen Erfordernissen ebenso wie den praktischen Forderungen entgegen. Die vorne stumpf, nach rückwärts schlank abfließende „Tropfenform" des Körpers kleinsten Luftwiderstandes ergibt sich ohne unorganisch lange Ueberbauung der Hinterachse beim Heckmotor zwanglos. Der eigentliche Nutzraum verlagert sich nach vorn in den größten zulässigen Querschnitt des Fahrzeugkörpers, das breite Halbrund der Sichtscheiben liegt im vorderen Drittel vor dem abgerundeten, abfallenden Vorderteil und ergibt Sichtverhältnisse, wie sie idealer, besonders für ein schnell fahrendes Fahrzeug, nicht gedacht werden können. ● Das Hecktriebaggregat ist mit dem eigentlichen Fahrzeugkörper in drei Punkten unter Zwischenlage von Gummi vereinigt und damit in allem, was Geräusch-, Schall- und Schwingungsübertragung angeht, völlig vom Fahrzeugkörper isoliert. Eine durchgehende, schall- und luftdicht ausgeführte Wand zwischen Sitzraum und Triebwerkraum macht jedes Geräusch und jede

Geruchbelästigung der Insassen durch das Triebwerk unmöglich. ● Der überaus kurz gebaute Achtzylinder mit je zwei unter 45 Grad stehenden, in Reihe angeordneten Vierzylindern gibt völlig erschütterungsfreien Lauf. Er arbeitet über die Kupplung durch die hohle Welle des Hinterachsgetriebes auf das Wechselgetriebe mit drei geräuschlosen Gangstufen. Im direkten Gang sind Motor und Hinterachs-Triebwerk unmittelbar starr miteinander gekuppelt. ● Die Kraftübertragung findet mit dem höchsten erdenklichen Wirkungsgrad, frei von allen Schwingungen, Reibungen und dergl. langgestreckter Uebertragungsorgane statt. Der bewährte gelenklose Antrieb der schwingenden Achshälften durch sich abwälzende Kegelräder ergibt unabhängig von der Radstellung stets gleichen und höchsten Wirkungsgrad. ● Tatra-**Luftkühlung** ist das Kennzeichen auch dieses hochentwickelten 3-l-Motors. Zwei geräuschlos durch Gummiriemen angetriebene Gebläse umspülen die Zylinderreihen mit ausreichender Kühlluft. Luftkühlung ist für den Hecktrieb unerläßlich und von grundsätzlicher Bedeutung im „Stromlinienwagen", da sie unabhängig macht von dem nur im Fahrwind bei großen Luftgeschwindigkeiten mit hohen Luftwiderständen arbeitenden Kühler der Wasserkühlung. ● Die Halbachsen des Hecktriebes schwingen um Achsmitte. Die abrollende Spuränderung der Lauffläche der Hinterräder mit ihrer hohen und wünschenswerten schwingungdämpfenden Wirkung erfolgt innerhalb der zulässigen Deformationsgrenzen der Bereifung. Sehr im Gegensatz zu jenen Tatra-Epigonen, die den Antrieb der schwingenden Halbachsen durch **Gelenke** bewirken, die weit außerhalb Achsmitte liegen. Hier wird die Bereifung bis an die Grenze der zulässigen Deformationen durch übermäßige Spuränderung bei gleichzeitig hohen Arbeitsverlusten und ungleichförmigen Triebkräften (Gelenkwirkung) beansprucht. ● Die **Hinterräder** stützen sich auf eine kräftige Querfeder mit progressiver Wirkung. Die Massenkonzentration ermöglicht Einbau einer verhältnismäßig harten Feder bei ausreichendem Federweg, so daß im Gegensatz zu übermäßig weicher Federung feste Haftung der Räder an der Fahrbahn und damit hervorragende Straßenlage gewährleistet ist, trotz völlig erschütterungsfreien Fahrens, auch auf schlechtester Fahrbahn ● Die Vorderräder sind kugelig

in parallelen Schwingarmen besonders stabiler Bauart gelagert und durch eine Querfeder gestützt. Lenk- und Federwirkung werden beide in der kugeligen Lagerung aufgenommen. Die hervorragend bewährte Tatra-**Zahnstangenlenkung** wirkt unabhängig mit geteilter Spurstange auf die Räder. ● Drei bequeme Sitze nebeneinander lassen sich in dem fast auf volle Spurweite verbreiterten Fahrzeugkörper in zwei Reihen hintereinander anordnen. Hinter den Rücksitzen zwischen den Mulden der Hinterräder liegt ein geräumiger **Kofferraum**. Zwischen den Mulden der Vorderräder sind Reserveräder, Akkumulator und Werkzeug untergebracht. Ein weiterer Gepäckraum ist vorgesehen und durch eine hochstellbare Haube leicht zugänglich gemacht. Zwei getrennte, durch Dreiwegehahn in Verbindung stehende Brennstofftanks liegen völlig außerhalb jeden Brandbereiches, frei von Erwärmung und Auspuffgasen, unter den Vordersitzen. **Hydraulische Bremsen** und **hydraulische Stoßdämpfer** wirken auf alle vier Räder. ● Und nun die **Fahreigenschaften!** ● Der auf dem niedrigsten, überhaupt denkbaren Abstand von der Fahrbahn liegende Schwerpunkt, die Konzentration der Massen im hinteren Wagendrittel, die vier unabhängig gefederten Räder — sie ergeben eine Dynamik des Fahrvorgangs, wie sie bisher niemals auch nur annähernd erreicht wurde. Die Insassen der hinteren Sitzreihe sitzen im Schwerpunkt völlig schwingungsfrei. Die Hinterachse arbeitet mit höchstem Adhäsionsdruck und einer Straßen- und Kurvenhaftung, die ans Unglaubliche grenzen. Die stark gedämpft wirkende Aufhängung der Vorderräder läßt die Vorder-

achse das Gelände gewissermaßen abtasten. Spielend leicht gehorcht die Lenkung jedem Steuerdruck, und selbst auf schlechtester Fahrbahn, bei höchsten Geschwindigkeiten ist kaum mehr als ein leises Wiegen für die Insassen zu spüren. Das Fahren wird zum rollenden Schweben, zu einem geräuschlosen Ueber-die-Landstraße-Stürmen, zu einem völlig neuen Erlebnis! Nur noch vergleichbar mit dem Naturgenuß, den eine Segelfahrt auf stillem Wasser bietet. ● Und welche **Fahrleistungen!** ● Der mit 6 Personen besetzte Wagen erreicht mit seinem 60 Pferde leistenden, also gering belasteten 3-l-Motor eine Spitzengeschwindigkeit von mehr als 150 km/h. Der Luftwiderstand ist beseitigt, seine kraftverzehrende Wirkung ausgeschaltet. ● Das äußert sich nicht nur in dieser enormen Spitzengeschwindigkeit, sondern in einem bisher unerreicht niedrigen **Brennstoffverbrauch**. Trotz mühelos erreichbarem Stundendurchschnitt von 80 km und darüber auf normalen Straßen werden wenig über 14 l Brennstoff für 100 km Fahrstrecke benötigt. Mit Verbrauchszahlen, die heute ein besonders günstig konstruierter Wagen normaler Bauweise mit einem 2-l-Motor und 4 Insassen erreicht, werden 6 Personen mit ausreichendem Gepäck in unerhörtem Stundendurchschnitt befördert. Der Kraftüberschuß aber, der noch bei Geschwindigkeiten um 100 km/h im Motor steckt, steht dem Fahrer als Reserve in Bergen und im Stadtverkehr zur Verfügung. ● Tatra hat in dieser Type 77 nicht nur dem konstruktiven Fortschritt neue Wege geebnet, sondern den Begriff **Wirtschaftlichkeit** neu gestaltet. ● Aber welches Maß von **Komfort** bietet dieses wirtschaftliche Fahrzeug seinem Besitzer: Der Kampf zwischen Fahrzeug und Luft, der als Chaos von Geräuschen den Wagen einhüllte, durch alle Ritzen pfiff und unleidlichen und unabstellbaren Zug auch im fest geschlossenen Wageninnern hervorrief — all diese Erscheinungen sind verschwunden. Selbst bei Höchstgeschwindigkeit ist nur ein weiches Rauschen der vorüberfließenden Außenluft zu hören. Im Wageninnern herrscht Ueberdruck, der jede Zugerscheinung vollkommen ausschließt. Während bisher die Sichtscheiben sich mit allen in der Luft fliegenden Fremdkörpern bedeckten, während Sogerscheinungen ganze Teile der Wagenoberflächen mit Staub und Kot überzogen, bleiben beim neuen Tatra die Scheiben völlig klar, der Fahrzeugkörper völlig sauber, auch nach langer Fahrt unter ungünstigen Bedingungen ● Dieser von jedem überflüssigen Zierat, von jeder sinnlosen Ornamentik und Rudimenten der Karossenzeit befreite Fahrzeugkörper ist mühelos zu reinigen und zu pflegen. Genau so wenig wie er der Luft Widerstand und Angriffspunkte bietet, genau so unempfindlich bleibt er gegen Einflüsse des Wetters, der Atmosphäre und der Verschmutzung. Bestimmte Seitenscheiben und in gewissen Zonen des Daches angebrachte Öffnungen lassen sich aufmachen, ohne daß Wirbelvorgänge auftreten. Sie liegen im Fahrwindschatten, der Luftstrom streicht daran vorüber - ohne Rückwirkung auf das Wageninnere. ● Der Tatra 77 ist damit im besten Sinne des Wortes ein Allwetter-Fahrzeug; er

schützt in einer bisher nie erreichten Weise die Insassen vor Kälte, Zugluft und Nässe, ohne sie räumlich zu behindern; bei schönem Wetter, bei Wärme und Sonnenschein bringt er sie in unmittelbaren Kontakt zur Aussenluft, ohne auf die Dauer unerträgliche Zugerscheinungen im raschen Wechsel von Ueberhitzung und starker Abkühlung. ● Es ist nicht zuviel behauptet, daß der neue Achtzylinder Tatra die Begriffe **Fahrsicherheit, Fahrkomfort** und **Wirtschaftlichkeit** völlig neu gestaltet hat. So wie der weltbekannte Zweizylinder Tatra 12 Jahre lang seiner Zeit voran war und als einziger Wagen der Weltproduktion 12 Jahre hindurch ohne wesentliche Änderungen in Serien produziert wurde — genau soweit eilt der neue Tatra 77 seiner Zeit voraus! ● Während geredet und diskutiert wird, während sich die Begriffe mit Schlagworten verwirren und Karosserie-Architektur getrieben wird, hat Tatra gearbeitet, geforscht, konstruiert und gebaut. Zum ersten Male ist die **Einheit** des Kraftfahrzeugs geschaffen: der aus sich selbst gewachsene **Organismus,** der über die Erdoberfläche rollt, die Luft durchschneidet und das Fahren zum Schweben macht:

TATRA Type 77, der Wagen der Zukunft!

TATRA baut alle Arten von Personen- und Nutzfahrzeugen serienmäßig mit torsionsfestem Fahrgestell, unabhängiger Radfederung und Lenkung gelenkloser Kraftübertragung.

TATRA baut **Personenwagen** von 1,2 l bis 6 l Zylinderinhalt, vom kleinen Volkswagen, bis zur großen Welt-Luxusklasse.

TATRA baut **Nutzfahrzeuge** vom kleinen Dreirad-Lieferwagen bis zum 10-Tonnen-Sechsradwagen. Unerreicht geringes Totgewicht bei höchster Stabilität und Tragfähigkeit, also vorbildlicher **Wirtschaftlichkeit!**

TATRA baut **Schienenomnibusse** und **Triebwagen** mit Benzin- und Dieselmotoren bis zu den schwersten Einheiten, mit mechanischem und elektrischem Antrieb.

TATRA baut **Spezialfahrzeuge** vom kleinen geländegängigen Sechsradwagen bis zum schweren Traktor und zur Straßenwalze.

TATRA beschäftigt 6000 Arbeiter und Angestellte und stellt sämtliche Teile der Fahrgestelle und Fahraufbauten in den eigenen Werksanlagen in **Kopřivnice, Stauding** und **Böhm. Leipa** her.

TATRA ist die älteste osteuropäische Automobilfabrik seit 1896.

TATRA-WERKE A.G.
GENERALDIREKTION PRAG-SMICHOV / FABRIK KOPŘIVNICE
Generalvertretung für Deutschland: Detra G.m.b.H., Frankfurt am Main, Franken-Allee 98-100

1934 TATRA T77 BROCHURE WITH IMAGES DRAWN BY PETR FLENYKO, AUR STUDIO, PRAGUE-SMÍCHOV. FLENYKO WAS THE AUTHOR OF THE FAMOUS POSTER FOR THE 25TH INTERNATIONAL AUTOMOBILE EXHIBITION, PRAGUE 1935. (COURTESY GARY CULLEN)

IN JEDER HINSICHT NEUARTIG

Die Abkehr vom Althergebrachten ist nicht willkürlich, im Gegenteil durch theoretische Erkenntnisse bedingt. Soll aber alles das, was moderne wissenschaftliche Forschung als praktisch durchführbar erkennt, auch konsequent in die Tat umgesetzt werden, dann dürfen Äußerlichkeiten und Gewohnheiten keine Hemmschuhe bilden, dann muß auch der Mut groß genug sein, die Fesseln des Herkömmlichen zu zerreißen.

Diesem Willen dankt der Tatra 77 seine Entstehung. Völlig neu ist seine Konstruktion. Sein Fahrzeugkörper und sein Triebwerk bilden eine Einheit, deren Außenform von den Gesetzen des kleinsten Luftwiderstandes gestaltet wurde. Mit einem geringstmöglichem Aufwand konstruktiver Hilfsmittel ist ein so hohes Maß an Fahrsicherheit, Schnelligkeit und Fahrkomfort erreicht worden, das alles in dieser Beziehung bisher Erreichte weit hinter sich läßt.

DAS TRIEBWERK des Tatra 77 ist im Heck — dem rückwärtigen Teil —

des Wagens untergebracht und zu einem kompakten Block zusammengeschrumpft. Motor, Kupplung und Getriebe sind miteinander vereinigt und mit der Hinterachse direkt verbunden. Der luftgekühlte 8-Zylinder-Motor, dessen Zylinder zu je 4 in einer Reihe unter 90° angeordnet sind und auf eine gemeinschaftliche Kurbelwelle arbeiten, ist freitragend auf dem Triebachsgehäuse angeblockt. Zwei Ventilatoren bewirken intensive Luftkühlung. Die Nockenwelle liegt zwischen den Zylinderreihen und betätigt durch einfache Schwinghebel die schräg im Zylinderkopf angeordneten hängenden Ventile. Ein Fallstrom-Doppelvergaser führt durch zwei Viererleitungen das Gemisch den Zylindern zu. Der ganze Vergaser samt Ansaugleitungen kann durch Betätigung von

Klappen mit der abströmenden warmen Kühlluft umspült oder mit kalter Frischluft versorgt werden. Über eine trockene Einscheibenkupplung bewährter Bauart arbeitet der Motor auf eine elastische Welle aus Spezialfederstahl, durch die hohle Ritzelwelle des Hinterachsantriebs hindurch auf das Vierganggetriebe, dessen zweiter und dritter Gang mit geräuschloser Schrägverzahnung versehen sind. Die Hinterachse selbst zeigt die tausendfach bewährte Tatra-Konstruktion mit gelenklosem Antrieb der Achshälften durch aufeinander abwälzende Kegelräder und Aufnahme der von den Hinterachsrädern ausgehenden Schub- und Bremskräfte in der praktisch abnutzungsfreien Gabellagerung der Achshälften.

DER FAHRZEUGKÖRPER ist als Einheit gebaut, eine Unterteilung in Fahrgestell und Karosserie ist nicht mehr vorhanden. Der Unterteil des Fahrkörpers, der zugleich den Fußboden bildet, zeigt einen zentralliegenden Hohlkörper, der die Verbindung zwischen dem rückwärtigen Triebwerkblock und der Vorderachse darstellt. Das Heck des Wagens

ist ein in sich geschlossener und vom eigentlichen Fahrzeug-
körper luftdicht abgeschlossener Raum, der die Führung der
Luftkanäle enthält und durch eine türartige Klappe freien
Zugang zum Motor schafft. Schalt-, Gas- und Bremsgestänge
sind an den zentralen Hohlkörper gelagert, an dessen Vorderseite die Einheit der Vorderachse samt Federung und
Lenkung befestigt ist. Die Vorderräder sind dabei in parallelen Schwingarmen kugelig gelagert, so daß Federungs- und
Lenkbewegungen im gleichen Gelenke aufgenommen werden.
Die Lenkung — Schraubenspindel — wirkt mit Einzel-
stangen auf jedes Rad, ist also als sogenannte Einzelradlenkung ausgebildet. Die Außenform ist den aerodynamischen
Bedingungen — der Überwindung des Luftwiderstandes —

völlig angepaßt. Ihre Grundform wird ausschließlich durch Spurweite und Radstand bestimmt. Die
den günstig geformten Bug umströmende Luft — Fahrwind — findet wirbelfreien Abfluß an den
glatten Seitenwänden mit dem verjüngten Heck, an der völlig glatten Unterseite und dem Dach.
Die Hinterräder sind seitlich durch leicht abnehmbare Verkleidungen verdeckt.

DIE RAUMAUFTEILUNG war durch Fortfall des Chassis beson-
ders glücklich lösbar. Der ganze zwischen den 4 Rädern liegende Raum konnte unbeschränkt als
Nutzraum dienstbar gemacht werden. Die Hintersitze liegen unmittelbar vor den Kotflügelmulden
der Hinterräder, haben also mehr als die volle Spurbreite und bieten bequemen Sitz für 3 Personen.
Sämtliche Scheiben sind nach innen geneigt, so daß die gefürchteten Spiegelungen von rückwärts
und der Seite unmöglich sind. Vier breite Türen gewähren bequemen Ein- und Ausstieg. Der Bug —
der vordere Teil des Wagens — ist durch eine hochstellbare Haube zugänglich. Er enthält den Brenn-
stoffbehälter und genügend Raum für die Unterbringung der Reserveräder, des Akkumulators,
des Werkzeugs und anderen Zubehörs.

DIE SCHWERPUNKTLAGE
ist von ausschlaggebendem Einfluß auf die Fahrsicherheit
und Fahreigenschaften eines Wagens. Bestimmend für die
Schwerpunkthöhe des Tatra 77 war ausschließlich der Bodenabstand, d. h. in diesem Falle der Abstand des Fußbodens
von der Fahrbahn. Er ist somit auf den praktisch tiefstmöglichen Punkt verlegt, so daß die absolut niedrigste Lage des
Schwerpunktes erzielt ist und beim Kurvenfahren die geringstmöglichen Kippmomente auftreten. Der Schwerpunkt
der Type 77 liegt etwa in den Hintersitzen, so daß die an
dieser Stelle sitzenden Insassen sich im Zentrum aller Massenschwingungen befinden, also von ihnen selbst unberührt
bleiben. Im vollbesetzten wie im leeren Wagen ist diese
Schwerpunktlage annähernd unverändert, so daß die Ab-

stimmung der Federn bei gleichbleibender Wirkung einwandfrei erfolgen kann. Die unabhängige
Federung sorgt für geringste Rückwirkung der Straßenunebenheiten auf die Fahrzeugmasse. Das
ist eine Tatsache, die seit mehr als einem Jahrzehnt von Tatra verfochten wird.

DIE FAHREIGENSCHAFTEN und alles, was unter Fahr-
komfort verstanden wird, liegen weit über dem bisher Gewohnten und Bekannten. Der Fahrzeugkörper liegt auch bei höchsten Geschwindigkeiten auf schlechter Fahrbahn vollkommen ruhig. Fast
ohne Lenkungskorrekturen hält der Wagen die Gerade und gehorcht willig dem leisesten Steuerdruck, zeigt eine bisher nie erreichte Kurvenhaltung, eine unbeschreibliche Anpassungsfähigkeit an
das Fahrterrain und eine ebenso erstaunliche Bremsfähigkeit. Die Maschinenanlage im Heck bleibt
unhörbar und geruchlos, ohne daß Kraft verzehrende Schalldämpfungen erforderlich wären. Die
überaus bequeme Sitzanordnung und Sitzlage, die schräg stehenden großen Seitenscheiben und
breiten Vorderscheiben in Verbindung mit dem schmalen zurücktretendem Dach ergeben eine Sicht,
die alle, Fahrer und Fahrgäste, in engstem Kontakt zur Landschaft bringt.

Die WIRTSCHAFTLICHKEIT

der Type 77 ist trotz der überlegenen Leistung, trotz dem Höchstmaße an Fahrkomfort geradezu vorbildlich. Der 3-Liter-Achtzylindermotor arbeitet — befreit von den Fesseln des Luftwiderstandes — mit höchstem Wirkungsgrad wie ein normaler 2-Liter-Motor auf ebenem Gelände. In den Bergen aber und in schwierigem Fahrterrain steht die volle Kraft des 3-Liter-Motors zur Verfügung, und nur hier wird bei Höchstgeschwindigkeiten der Motor auf volle Leistung beansprucht. Um ein Optimum an Wirtschaftlichkeit zu erreichen, war die neuartige Konstruktionsweise des Tatra 77 an keine schönheitsmindernde Formen oder Linien gebunden. Die Gesetze des kleinsten Luftwiderstandes diktierten Kraftmaß und Form! So steht ein Wagen vor Ihnen, dessen wahre wirtschaftlichen Grundlagen der geringstmögliche Verbrauch und die längste Lebensdauer sind!

MOTOR UND ÜBRIGES TRIEBWERK

ZYLINDERZAHL:	8	KOLBEN:	Leichtmetall
BOHRUNG UND HUB:	75 × 84 mm	ZÜNDUNG:	Batterie
INHALT:	2970 cm³	SCHMIERUNG:	Druckumlauf mit Filter
ZYLINDERKÖPFE:	abnehmbar	VERGASER:	Doppelfallstrom
STEUERUNG:	geräuschloser Kniehebel	BRENNSTOFFZUFUHR:	mechanische Pumpe
STEUERWELLE UND ANTRIEB:		zwischen den Zylinderreihen mit geräuschloser Rollenkette	
KURBELWELLE:		3-fach gelagert,	
KÜHLUNG:		Luftkühlung durch 2 Gebläse, Keilriemenantrieb	
DREHZAHL BEI 100 St/km:	2720 U/min.	ZÜNDFOLGE:	1, 2, 7, 8, 4, 5, 6, 3
BREMSLEISTUNG BEI 3500 U/min.:	60 PS	KUPPLUNG:	Einscheiben-Trockenkupplung
GETRIEBE: Übersetzungsverhältnis (1:4·14, 1:2·7, 1:1·58, 1:1)			
SCHALTUNG:	Kugelschaltung	KRAFTÜBERTRAGUNG:	gelenklos
DIFFERENTIAL:	Stirnanordnung	FEDERUNG:	Querfedern hinten und vorn
FUSSBREMSE:	hydraulische Vierradbremse	HANDBREMSE:	an die Hinterräder, mechanisch
RÄDER, FELGEN:	Vollscheiben, 16 × 45	HINTERACHSE:	geteilt, spiralverzahnte Kegelräder
VORDERACHSE: Parallelschwingarme mit kugeliger Lagerung des Lenkzapfens			Übersetzungsverhältnis, 1:3·75
LENKUNG:	Einzelradlenkung mit Schraubenspindel		
AUSRÜSTUNG: 2 bereifte Reserveräder, Stoßstangen, hydraulische Stoßdämpfer, Zentralschmierung.			

HAUPTABMESSUNGEN

SPURWEITE: 1300 mm	GRÖSSTE WAGENLÄNGE: ca. 5150 mm
RADSTAND: ca. 3150 mm	GRÖSSTE WAGENBREITE: ca. 1700 mm
HÖHE: ca. 1520 mm	BODENFREIHEIT: 220 mm
KOFFERRAUM:	ca. 250 dm²
KRAFTSTOFFVERBRAUCH bei Fahrten auf freier Strecke:	14 - 16 l/100 km
ÖLVERBRAUCH:	0·3 - 0·4 l/100 km
HÖCHSTGESCHWINDIGKEIT:	150 km/St.
GEWICHT:	ca. 1700 kg fahrbereit

TATRA - WERKE
AKT. GES. FÜR AUTOMOBILBAU
PRAG - SMÍCHOV, KARTOUZSKÁ 3

TATRA-WERKE
PRAG-SMÍCHOV

1934 TATRA T77
BROCHURE, INCLUDING
FIVE PHOTOGRAPHS
BY JOSEF SUDEK, THE
WORLD-RENOWNED
PHOTOGRAPHER, OF THE
T77 PROTOTYPE SHOWN
OUTSIDE RUDOLFINUM, ON
VALDŠTEJNSKÁ STREET, IN
THE COUNTRY, AT MÁNES
BRIDGE, AND ON SKALNÍ
STREET, BARRANDOV,
PRAGUE. COVER DESIGN BY
AUR STUDIO. (COURTESY
GARY CULLEN)

TATRA 77

TATRA TYPE 77.

Tradition heißt: Fest verwurzelt sein in der Vergangenheit und ihrer Entwicklungsgeschichte, um sicher in der Gegenwart zu stehen und der Zukunft kraftvoll entgegen zu wachsen.

Die Zeit der Karosse und langsamen Beschaulichkeit ist vorüber. Die Gegenwart hat Fahrzeuge geschaffen, die schneller als Sturmwind das Land durcheilen, die einen Sturmwind in der Luft erzeugen, der sich ihnen entgegenstemmt, mit Kräften, mächtiger als ein Orkan.

Das Tempo der Zeit kommt in diesen schnellen Gefährten zum Ausdruck. Fahren wird zum Kampf gegen die Atmosphäre. Schnell sein heißt: Den trägen Widerstand der Luft überwinden. Noch versucht die Gegenwart die Führung dieses Kampfes mit brutaler Kraft. Doch so wie rohe Gewalt, stets geistigen Waffen unterlegen war, so gilt es heute, den Kampf gegen den Luftwiderstand mit den Waffen der jüngsten Wissenschaft — der Aerodynamik — aufzunehmen.

Zwölf Jahre zuvor haben die Tatrawerke in völliger Abkehr von den damals geltenden Konstruktionprinzipien dem Fahrgestell des Automobils die Eigenschaften des „rollenden Organismus" gegeben. Diese von Tatra zum erstenmale verwirklichten Bauprinzipien der unabhängigen Radfederung und Radlenkung in Verbindung mit dem verwindungssteifen Fahrgestell, sind heute Kennzeichen moderner Konstruktion.

Die von Tatra im Jahre 1934 herausgebrachte Type 77 vollzieht einen ebenso einschneidenden Bruch mit diesen modernsten Bauprinzipien: Sie schafft die völlige Vereinheitlichung und Vereinigung von Fahrzeugkörper, rollenden und treibenden Organen und paßt die Außenform dieser Einheit den Gesetzen des kleinsten Luftwiderstandes an.

Nicht das „Modeschlagwort" Stromlinie war maßgebend für diese Bauweise. Ebenso wenig ist der Versuch gemacht worden, eine gegebene Fahrgestellkonstruk-

1

TATRA 77

tion aerodynamisch richtig zu „verkleiden". Nein — die Tatra Type 77 ist eine Einheit, deren Einzelheiten untrennbar voneinander sind und die in allen Punkten den Grundsätzen höchster Zweckmäßigkeit unbedingt gehorcht.

So entstand ein Fahrzeug, das innerlich zu Höchstleistungen befähigt ist, das mit dem geringstmöglichen Aufwand konstruktiver Hilfsmittel und Todgewicht ein Maß von Fahrtsicherheit, Schnelligkeit, Fahrkomfort und Kraftreserve bietet, das alles bisher Erreichte weit hinter sich läßt.

Und diese überlegenen Eigenschaften sind hier bei einem Fahrzeug zu finden, das an Stelle brutaler Kraftentfaltung den Luftwiderstand spielend überwindet und daher als 6-sitziges Fahrzeug mit einem Kraft- und damit Brennstoffverbrauch auskommt, der heute für kleine 4-sitzige Wagen üblich ist.

Hier ist ein Fahrzeug geschaffen, das Zukünftiges verwirklicht und das gegenwärtige Höchstleistungen mit der Selbstverständlichkeit eines Gebrauchsfahrzeuges vollbringt.

DAS TRIEBWERK

zeigt in seiner eigenwilligen Gestaltung den ersten grundlegenden Unterschied, den üblichen Bauarten gegenüber. Die sonst den ganzen Wagen durchsetzende Triebwerksreihe ist zu einem einzigen kompakten Triebwerkblock zusammengeschrumpft. Treibender Teil (Motorkupplung, Getriebe) und getriebener Teil (schwingende Halbachsen) sind nicht nur völlig vereinigt, sondern der getrie-

bene Teil (die Hinterachse) liegt in der Mitte dieses Blockes. Ein luftgekühlter Achtzylindermotor, dessen Zylinder zu je 4 in Reihe unter 90° angeordnet sind und auf eine gemeinschaftliche Kurbelwelle arbeiten, ist rückwärts freitragend auf das Triebachsgehäuse angeblockt. Zwei rechts und links unter den Zylinderreihen liegende, durch Keilriemen geräuschlos angetriebene Ventilatoren bewirken intensive Luftkühlung. Die Nockenwelle liegt zwischen den Zylinderreihen und betätigt durch einfache Schwinghebel die schräg im Zylinderkopfe angeordneten hängenden Ventile. Ein Fallstrom-Doppelvergaser führt durch zwei Vierzylinderleitungen das Gemisch den Zylindern zu. Der ganze Vergaser samt Ansaugleitungen kann durch Betätigung von Klappen mit der abströmenden warmen Kühlluft umspült oder mit kalter Frischluft versorgt werden.

Über eine trockene Einscheibenkupplung bewährter Bauart arbeitet der Motor auf eine elastische Welle aus Spezial-Federstahl, durch die hohle Ritzelwelle des Hinterachsantriebs hindurch auf das Vierganggetriebe, dessen zweiter und dritter Gang mit geräuschloser Schrägverzahnung versehen sind. Ein ein- und abstellbarer Freilauf vor dem Getriebe sichert müheloses und geräuschloses Schalten.

Die Hinterachse selbst zeigt die tausendfach bewährte Tatra-Konstruktion mit gelenklosem Antrieb der Achshälften durch aufeinander abwälzende Kegelräder und Aufnahme der von den Hinterrädern ausgehenden Schub- und Bremskräfte in der praktisch abnutzungsfreien Gabellagerung der Achshälften.

2

TATRA 77

TATRA 77

DER FAHRZEUGKÖRPER

ist als Einheit gebaut, eine Unterteilung in Fahrgestell und Karosserie ist nicht vorhanden.

Der Unterteil des Fahrkörpers, der zugleich den Fußboden bildet, zeigt einen zentralliegenden Hohlkörper, der die Verbindung zwischen Triebwerkblock und Vorderachse darstellt. Der Triebwerkblock selbst ist im Heck angeordnet, und zwar in Dreipunktaufhängung gummi-

gelagert mit dem Fahrzeugkörper verbunden. Das Heck des Wagens ist als in sich völlig geschlossener und vom eigentlichen Fahrzeugkörper luftdicht abgeschlossener Raum ausgebildet, der die Führung der Kühlluftkanäle enthält und durch eine türartige Klappe im oberen Rückteil freie Zugänglichkeit zum Motor bietet. Schalt-, Gas- und Bremsgestänge sind an dem zentralen Hohlkörper gelagert, an dessen Vorderseite die Einheit der Vorderachse samt Federung und Lenkung befestigt ist. Die Vorderräder sind dabei in parallelen Schwingarmen kugelig gelagert, so daß Federungs- und Lenkbewegungen im gleichen Gelenke aufgenommen werden. Die Lenkung (Schraubenspindel) wirkt mit Einzelstangen auf jedes Rad, ist also als sogenannte Radeinzellenkung ausgebildet.

DIE AUSSENFORM

ist den aerodynamischen Bedingungen des Körpers kleinsten Luftwiderstandes völlig angepaßt. Ihre Grundform wird ausschließlich durch Spurweite und Radstand bestimmt, Kotflügel und Fahrzeugkörper sind zu einer Einheit vereinigt, die den ganzen Raum unter Einschluß der Räder überdeckt. Die den günstig geformten Bug umströmende Luft — der Fahrwind — findet wirbelfreien Abfluß an den glatten Seitenwänden mit dem verjüngten Heck, ebenso wie an der völlig glatten Unterseite des Fahrzeuges. Eine Einschnürung im Vorderteil des geschlossenen Fahrzeugkörpers ermöglicht den organischen Einbau der Sichtscheiben, die nach innen geneigt das stark verjüngte Dach tragen.

3

TATRA 77

TATRA 77

Der Fahrwind umströmt diesen Oberteil und findet wiederrum wirbelfreien Abfluß im langgestreckten, abwärtsgezogenen Heckteil des Wagens. Die Scheinwerfer sind vollständig eingebaut und passen sich der Wagenoberfläche an. Die Hinterräder sind seitlich durch leicht abnehmbare Verkleidungen verdeckt. Diese Formgebung wurde nach umfassenden aerodynamischen Versuchen als besonders günstig ermittelt.

DIE RAUMAUFTEILUNG

des Fahrzeugkörpers bietet bisher unerreichte Vorteile.

Zum ersten ist der ganze zwischen den 4 Rädern liegende Raum unbeschränkt als Nutzraum dienstbar gemacht. Die Hintersitze liegen unmittelbar vor den Kotflügelmulden der Hinterräder, haben also mehr als die volle Spurbreite und bieten bequemen Sitz für 3 Personen. Hinter den Hintersitzen über dem Getriebe des Maschinenaggregates ist ein überaus geräumiger Kofferraum im Wageninnern vorgesehen.

Der Führer sitzt in der Mitte des Wagens. Tatra hat die ewige Streitfrage „Rechts- oder Linkslenkung?" so entschieden, indem es den Führer an die Stelle des Wagens setzt, wo er unbehinderten, idealen Überblick über Fahrbahn und Fahrzeug erhält. Die Instrumente liegen vor ihm, die Pedale sind rechts und links vom Mittelträger angeordnet. Sämtliche Scheiben sind nach innen geneigt, so daß die gefürchteten Spiegelungen von rückwärts und der Seite unmöglich sind.

Zwei weitere Vordersitze sind vorgesehen, die im solchen Maße versetzt hinter dem zentralen Führersitz

liegen, daß eine Behinderung des Führers durch die Mitfahrenden niemals eintreten kann, ohne daß der Kontakt mit den übrigen Insassen verloren geht.

Vier breite Türen bilden bequemen Ein- und Ausstieg.

Der Bugteil des Wagens ist durch eine hochstellbare Haube zugänglich. Er enthält den Raum für die Unterbringung der Reserveräder, des Akkumulators, des Werkzeugs und anderen Zubehörs.

4

TATRA 77

TATRA 77

Der Brennstoff ist in zwei getrennt durch Dreiwegehahn schaltbaren Tanks weit außerhalb des Bereichs von Motor und Auspuffgasen in der Wagenmitte unter den Vordersitzen angebracht und sind von einer Stelle außerhalb des Fahrgastraumes zu füllen.

DIE SCHWERPUNKTLAGE

ist von ausschlaggebendem Einfluß auf Fahreigenschaften und Fahrsicherheit. Während bei der üblichen Bauart die Schwerpunkthöhe maßgebend von der Mitte des Achsantriebes bestimmt wurde, da die Triebswerkorgane in der Ebene dieser Mittellinie liegen mußten und den Wagen der Länge nach durchsetzen, bleibt die Type 77 von diesen Maßbindungen frei. Bestimmend für die Schwerpunkthöhe war ausschließlich der Bodenabstand, d. h. in diesem Falle der Abstand des Fußbodens von der Fahrbahn. Er ist auf den praktisch tiefstmöglichen Punkt verlegt, so daß die absolut niedrigste Lage des Schwerpunktes erzielt ist und beim Kurvenfahren die geringstmöglichen Kippmomente auftreten.

Der Schwerpunkt der Type 77 liegt etwa in den Hintersitzen, so daß die an dieser Stelle sitzenden Insassen sich im Zentrum aller Massenschwingungen befinden, also unberührt von diesen Vorgängen bleiben.

Im vollbesetzten wie im leeren Wagen ist diese Schwerpunktlage annähernd unverändert, so daß die Abstimmung der Federn bei gleichbleibender Wirkung einwandfrei erfolgen kann.

DIE UNABHÄNGIGE FEDERUNG

sorgt für geringste Rückwirkung der Straßenunebenheiten auf die Fahrzeugmaße. Es ist dies eine Tatsache, die von den Tatra-Werken seit über einem Jahrzehnt verfochten wird. Wie gut dieses Konstruktionsprinzip ist, beweist am besten der Umstand, daß heute der weitaus größte Teil der Autofabriken auf dasselbe übergeht.

Ebenso wie die Tatra-Type 77 in ihrem Gesamtauf-

5

TATRA 77

 TATRA 77

bau von jeder Norm abweicht — ebenso liegen die

FAHREIGENSCHAFTEN

und alles, was unter Fahrkomfort verstanden wird, ausserhalb des Gewohnten und Bekannten.

Die Dynamik des Fahrvorganges wird von der Konstruktion völlig beherrscht. Der Fahrzeugkörper liegt auch bei höchsten Geschwindigkeiten auf schlechter Fahrbahn vollkommen ruhig. Fast ohne Lenkungskorrekturen hält der Wagen die Gerade und gehorcht willig dem leisesten Steuerdruck, zeigt eine bisher nie erreichte Kurvenhaltung, eine unbeschreibliche Anpassungsfähigkeit an die Fahrbahn und eine ebenso erstaunliche Bremsfähigkeit.

Fast ebenso sehr aber ist der Fahrer dieser neuen Type von den Wirkungen der aerodynamisch richtig gebauten Karosserie überrascht. Die Beschleunigungsfähigkeit bleibt in höheren Geschwindigkeitsbereichen fast gleichmäßig groß. Völlig verschwunden sind die überaus lästigen und unvermeidlichen Zugerscheinungen — jeder gewünschte Grad der Ventilation kann ohne Zugerscheinung erreicht werden durch Öffnen bestimmter Klappen- oder Seitenfenster, an denen der Fahrwindstrom vorüberstreicht.

Die Maschinenanlage im Heck des Wagens bleibt ebenso unhörbar wie geruchlos, ohne das Kraft verzehrende Geräusche- und Schalldämpfungen erforderlich sind.

Die überaus bequeme Sitzanordnung und Sitzlage in diesem tief an die Straße geduckten Fahrzeugkörper, 6 die schräg stehenden großen Seitenscheiben und breiten

Vorderscheiben in Verbindung mit dem schmalen Dach ergeben eine Sicht, die den Fahrer wie die Mitfahrenden in den engsten Kontakt zur Landstraße und Landschaft bringen.

Der in der Tatra-Type 77 Fahrende hat nicht mehr den Eindruck in einem Automobil zu sitzen, sondern das Fahren wird zu einem Erlebnis, zu der Gewißheit, daß hier Zukünftiges Wirklichkeit geworden ist.

 TATRA 77

TATRA 77

DIE WIRTSCHAFTLICHKEIT.

Während Fahrkomfort bisher zum guten Teil auf Kosten der Wirtschaftlichkeit ging, ist die neue Tatra-Type 77 trotz ihrer überlegenen Leistungen, trotz ihres Höchstmaßes an Fahrkomfort von vorbildlicher Wirtschaftlichkeit.

Der 3 L Achtzylindermotor arbeitet mit höchstem Wirkungsgrad, befreit von den Fesseln des Luftwiderstandes mit dem gleichen Kraftstoffverbrauch beim sechssitzigen Wagen wie ein normaler 2 L Motor in normalem Gelände. In den Bergen aber und in schwierigem Gelände steht die volle Kraft des 3 L Motors zur Verfügung, und nur hier bei Höchstgeschwindigkeit wird der Motor auf volle Leistungen beansprucht. Geringer Verbrauch und lange Lebensdauer — sie sind die wahren Grundlagen der Wirtschaftlichkeit!

TECHNISCHE DATEN.

MOTOR.

Zylinder :	8, einzeln stehend, 2×4 in Reihe, V-Form 90⁰
Bohrung und Hub :	75×84 mm
Inhalt :	2970 cm³
Zylinderköpfe :	abnehmbar
Verdichtungsverhältnis :	1:5,3
Kurbelwelle :	5-fach gelagert, statisch-dynamisch ausgewuchtet
Ventilatoranordnung :	seitlich stehend
Steuerung :	gestängeloser Kniehebel
Steuerwelle und Antrieb :	zwischen den Zylinderreihen mit geräuschloser Rollen-Kette
Kolben :	Leichtmetall
Zündung :	Batterie
Schmierung :	Druckumlauf mit Filter
Vergaser :	Doppelfallstrom Zenith
Kühlung :	Luftkühlung durch 2 Gebläse je Zylinderreihe Keilriemenantrieb mechanische Pumpe
Brennstoffzufuhr :	
Drehzahl bei 100 km/St. :	2720 U/min.
Bremsleistung bei 3500 U/min. :	60 PS
Zündfolge :	1, 2, 7, 8, 4, 5, 6, 3

ÜBRIGES TRIEBWERK.

Kupplung :	Einscheiben-Trockenkupplung
Getriebe :	4 Vorwärts-, 1 Rückwärtsgang (1:4,14, 1:2,7, 1:1,58, 1:1)
Schaltung :	Kugelschaltung
Kraftübertragung :	gelenklos
Hinterachse :	geteilt, spiralverzahnte Kegelräder, 1:3,75
Differential :	Stirnradanordnung, Freilauf zwischen Getriebe und Motor, ausrückbar
Vorderachse :	Parallelschwingarme mit kugeliger Lagerung des Lenkzapfens
Federung :	Querfeder vorn und hinten
Lenkung :	Einzelrad-Lenkung, mit Schraubenspindel
Fußbremse :	hydraulische Vierradbremse
Handbremse :	auf die Hinterräder mechanisch
Räder, Felgen :	16×45 Vollscheiben
Ausrüstung :	2 bereifte Reserveräder, vordere Stoßstange, hydraulische Stoßdämpfer vorn.
Besondere Ausstattung :	Zentralschmierung.

7

TATRA 77

TATRA 77

HAUPTABMESSUNGEN.

Spurweite :	1300 mm	Größte Wagenlänge 6-sitzer :	5200 mm
Radstand 4-sitzer :	3050 mm	Größte Wagenbreite :	1650 mm
6-sitzer :	3250 mm	Bodenfreiheit :	220 mm
Höhe 4-sitzer :	1420 mm	Kraftstoffverbrauch :	14—16 Liter/100 km
6-sitzer :	1500 mm	Ölverbrauch :	0,3—0,4 L/100 km
Größte Wagenlänge 4-sitzer :	5000 mm	Höchstgeschwindigkeit :	150 km

8

TATRA 77

TATRA 77

TATRA 77

1936 TATRA T77 BROCHURE. SEVERAL PHOTOGRAPHS SHOW THE NEXT TATRA MODEL T77A WITH THREE HEADLAMPS. THE V8 ENGINE OFFERED HERE IS THE LARGER 3.4-LITRE, INSTALLED IN THE LATTER T77 SERIES AND IN T77A. INTERESTINGLY THE RESALE VALUE OF THE CAR IS EMPHASISED. (COURTESY GARY CULLEN)

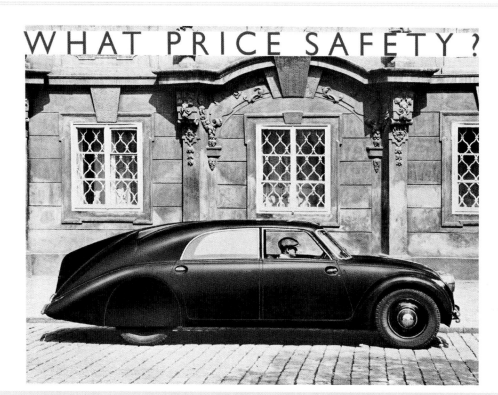

WHAT PRICE SAFETY?

YOU ARE ACTUALLY SAFER WHEN RIDING IN A TATRA 77

WE DON'T OFFER YOU JUST ANOTHER AUTOMOBILE

WE OFFER YOU THE TATRA 77

Made by

TATRA WORKS LTD

Prague Czechoslovakia

WHERE YOUR TATRA 77 WAS MADE

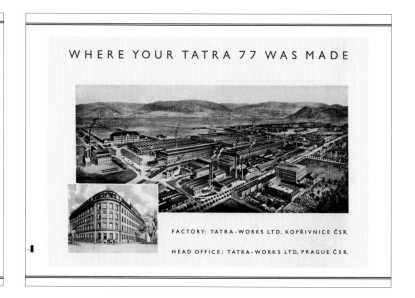

FACTORY: TATRA-WORKS LTD, KOPŘIVNICE ČSR.

HEAD OFFICE: TATRA-WORKS LTD, PRAGUE ČSR.

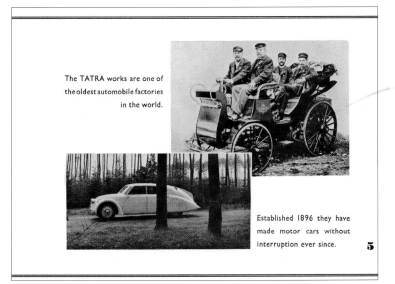

The TATRA works are one of the oldest automobile factories in the world.

Established 1896 they have made motor cars without interruption ever since.

5

6

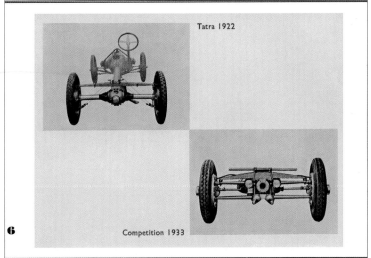

Tatra 1922

Competition 1933

TATRA

certainly responsible for many features now standard on every automobile, has always been known for engineering leadership.

Major Tatra features have been universally adopted and constructive ideas pioneered by us have become commonplace.

This engineering leadership, of which we are justly proud, has induced three major automobile factories to build Tatra cars for their markets under their national trademark, in licence agreement with Tatra.

There is no modern car built anywhere, not embodying some feature pioneered by us.

7

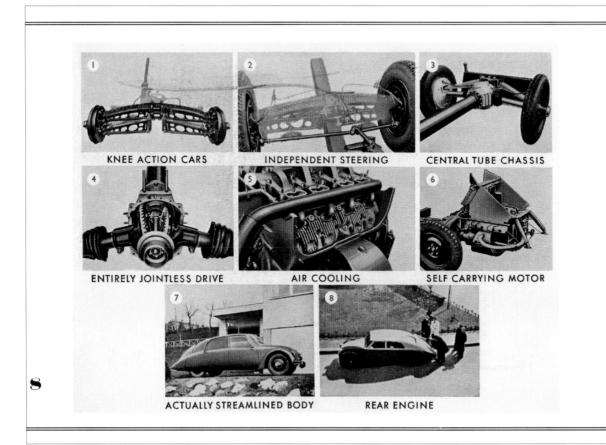

KNEE ACTION CARS   INDEPENDENT STEERING   CENTRAL TUBE CHASSIS

ENTIRELY JOINTLESS DRIVE   AIR COOLING   SELF CARRYING MOTOR

ACTUALLY STREAMLINED BODY   REAR ENGINE

8

And we are again in the lead because of
     Mr. Hans Ledwinka

DEAN OF AUTOMOTIVE ENGINEERS
has more radically changed automobile design than any
other man.

Some of the things this man takes credit for:

1. Knee action cars
2. Independent steering
3. Central tube chassis
4. Entirely jointless drive
5. Air cooling
6. Self carrying motor
7. Actually streamlined body
8. Rear Engine

And his crowning effort 5 years ahead of the industry
     TATRA 77

9

10

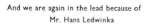

GROUND VIEW AT 14 m (46')

GROUND VIEW AT 5 m (16')

The TATRA 77 gives you everything any other high priced car will give and:

„MORE SAFETY": Because no other car has such a low center of gravity:

Bacause knee action on all four wheels prevents any wheel to ever leave the ground.

Each wheel is independently pressed to the road to steady tire contact.

Because the placing of the biggest weight near the driving wheels, the rear wheels, makes taking of curves and corners vastly safer by best adhesion.

Because the engine being placed on the back prevents valuable parts from damage and protects you from evil smelling and poisonous gases.

Because you have the finest visibility in all directions when driving.

Because there is a rubber cushion of two spare tires in front to protect you.

11

12

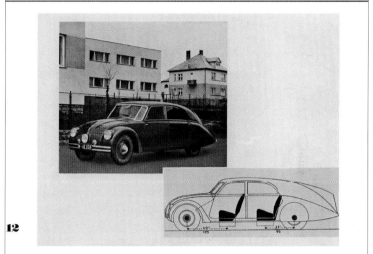

GREATER RIDING COMFORT:

Because of better suspension with knee action on all four.

Because you dont have to ride on the axle or anywhere near it.

All five seats on a Tatra 77 are much further away from the axle than the seats of any other car now built.

You get Roadster comfort in a closed Sedan.

Because of complete absence of shocks even over uneven roads and at high speeds, the independently hung wheels with knee action, absorbing all of them.

BETTER PERFORMANCE:

The 8 cyl. engine, placed in the back will give you a comfortable cruising speed of 80 miles per hour, a fast pickup to 100 miles per hour if desired. This without laboring and effort.

You will feel the ability of this engine to do its job under all conditions.

Four speeds in front, one in back.

13

14

BETTER APPEARANCE:

Ajudged the best looking car at the Paris show.

Bought by prominent society matrons because of its elegance in appearance.

Beautiful in the pure streamlining of its design.

Radically breaking with traditional body design giving the impression of effortless

speed.

Truly the car of to-morrow.

15   16

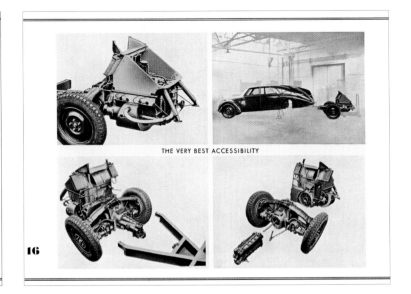

THE VERY BEST ACCESSIBILITY

SERVICE

We are providing an ever increasing network of dealers, for customers abroad. In a short space of time there will be no country in which original Tatra parts and genuine Tatra service will not be available.

Your Tatra dealer has been chosen because of his standing in his community and we are satisfied that your car will get the attention it deserves.

Our standard factory guarantee provides for 90 days free service from date of delivery.

All the vital parts on Tatra 77 are easily accessible for repairs.

Every part individually made and fitted your service bill should be a minimum as compared with conventional automobiles.

17 **18**

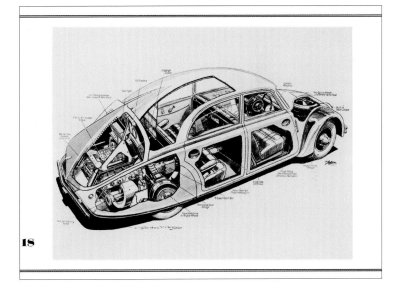

Now lets discuss the cost of transportation in a Tatra 77.

RESALE VALUE:

A look at any used car dealers stock will convince you that the cars of only yesterday are totally obsolete and therefor worth only a fraction of their original cost.

The day of aerodynamic streamline design is here and here to stay.

Therefor the investment in a high priced conventional car is a poor one.

There are practically no buyers for second hand high priced cars unless sold at a sacrifice.

The deduction is clear: Your Tatra 77 now 5 years ahead will be worth considerably more in three years from now than any other car of the same price.

COST OF OPERATION:

Wear and Tear: Custom built. Therefor longer wear.
100.000 Tatra miles equal 50.000 miles any conventional car in wear.

Petrol: 18—20 miles to the gallon, with a big 8 cylinder car.

Oil: 680—950 miles to the gallon.

19

SPECIFICATIONS

Cylinders:	8 in V-Type
Bore and stroke:	80 × 84 mm — $3^1/_8'' \times 3^1/_{16}'$
Cubic capacity:	3400 ccm — 207 cub in.
Cylinder heads:	Detachable
Pistons:	Light metal
Camshaft and drive:	Between cylinder rows by silent chain
Crankshaft:	In three bearings
Engine revolutions:	2700 r. p. m. at 100 km./h. - 80 m. p. h.
Brake horse power:	70 B. H. P. at 3500 r. p. m.
Firing order:	1, 2, 7, 8, 4, 5, 6, 3
Ignition:	Battery
Lubrication:	Pressure feed to all bearings by gear pump
Cooling system:	Aircooled by means of two fans
Carburettor:	Double down draught
Fuel feed:	Mechanical pump
Change-speed gears:	Ratios 1 : 4,14 — 1 : 2,7 — 1 : 1,58 — 1 : 1
Change-speed mechanism:	Ball type
Clutch:	Single plate dry clutch
Power transmission:	Jointless drive.
Differential:	Spur-gear differential
Brakes:	Hydraulic four wheel brake, Emergency: mechanical on rear wheels
Wheels:	Steel disc wheels 16''
Tires:	16 × 45
Front axle:	Independently sprung half axles
Rear axle:	Independently driven and independently sprung half axles, jointless drive by two pairs of spiral bevel gears (Special Tatra Design), ratio 1 : 3,75
Steering:	Independent steering for each wheel by dealt track-rod
Springs:	Transvers springs both front and rear
Fuel tank capacity:	80 Liters — 18 gallons
Wheel track:	1300 mm — 4' 3''
Wheel base:	3150 mm — 10' 4''
Height:	1520 mm — 5'
Overall length:	5150 mm — 17'
Overall width:	1700 mm — 5' 7''
Ground clearance:	220 mm — $8^5/_8''$
Lugage room:	ca 250 cdm — 9 cb feet
Fuel consumption:	14—16 l/100 km 18—20 m. p. g.
Oil comsumption:	0,3—0,4 l/100 km 680—950 m. p. g.
Maximum speed:	150 km/h — 95 m. p. h.
Weight:	1700 kg — 33 cwt

EQUIPMENT

On instrument panel: Speedometer for 160 kilometers, automobile watch, fuel indicator, oil pressure indicator, instrument board light, fuse plug box, plug switch for hand lamp.
Electric horn for the town, special twin horn for highways, direction indicators. two head lamps, one long distance, electric dual screen wippers. 12 V starting and lighting.
Central chassis lubrication, hydraulic shock absorbers, bumpers in front and in the rear, two spare wheels with tires, jack and tire pump, tools and spare parts. Hand throttle control.
Bodywork equipment: Leather upholstery or corded material (cloth) according to order, safety glasses throughout, interior mirror, inside lamps, sun protecting glasses, car heating with fresh air.

20

Every Tatra 77 is hand made, every part is fitted by hand, every body is custom built.

Price   fully equipped,

it is the best automobile investment you ever made.

21

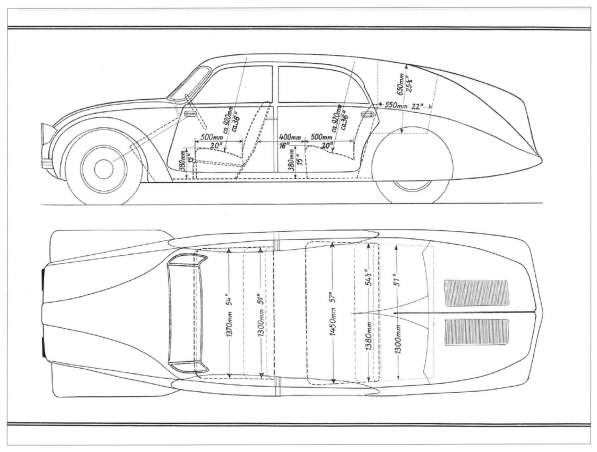

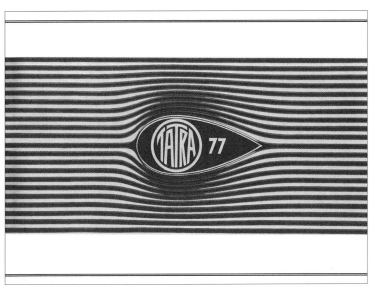

1948 TATRA
T87 BROCHURE
ILLUSTRATING THE
RARE POSTWAR
TWO HEADLAMP
MODEL WITH THE
CLASSIC COVER
DESIGN. (COURTESY
GARY CULLEN)

STREAMLINED EIGHT-CYLINDER PASSENGER CAR WITH AIR COOLED REAR-ENGINE 100 miles/h

The Tatra-Works Factory at Kopřivnice, Czechoslovakia

began building motor cars as early as 1896 and has for many years occupied a leading position founded on the technical progress in the design of the Tatra Cars. Backed by a staff of experienced designers under the leadership of prominent experts, the names of Kopřivnice and Tatra embody the best tradition of pioneers in the building of motorcars, having gained an excellent reputation not only for the Tatra Cars but for automobile technique in general. Since the first series of cars left the factory at Kopřivnice—the first automobile factory in the former Austria-Hungarian Monarchy—constant progress has been made, and the untiring research-work and continuous efforts have gained world renown for Tatra Cars. Many of the sweeping innoviations which may now be found in all motorcars were originally conceived by Tatra designers at a time when even in the Technical World the conception of a single backbone bearer, swinging axle, air cooled engine, etc. received but very little appreciation. Thus the proverbial reliability and performance of the Tatra Cars are the results of technical perfection, as well as precision and economy in the Tatra manufacturing methods.

The owner of a Tatra 87 knows that he has a thoroughly efficient, economical and modern car which will not be out-of-date in a year or two.

The streamlined all-steel construction of the Tatra 87 with its pleasing exterior appearance is in itself a sufficient proof of the progress made. It represents a novel idea of beauty in the bulding of passenger cars and a perfect technical solution of the streamlined shape. It is the result of the work of the Tatra designers and of the many exhaustive experiments that had been conducted in a special wind-tunnel to reduce air resistance. When the designers chose this special shape they had in mind not only the resulting higher speed but also the economies in petrol, oil and maintenance costs resulting from the lessened load on the engine. The mudguards form an integral part of the body thus widening the interior space of the car. Another great advantage of the new design is the housing of the engine in the rear, which has made it possible to push the seats forward. Thus, unlike any other car, both the front and back seats are placed between the axles which being the most favourable position for springing, ensures that the unevenness of the road is hardly felt by the passengers. Consequently, many hundreds of miles can be covered in the car without the least fatigue to the passengers so that travelling in this car has become a real pleasure. The curved shape of the streamlined car body in conjunction with the all-steel selfsupporting body provides the car with a stability and reliability that fully justifies the adoption of the streamlined shape.

The interior of the Tatra 87, has its individual characteristics. The streamlined design has enabled the designers to find new and brilliant solutions to old problems of comfort. These solutions combined with many technical advancements justify the makers claim to have set a new standard for interiors. The instrument panel placed clear of the knees has been carefully arranged so that all levers and switch buttons are within easy reach of the driver and enable that the instruments are clearly visible. Under the windscreen there are two scuttle ventilators for letting fresh or warm air into the interior of the car without draught so that frost screen may be dispensed with. The steering column is provided with an ignition lock and the steering wheel is spring mounted. In all cars of this type provision has been made for the installation of a wireless set.

The high-backed seats which are adjustable under way, have been adapted to the natural position of human body and so constructed as to make full use of the width of the car body, thus providing ample accomodation for 5 passengers. The richly upholstered seats offer pleasant relaxation and with the front seats folded provide comfortable sleeping accomodation for 2 passengers. All doors are provided with arm rests which nevertheless do not restrict the space available for entering or leaving the car. The spacious luggage compartment takes an unusual amount of luggage and is dust-proof and easily accessible from the interior of the car when the backs of the rear seats are folded. All window-panes are of splinter-proof glass, the floor is covered with thick carpets and the interior of the car is properly ventilated without any draught. The engine is housed in the rear thus preventing oil and petrol vapours entering the interior of the car. In winter the interior of the car can be heated with warm air. To satisfy the friends of convertibles the car is fitted with a sliding roof which is in perfect keeping of the streamlined shape of the car. The steering wheel being spring-mounted does not transmit any road shocks. The clutch, brakes and synchronmesh gearbox operate smoothly and can be handled with ease.

The Tatra 87 has a maximum speed of 100 miles per hour. The hydraulic brakes are adapted to the highest speeds attainable and enable stopping the car in the shortest distance possible. The rear end of the body is the ideal position for the engine, not only for reasons of comfort as already explained, but also for technical reasons. By placing the driving mechanism at the rear a one-block driving unit has been created which eliminates

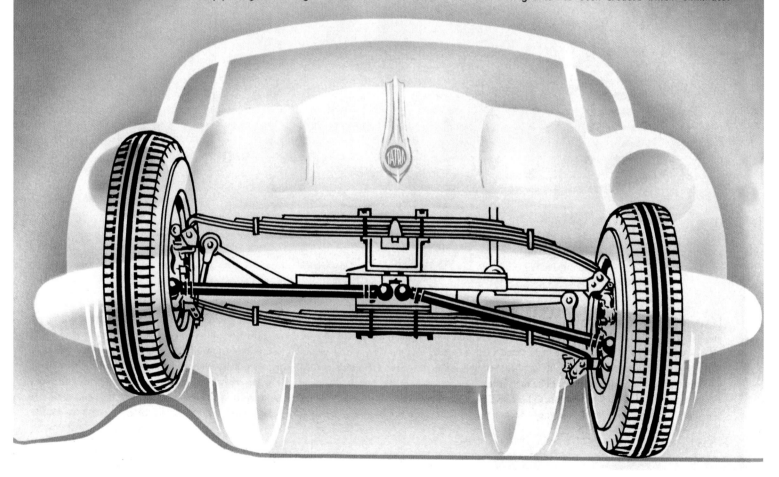

losses due to transmission of power. The air cooled Tatra engines are of light weight metal so that their power-weight ratio is almost that of aircraft engines. The engine itself is of unique construction. It is an eight-cylinder air-cooled engine, cylinders arranged in two rows of 4 each in the shape of a ,,V" at an angle of 90⁰. The gear box is fitted with 4 speeds, this number having proved most suitable for all gradients and traffic conditions. Gear changing is very easy. The engine is quite inaudible inside the car and this with its quick starting, acceleration and climbing capacity are among its main features serving as a proof of its excellent performance. Another special advantage of the air-cooled Tatra 87 engine is that it may be easily taken out and placed back in position. Oil is conveyed under pressure from the oil pump to all main bearings, connecting rod bearings and camshaft bearings. The high degree of efficiency, economy and vitality of the engine which are the results of thorough technical experience have gained

general recognition. Each individual part of the body is constructed in full harmony with the engine. The maintenance of a high speed in the open country, quick acceleration in traffic and climbing capacity with full load and a sufficient reserve of power—are features offered by the air-cooled engine of the streamlined Tatra 87 Car.

The soft springing of the Tatra 87 provides efficient and reliable road stability and enables the car to take rough roads smoothly. The stable equilibrium of the car, no matter whether one or 5 passenger occupy it, and the low centre of gravity provide the streamlined Tatra 87 with surprising stability in curves. The soft springing and perfect road holding has greatly increased the braking capacity of the Tatra 87, as shown in the diagram. The excellent road holding and security on curves ensure higher average speads.

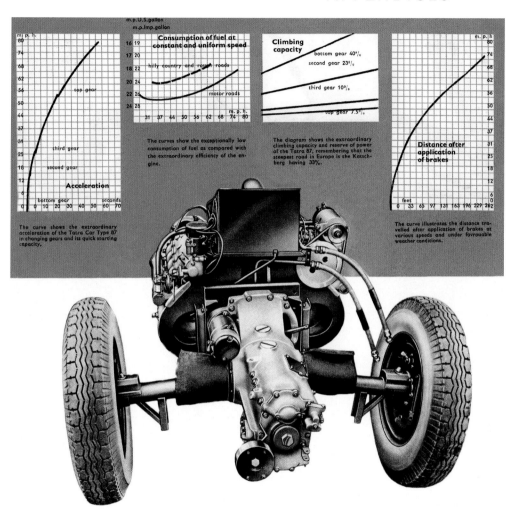

m.p.h.
80
74
68
62
56
50
44
37
31
25
18
12
6
0

top gear

third gear

second gear

bottom gear   seconds

0 10 20 30 40 50 60 70

The curve shows the extraordinary acceleration of the Tatra Car Type 87 in changing gears and its quick starting capacity.

Acceleration

m.p.U.S.gallon
m.p.Imp.gallon

Consumption of fuel at constant and uniform speed

16 19
17 20
18 22
20 24
22 26
24 28

hilly country and rough roads

motor roads

m.p.h.
31 37 44 50 56 62 68 74 80

The curves show the exceptionally low consumption of fuel as compared with the extraordinary efficiency of the engine.

Climbing capacity

bottom gear 40%

second gear 23%

third gear 10%

top gear 7.5%

The diagram shows the extraordinary climbing capacity and reserve of power of the Tatra 87, remembering that the steepest road in Europe is the Katschberg having 33%.

Distance after application of brakes

m.p.h
80
74
68
62
56
50
44
37
31
25
18
12
6
0

feet
0 33 65 97 131 163 196 229 262

The curve illustrates the distance travelled after application of brakes at various speeds and under favourable weather conditions.

TECHNICAL DATA

DRIVING UNIT:

Engine, rear-axle and gear-box forming one rigid unit mounted on rubber blocs.

ENGINE:

housed in the rear—air cooled—output 75 HP—eight-cylinder—bore 75 mm—stroke 84 mm—,,swept" volume 2958 ccm—compression ratio 1 : 5,6—five-bearing crankshaft—light-metal pistons—double-chain camshaft drive—over-head valve—forced lubrication—double carburetor with acceleration pump device—fuel pump—fuel tank in front, capacity 15 U. S. gallons (12 Imp. gallons)—constant speed 3500 r. p. m.

COOLING:

air cooled by blow air—,,V" belt drive.

Electrical installation:

12 V electric starter—battery ignition—capacity of battery 60 amp. hours—2 main headlights—1 spotlight—foot operated dimmer switch.

CLUTCH:

dry, single-plate.

GEARS:

four gears—bottom gear 4,7 : 1, second gear 2,95 : 1, third gear 1,56 : 1, top gear 1,04 : 1, reverse 5,92 : 1; silent second, third and top gear, synchronized third and top with helical tooth gears.

BRAKES:

four wheel hydraulic brakes, cable-hand-brake on the rear wheels.

STEERING :

on the left-hand side by rack and pinion, separate tie rods.

FRONT-AXLE:

parallel transverse semi-eliptic springs—hydraulic shock absorbers-steering knuckle carried in conical bearings.

REAR-AXLE:

spiral bevel gears—cantilever springs—hydraulic shock-absorbers—ratio of gearing 3,15 : 1.

WHEELS AND TIRES:

5 star-shaped spoke-wheels—tires 6,50 by 16".

CAR BODY:

self-supporting—all steel—streamlined—4 doors—sliding top.

LUBRICATION OF CHASSIS:

central lubrication.

GENERAL DETAILS:

wheel-base 112 in.—tread front and rear 49 in. ground clearance 9 in.—lenght over-all 186 in.—width over-all 66 in.—height 59 in.—weight 3014 lbs.

EQUIPMENT

double windscreen wiper—oil thermometer—speedometer—fuel gauge—clock—cubby hole—rear-view mirror—adjustable front seats—sleeping seats—perfect ventilation—warm air heating—front and rear bumpers—ash-tray—sun-blinds—ignition lock—foot switch for headlights— electric horn—,,Vigot" two wheel jack—tools and spare parts.

DRIVING DETAILS:

Maximum speed 95—100 mph—cruising speed on roads 85 mph—fuel consumption 24 miles/Imp. gallon, (19 miles/U. S. gallon) oil consumption approx. 0,7 pint per 100 miles.

TEXT AND ILLUSTRATION WITHOUT OBLIGATION ● SUBJECT TO CHANGE

TATRA NATIONAL CORPORATION **PRAHA** CZECHOSLOVAKIA

TIMELINE

1822	Ignaz Schustala was born on December 6th in Nesselsdorf, Austria-Hungary.
1850	Schustala set up a workshop in Nesselsdorf.
1852	Schustala obtained permission to erect factory buildings.
1858	Schustala & Comp. founded.
1878	Hans Ledwinka was born on February 14th, in Klosterneuburg near Vienna.
1881	Nesselsdorf became a station on Stauding – Stramberg railway line.
1884	Leopold Sviták started to work for Schustala & Comp.
1886	Karl Benz showed his first motor vehicle in public.
1890	Hugo Fischer von Röslerstamm became director at Schustala & Comp.
1891	Schustala & Comp. was incorporated becoming Nesselsdorfer Wagenbau-Fabriks-Gesellschaft A. G. vormals k.k. priv. Wagen-Fabrik Schustala & Comp. NW marque in use. Ignaz Schustala died in Vienna on January 29th.
1893	The first motor car arrived in Bohemia.
1895	Schustala brothers sold their shares in Nesselsdorfer Wagenbau and founded a rival company Moravskoslezská vagónka in Stauding. Nesselsdorfer Wagenbau decided to manufacture cars.
1897	Benz Phaeton, later renamed Instruktor, arrived in Nesselsdorf. Sviták, Rumpler, Sage, Kuchař and others produced the first Nesselsdorfer car – Präsident. Ledwinka started at Nesselsdorfer in September.
1898	Präsident was driven to Vienna. First Nesselsdorfer goods vehicle was produced.
1899	First series of Nesselsdorfer cars was made. First Nesselsdorfer racing victories.
1900	Kuchař died and Sviták lost a leg in an automobile accident.
1902	Ledwinka left Moravia to work for Alexander Friedmann and Gräf & Stift in Vienna. Ledwinka's first interest in small car design. Worldwide crisis in the automobile industry.
1904	The main company headquarters was located in Vienna.
1905	Ledwinka returned to Nesselsdorfer and was appointed director of the automobile workshop.
1906	Serious factory strike demanding trade union recognition.
1912	Another strike for increased wages. Sviták retired.
1913	Fischer von Röslerstamm retired.
1914	The First World War started with the assassination of Archduke Franz Ferdinand in Sarajevo.
1916	Ledwinka left Nesselsdorfer to become chief designer at Steyr.
1918	End of the war. Austria-Hungary dissolved into several independent states. Czechoslovakia became a republic.
1919	The first use of Tatra sign on the TL4 truck.
1921	NW marque was replaced by the Tatra emblem. Nesselsdorfer Wagenbau-Fabriks was renamed Kopřivnická vozovka a s Ledwinka returned to Moravia for good. Ledwinka designed the revolutionary type 11 'people's car' – a major date in the factory history. The company headquarters moved from Vienna to Prague.

1923	Baron Hans Ringhoffer became the general director of the factory.
1924	Company name changed to Závody Tatra akciová společnost pro stavbu automobilů a železničních vozů.
1925	The first Auto Tatra showroom in Prague, Adriatica Palace, Jungmannova Street, later moving to Dunaj Palace, Národní Avenue.
1927	Company name changed to Závody Tatra a s Übelacker started working at Tatra.
1931	The first Tatra rear engine prototype.
1932	Design of the first Tatra aerodynamic rear engine prototype commenced.
1933	Hitler and Ledwinka discussed air-cooled rear engine car design.
1934	Tatra T77 introduced to journalists, March 5th. Ledwinka became director of the Tatra automotive division.
1935	Baron Hans Ringhoffer combined Tatra with his works Ringhofferovy závody in Prague-Smíchov and the company became Závody Ringhoffer-Tatra a s.
1936	Company marque became either Ringhoffer-Tatra or Tatra-Ringhoffer. T87 and T97 models produced.
1938	Sudetenland including the Tatra factory was occupied by the Third Reich.
1939	The rest of Bohemia and Moravia was taken over by the Third Reich. The Second World War started.
1940	Ringhoffer-Tatra continued production throughout the war years.
1944	Ledwinka received an honorary doctorate from University of Technology, Vienna.
1945	End of the war. Kopřivnice liberated by the Soviet Army, May 6th. Wagon works resume production on May 8th. Ledwinka was imprisoned on June 3rd.
1946	Resumption of automobile/truck production with T57, T87 and T111 models. Ringhoffer-Tatra nationalised and named Tatra, národní podnik, Kopřivnice.
1947	Hanzelka and Zikmund started their journey through Africa and South America in a T87.
1948	Czechoslovakia became a Communist state in February. Ledwinka was tried and sentenced to six year imprisonment.
1949	Julius Mackerle became the chief designer at Tatra.
1951	Ledwinka was released and left Czechoslovakia to live in Austria and later in Munich, West Germany.
1964	Klub Tatra Praha founded.
1967	Ledwinka died on March 2nd in Munich.
1981	Club der Tatra Freunde e.V. now Tatra-Freunde International, was founded in Salzburg.
1982	Tatra Register Schweiz founded.
1986	Tatra Register Netherland founded.
1988	Tatra T815 4x4 truck driven by Loprais, Stachura and Krpec won the 10th Paris Dakar Rally. Victories followed in 1994, 1995, 1998, 1999 and 2001.
1990	Annual production of over 15,000 commercial vehicles.
1992	Ledwinka was fully rehabilitated by the High Court of the Czech Republic. Tatra a s founded.
1993	Tatra Register UK founded.
1995	Tatra Register Deutschland founded.
1998	Tatra Klub CZ founded.
1999	Last two T700 passenger cars made at Kopřivnice. Truck manufacture continues to the present day by Tatra Trucks a s.

NESSELSDORFER/TATRA VEHICLES TECHNICAL INFORMATION

Passenger cars

Type	Year	Number of passengers	Engine position	Cylinders	Bore/stroke mm	Capacity cc	Cooling	rpm	bhp	Valves	Wheelbase mm	Front track	Rear track	Tyres	Fuel content lts	Max speed kph	Number made	Engine type
Präsident	1897	4	rear	2	120x120	2714	water	600	6.5	SV	1780	1150	1150			20.7	1	Benz
Meteor	1899	4	rear	2	120x120	2714	water	600	6	SV	1850	1250	1250			30	1	Benz
Nesselsdorf	1899	4	rear	2	120x120	2714	water	820	6 -9	SV	1850	1250	1250	800x55, 1100x90		35	1	Benz
Wien	1899	4	rear	2	120x120	2714	water		6	SV	1790	1250	1250			32	1	Benz
Bergsteiger	1899	4	rear	2	120x120	2714	water		6	SV	1780	1260	1260			32	1	Benz
Versucher	1899	4	rear	2	120x120	2714	water		6	SV	1850	1250	1250	800x90, 1110x90		32	1	Benz
Auhof	1899	4	rear	2	120x120	2714	water		6	SV	1780	1250	1250			48	1	Benz
Spitzbub	1899	4	rear	2	120x120	2714	water		6	SV	1780	1250	1250	800x65, 1110x90		36	1	Benz
Rennzweier	1900	2	rear	2	130x160	4520	water	1360	12	SV	1850	1375	1375	800x90, 880x120		82	1	Benz
A-Vierer	1900	4	rear	2	120x120	2714	water	1400	9-12	SV	1850	1375	1375	700x90, 950x90		55	14	Hardy
Tourenwagen	1900	4	rear	2	120x120	2714	water	1400	9	SV	1850	1250	1250	700x90, 950x90		55	1	Benz
Electromobil	1900	4	rear						2x3		2075	1240	1240	760x90, 920x120		21	2	2 x EAG
Neuer Vierer	1901	4	rear	2	125x130	3188	water		12	SV	1850	1250	1250	800x900		40	4	NW
B	1902-04	2-8	centre	2	125x130	3188	water		12	SV	1850	1250	1250	750x90, 810x90		45	36	NW
C/D	1902-04	4	centre	4	120x130	5878	water	1300	24	SV	2300	1250	1250	910x90, 920x120		50	1	NW
E	1904-06	2-4	centre	2	136x130	3775	water		18	SV	2470			820x120		52	6-7	NW
F	1905-06	4	centre	4	136x130	7550	water		33.5	SV				915x105, 920x120		60	5	NW
J	1906-11	6	front	4	120x130	5878	water		30	SV	3140	1380	1380	915x1050, 920x120		80	22	NW
S4 (18/24)	1910-12	2-6	front	4	90x130	3306	water	2200	20	OHC	varied	1280	1280	820x120		80	18	NW
S4 (20/30)	1913-17		front	4	90x130	3306	water	2200	30	OHC	3100	1280	1280	820x120		90	47	NW
S6	1912-15	4-6	front	6	90x130	4959	water	2600	50	OHC	3450	1400	1400	895x135		110	12	NW
T	1914-26	4-6	front	4	90x140	3562	water	2200	44	OHC	3370	1280	1280	820x120		90	350	NW
U	1915-18	4-6	front	6	90x140	5340	water	2230	64	OHC	3635	1400	1400	895x135		120	15	NW
10	1920-27	6	front	6	90x140	5340	water	2230	67	OHC	3635	1400	1400	895x150	17-19	120	129	Tatra
11	1923-27	2-6	front	2	82x100	1056	air	2500	12	OHV	varied	1200	1200	710x90	9-10	70	3767	Tatra
12	1926-36	2-6	front	2	82x100	1056	air	2800	12-14	OHV	2635	1200	1200	710x90	9-10	70	7222	Tatra
17	1925-28	4-6	front	6	64x100	1930	water	3000	34	OHC	varied	1350	1350	6,00x20, 6,50x20	13-15	110	378	Tatra

Type	Year	Number of passengers	Engine position	Cylinders	Bore/stroke mm	Capacity cc	Cooling	rpm	bhp	Valves	Wheelbase mm	Front track	Rear track	Tyres	Fuel content lts	Max speed kph	Number made	Engine type
17/31	1928-31	4-6	front	6	70x100	2310	water	3000	40	OHC	varied	1350	1350	6,00x20, 6,50x20	13-15	115	318	Tatra 31
30	1926-31	4-6	front	4	75x95	1680	air	3000	24	OHV	varied	1300	1300	45x13, 45x14	11-12	90	3847	Tatra
30/52	1929-31	4	front	4	80x95	1910	air	3000	30	OHV	varied	1300	1300	45x13, 45x14	13.5	90	94	Tatra 52
52	1931-39	4-6	front	4	80x95	1910	air	3000	30	OHV	varied	1300	1300	160x40	13-15	90	1684	Tatra
54	1931-36	4	front	4	70x95	1465	air	3000	22	OHV	2820	1300	1300		10-11	90	486	Tatra
54/30	1931-36	4	front	4	75x95	1680	air	3000	24	OHV	2820	1300	1300		12.5	90	928	Tatra 30
57	1931-35	2-4	front	4	70x75	1155	air	3000	18	OHV	2550	1200	1200	5.25x16	8-9	80	6851	Tatra
57A	1935-38	2-4	front	4	70x75	1155	air	3500	20	OHV	2550	1200	1200	5.25x16	8.5	90	6854	Tatra
57B	1938-48	4	front	4	73x75	1256	air	3500	25	OHV	2550	1200	1200	5.25x16	10	90	6667	Tatra
57K (military)	1941-48	4	front	4	73x75	1256	air	3500	23	OHV	2550	1220	1200	6.00x16	9.4	90	6494	Tatra
70	1931-34	4-6	front	6	80x113	3406	water	3000	64	OHC	3800	1450	1450	17x50	20	110	51	Tatra
70A	1935-41	4-6	front	6	85x113	3845	water	3500	69	OHC	3800	1450	1450	17x50	22	130	66	Tatra
75	1934-39	2-6	front	4	80x84	1688	air	3500	30	OHV	2700-3200	1250	1250	4.00x16	12.5	100	4054	Tatra
57 - V570	1931	2	rear	2	80x85	854	air	3500		OHV	2320	1120	1120	710x90	9	75	2	Tatra
V570	1933	4	rear	2	80x85	854	air	3500		OHV	2320	1120	1120	5.00x16	10	80	1	Tatra
77	1933-35	4-6	rear	V8	75x84	2968	air	3500	60	OHC	3150	1300	1300	45x18	14-16	150	106	T77 & T77A
77A	1936-39	4-6	rear	V8	80x84	3380	air	3500	70	OHC	3250	1300	1300	45x18	14-16	150	167	Tatra
80	1932-38	4-6	front	V12	75x113	5990	water	3000	120	SV	3800	1450	1450	50x17	25	140	26	Tatra
87	1936-50	5	rear	V8	75x84	2968	air	3500	75	OHC	2850	1250	1250	6.50x16	12.2	160	3102	Tatra
90	1935	6	front	4	90x98	2490	air	3200	54	OHC	3220	1450	1450		13.5	110	2	T82
97	1936-39	4	rear	4	75x99	1749	air	3500	40	OHC	2600	1250	1230	5.75x16	11	130	511	Tatra
107, 2-107	1946-47	5-6	rear	4	80x86	1750	air	4000	48	OHV	2700	1300	1300	6.00x16	12	125	2 + 5	Tatra
600 Tatraplan	1948-52	5-6	rear	4	85x86	1952	air	4000	52	OHV	2700	1300	1300	6.00x16	11	130	6335	Tatra
600D	1949-53	5-6	rear	4	85x86	1952	air	3300	42	OHV	2700	1300	1300	6.00x16	10	125	3	T913 Diesel
201	1949	2	front	4	85x86	1952	air	4000	52	OHV	varied	1300	1300	6.00x16	11	130	4	T107 & T600
601 Monte Carlo	1949-52	5	rear	4	85x86	1952	air	4000	52	OHV	2700	1300	1300	6.00x16	11	130	1	T600 & T603A
602 Tatraplan Sport	1949	2	ahead of rear axle	4	85x86	1952	air	4500	74	OHV	2400	1300	1300	5.50x16, 6.00x16		182	2	T600

Type	Year	Number of passengers	Engine position	Cylinders	Bore/stroke mm	Capacity cc	Cooling	rpm	bhp	Valves	Wheelbase mm	Front track	Rear track	Tyres	Fuel content lts	Max speed kph	Number made	Engine type
603	1955-62	6	rear	V8	75x72 (70)	2545 (2472)	air	5000	95	OHV	2750	1430	1400	6.70x15	13	170	5592	T603F & T603G
2-603	1962-75	6	rear	V8	75x70	2472	air	5000	105	OHV	2750	1485	1400	6.70x15	12.5	160	14,830	T603H
603A	1964	5	rear	V8	75x70	2472	air	5000	98	OHV	2780	1460	1400	6.70x15	12.5	160	1	T603H
603X	1966	5	rear	V8	75x70	2472	air	5000	95	OHV	2840	1460	1460	7.50x14	12.5	150	1	T603H
603 B5	1966-67	5	rear	V8	75x70	2472	air	6000	150	OHV	2750	1480	1430	185x15	25	200	8	T603H
604	1954	4	rear	4	60x65	635	air	4500	22	OHV	2150	1200	1200	5.00x14				Tatra
605 training racer	1957	2	ahead of rear axle	2	75x72	636	air	7000	54	OHV	2070	1200	1120	5.00x15		168	2	T910
607 Monopost	1950	1	ahead of rear axle	V8	72x61 (72)	1985 (2345)	air	7-8000	95 (132)	OHV	2250	1300	1300	5.50x15, 6.50x15		207	2	T603
607-2 Monopost	1953	1	ahead of rear axle	V8	75x72	2545	air	7-8000	198	OHV	2350	1300	1300	5.50x15, 6.50x15		215	3	T603
613	1969-97	5	above rear axle	V8	85x77	3495	air	5200	165	DOHC	2980	1520	1520	215/70 HR 14	18	190	8712	Tatra
613-S	1979-91	4	above rear axle	V8	85x77	3495	air	5200	168	DOHC	3130	1520	1520	205/70 HR 14	14.5	190	135	T613S1
613-3	1985-91	5	above rear axle	V8	85x77	3495	air	5200	168	DOHC	2980	1520	1520	205/70 HR 14	12.5	190		T613E1
613-4	1991-96	4	above rear axle	V8	85x77	3495	air	5750	200	DOHC	3130	1532	1532	205/70 R 14	12.5	230	118	T613
613-5 RHD	1993	4	above rear axle	V8	85x77	3495	air	5750	200	DOHC	3130	1532	1532	205/70 R 14	12.5	230	4	T613
700	1995-99	4	above rear axle	V8	85x77	3495	air	5750	200	DOHC	3130	1532	1532	205/65 R 15	12.5	230	69	T613
MTX V8 Král	1991-93	2	above rear axle	V8	90x77	3919	air	5800	217	DOHC	2700	1620	1640	245/40 ZR 17		245-60	3+1	T613
Ecorra Sport V8	1997	2	above rear axle	V8	95x78	4423	air		400	DOHC	2980	1552	1555	255/40-18		300	1	T613

Commercial vehicles

Type	Year	Engine position	Cylinders	Bore/stroke mm	Capacity cc	Cooling	rpm	bhp	Valves	Wheelbase mm	Front track mm	Rear track mm	Carrying capacity tonnes	Unladen weight tonnes	Max speed kph	Powered axles	Number made	Engine type
Goods wagon	1898	rear	2x2	120x120	5428	water	600	13.2	SV	2000	1200	1200	2.5		15	1	1	2 x Benz
Steam bus	1900	front	2	100-190x160				30		2850	1200	1300	12 persons	8.5	20	1	1	De Dion-Bouton
K	1909-11	front	4	110x130	4940	water		40	SV	3350	1280	1300			25	1	1	Kronfeld
M	1909	front	4	105x130	4500	water		25	SV	3350	1360	1310				1	5	Lang
O	1907-09	front	4	105x130	4500	water		30	SV	3350	1360	1310	20 persons	2.7	25	1	5	Lang
R	1908	front	4	105x120	4158	water		25	SV	3485	1540	1540	2.5		20	1	1	NW
4R Jaguár	1908	front	4	170x150	13,619	water		80	SV	3530	1450	1450	2.5			2	1	NW
SO	1910-14	front	4	90x130	3306	water		30	SV							1	8	NW
TL2	1915-23	front	4	90x140	3562	water	1600	45	SV	3700	1450	1450	2	2.1	35	1	351	NW
TO	1919-22	front	4	90x140	3562	water	2000	45	SV		1450	1450	14-16 persons	2.1	35	1	5	NW
TL4	1916-27	front	4	90x140	3562	water	2000	45	SV	3980	1450	1495	4 - 5		25-35	1	1,032	NW
13	1924-32	front	2	82x100	1056	air	2800	12-14	OHV	2763	1200	1400	1	1.2	45	1	716	T11/12
18 draisine	1925-27	centre	2	82x100	1056	air	2500	12	OHV	4500	1500	1500	5.5	4		2	7+9	T11
22	1934-38	front	4	100x150	4712	water	2100	60	OHV	3200	1700	1700		6.5	55	2	18	Tatra
23	1927-33	front	4	115x180	7480	water	1200	65	OHV	3957	1800	1800	4	4.35	55	1	35	Tatra
23/80	1930-33	front	4	120x180	8180	water	1500	80	OHV	3957	1800	1800	4	3	55	1	37	Tatra
24/67	1937-39	front	6	140x180	16,600	water	1400	140	OHV	4022	1800	1900	10	8.3	60	2	49	Tatra, diesel
25	1927-34	front	6	115x180	11,220	water	1200	105	OHV	3000	1840	1900	8	6.6		3	29	Tatra
26	1926	front	2	82x100	1056	air	2800	14	OHV	3000	1300	1300		1.3	60	2	3	T12
26/30	1930	front	4	75x95	1680	air	3000	24	OHV	varied	1300	1300	1.5	1.29	60-70	2	156	T30
26/52	1932	front	4	80x95	1910	air	3000	30	OHV	2900	1300	1400	1.5		60-70	2	4	T52
27	1931-39	front	4	95x150	4260	water	2100	52	OHV	4000	1700	1700	3 or 24 persons	3.95	55	1	1801	Tatra
27a	1937-40	front	4	100x150	4712	water	2100	63	OHV	4000	1700	1700	3	3.98	60	1	443	Tatra
27b	1940-46	front	4	100x150	4712	water	2100	63	OHV	3500	1700	1800	3.15	3.28	60	1	3365	Tatra
28	1932-35	front	4	100x150	4712	water	2100	63	OHV	3200	1700	1700	4.4		48	2	12	Tatra
29	1934-35	front	4	115x180	7478	water	1500	65	OHV	4022	1800	2050			50	2	116	Tatra
43	1929-31	front	4	75x95	1680	air	3000	24	OHV	3287	1300	1500	1.5	1.36	60	1	629	T30

Type	Year	Engine position	Cylinders	Bore/stroke mm	Capacity cc	Cooling	rpm	bhp	Valves	Wheelbase mm	Front track mm	Rear track mm	Carrying capacity tonnes	Unladen weight tonnes	Max speed kph	Powered axles	Number made	Engine type
43/52	1931-38	front	4	80x95	1910	air	3000	30	OHV	3287	1300	1500	1.5	1.38	60	1	492	T52
49 (3-wheeler)	1930-39	rear	1	82x100	528	air	2500	7	OHV	2265	1300		0.4	0.515	40-50	1 rear wheel	206	Tatra
72	1934-38	front	4	80x95	1910	air	3000	32	OHV	2200	1300	1300	1.5	0.95	60	2	320	T52
72 military	1934	front	4	75x95/ 80x95	1680/ 1910	air	3000	24/32	OHV	2145	1300	1300				2	75	T30/T52
81	1940-43	front	V8	115x150	12,460	water	2100	160	OHV	4000	2000	1800	6.5		65	2	200	Tatra, diesel
82	1935-38	front	4	90x98	2490	air	3500	55	OHC	2900	1450	1500	2	3.15	45	2	322	Tatra
84	1935	front	4	115x180	7475	water	1500	65	OHV							3	3	Tatra
85	1936-39	front	4	120x180	8130	water	1500	80	OHV	3500	1700	1700	4	5.96	60	2	418	Tatra
86 trolleybus	1936-38						2100	34		5150	1300	1300	80 persons	9.6	45	2	9	4 x Sousedík
92	1938-39	front	V8	80x99	3981	air	3000	74	OHC	2800	1500	1330	2	5.58	60-70	2	529	Tatra
93	1938-39	front	V8	80x99	3891	air	3000	74	OHC	2800	1500	1330	2	5.6	60	3	783	T92
111	1942-52	front	V12	110x130	14,825	air	2200	210	OHV	4175	2080	1800	8	8.46	75	3	33,691	Tatra, diesel
114	1947-48	front	4	110x130	4940	air	2200	65	OHV	3500	1700	1800	3.15	3.75	60	1	407	Tatra, diesel
115	1948-49	front	4	110x130	4940	air	2200	65	OHV	4000	1700	1800	3.15		60	1	602	T114
128	1951-52	front	V8	110x130	9883	air	2000	130	OHV	3950	1800	1800	3	6.02	80	2	4060	T108, diesel
138	1959-72	front	V8	120x130	11,762	air	2000	180	OHV	3690	1930	1752	13	9.5	71	3	48,222	Tatra, diesel
148	1969-82	front	V8	120x140	12,667	air	2000	212	OHV	3690	1966	1770	15.5	10.7	71	3	113,647	Tatra, diesel
805	1953-60	underfloor	V8	75x72	2545	air	4200	75	OHV	2700	1600	1600	2.25	2.75	70	2	13,625	T603A
813	1967-82	underfloor	V12	120x130	17,640	air	2000	270	OHV	varied	varied	varied	varied	varied	50-90	2-4	11,751	Tatra, diesel
815	1976-to date	underfloor	V8-V12	120x140	12,670-19,000	air	2200	230-320	OHV	varied	varied	varied	varied	varied	70-95	2-4	139,055 up to 1998	Tatra, diesel
815 4x4 Dakar	1988	underfloor	V8	120x140	12,670	air	2200	408	OHV	3900	2026	2030	2	8.5	150	2	1	Tatra, diesel
815 6x6 Dakar	1988	underfloor	V12	120x140	19,000	air	2200	476	OHV	3550	2026	2030	2	10.5	160	3	1	Tatra, diesel
M290	1936	within bogies	6	140x180	16,625	water	1400	165	OHV	18,500	1360	1360	42.580	36	150	2 x 4-wheel bogies	2	2x T67, petrol
V855	1942	rear	V8	75x84	2968	air	3500	75	OHC	2950	1600	1620	0.4		80	rear propeller	1	T87

SELECT BIBLIOGRAPHY

BOOKS:

Barker, Ronald & Harding, Anthony, *Automobile Design: Twelve Great Designers and Their Work*, Warrendale: Society of Automotive Engineers, 1992

Bauer, Zdeněk, *Profily Automobilů 1 – Tatra 11, 12*, Praha: NADAS 1974

Boddy, William, *Continental Sports Cars*, London: The Marshall Press, 1951

Bröhl, H P, *Paul Jaray – Stromlinienpionier von der Kastenform zur Stromlinienform*, Bern, 1978

Bruchhäuser, Alex, *Der Kragstuhl*, Berlin: Alexander Verlag, 1986

Clarke, R M, *Tatra Cars: Road Test Portfolio*, Cobham: Brooklands Books, 2005

Courtenay, Vincent R, *Ideas That Move ... The Budd Company at 75*, Troy: The Budd Co, 1987

Fersen, Hans-Heinrich von, *Klassische Wagen I*, Bern: Hallwag Verlag, 1978

Foster, Norman, *Buckminster Fuller*, London: Ivorypress, 2010

Fry, Robin, *The VW Beetle*, Newton Abbot: David & Charles, 1980

Gomola, Miroslav, *Historie automobilů Tatra 1850-1997*, Brno: AGM-Gomola, 1997

Gomola, Miroslav et al, *Automobiles Tatra – Aerodynamic cars from Kopřivnice*, Brno: AGM CZ, 1998

Gomola, Miroslav, *Automobily Tatra – závodní a sportovní vozy z Kopřivnice*, Brno: AGM CZ, 2003

Hanzelka, Jiří & Zikmund, Miroslav, *Afrika snů a skutečnosti*, Praha: Naše vojsko, 1957

Hanzelka, Jiří & Zikmund, Miroslav, *Tam za řekou je Argentina*, Praha: Orbis, 1956

Hausman, Ing Jaroslav, Kovařík, Miloš, *Vteřiny za volantem*, Praha: NADAS, 1968

Howard, Geoffrey, Automobile *Aerodynamics – Theory and Practice for Road and Track*, London: Osprey, 1986

Hucho, Wolf-Heinrich, *Aerodynamics of Road Vehicles*, London: Butterworth, 1987

Kieselbach, Ralf J F, *Stromlinienautos in Deutschland*, Stuttgart: Verlag W Kohlhammer, 1982

Kieselbach, Ralf J F, *Stromlinienautos in Europa und USA*, Stuttgart: Verlag W Kohlhammer, 1982

Kleinhampl, Z V, *70 Years of Tatra Motor Cars*, Praha: NADAS, 1967

Koenig-Fahsenfeld, Reinhard, *Aerodynamik des Kraftfahrzeugs*, Band I and II, Frankfurt a. M.: 1951 and Band III and IV, Heubach: 1984

Kovařík, Miloš, *Svět velkých závodů*, Praha: Novinář, 1984

Křesina, V et al, *Sedmdesát let výroby automobilů Tatra*, Kopřivnice, 1967

Kuba, Adolf, *Automobil v srdci Evropy*, Praha: NADAS, 1986

Kuba, Adolf & Spremo, Milan, *Atlas našich automobilů 1 – 4*, Praha: NADAS, 1988-1991

Lášek, Pavel & Vaněk, Jan, *Obrněná drezína Tatra T18*, Corona, 2002

Lichtenstein, Claude & Engler, Franz, *Streamlined: The Metaphor for Progress, Baden*: Lars Müller Publishers, 1996

Mackerle, Julius, *Air-Cooled Motor Engines*, Prague: SNTL, 1961

Mackerle, Julius, *Automobily s motorem vzadu*, Praha: SNTL, 1966

Norbye, Jan P, *German Car*, New York: Portland House, 1987

Norbye, Jan P, *Streamlining & Car Aerodynamics*, Blue Ridge Summit: Tab Books, 1977

Pauly, Jana a Kožíšek, Petr, editors, *100. Výročí zahájení automobilové výroby v Tatře Kopřivnice*, Praha: NTM, 1997

Oswald, Werner, *Deutsche Auto 1920-45*, Stuttgart: Motor Buch, 1985

Procházka, Hubert, Martof, Jan, *Automobily Tatra*, Brno: CPress, 2011

Ražnok, Jan & Zátopek, Radim, *Hans Ledwinka: Od Präsidenta do síně slávy*, Kopřivnice: Tatra Muzeum, 2009

Rosenkranz, Karel, *Tatra*, Brno: ZO Svazarm, 1987

Rosenkranz, Karel, *Tatra 603*, Corona, 2004

Rosenkranz, Karel, *Tatra Autoalbum*, Brno: MS Press, 2002

Rosenkranz, Karel, *Tatra Passenger Cars: 100 Years*, Praha: GT Club – Motormedia, 1998

Rosenkranz, Karel, *Tatra Trucks: 100 Years*, Praha: GT Club – Motormedia, 1999

Rosenkranz, Karel & Kozlovský, Jan, *Tatra Technické muzeum*, Kopřivnice 1985

Schilperoord, Paul, *The Extraordinary Life of Josef Ganz: The Jewish Engineer Behind Hitler's Volkswagen*, New

York: RVP Publishers, 2012

Schmarbeck, Wolfgang, *Hans Ledwinka: Seine Autos – Sein Leben*, Graz: H Weishaupt Verlag, 1997

Schmarbeck, Wolfgang, *Tatra: Die Geschichte der Tatra Automobile*, Lübbecke: Verlag Uhle & Kleimann, 1989

Seper, Hans, *Österreichische Automobil Geschichte 1815 bis Heute*, Wien: ÖRAC, 1986

Sloniger, Jerry, *The VW Story*, Cambridge: Patrick Stephens, 1980

Smit, Kees, *Tatra Onder De Zeespiegel*, Tatra Register Nederland, 2008

Sviták, Ivan, *The Freedom Machine: Absurdity on Wheels*, Chico, 1986

Šuman-Hreblay, Marián, *Aerodynamické automobily*, Brno: CPress, 2013

Šuman-Hreblay, Marián, *Tatra 600 Tatraplan*, Brno: CPress, 2013

Tatra, *Od kočáru k automobilu*, Kopřivnice, 1947

Tatra, *Technické novinky v automobilce Tatra*, Praha: Práce, 1956

Tichánek, Jiří, *Schustala – Kopřivnice Coaches*, Ostrava: Jiří Müller, 2000

Tuček, Jan, *Tatra 603*, Praha: Grada Publishing, 2005

Tuček, Jan, *Tatra 613*, Praha: Grada Publishing, 2011

Wilk, Christopher, *Modernism: Designing a New World 1914-1939*, London: V&A Publishing, 2008

Wood, Jonathan, *VW Beetle, A Collector's Guide*, Croydon: Motor Racing Publications, 1983, 1997

EXHIBITION CATALOGUES:

Czech Functionalism 1918-1938, The Architectural Association, London 1987

Motor Show 1933, Olympia, London, October 12-21, 1933

Ringhoffer Tatra Werke AG Presse-Informationen, Internationale Automobil – und Motorrad – Ausstellung, Berlin 1939

MAGAZINES AND SCIENTIFIC PAPERS:

Architectural Design, Ivan Margolius, 'Tatra 600 – Tatraplan: A Mass-Produced Teardrop Car,' Vol 71, no 5, September 2001

Auto, 1.11.1935

Autocar, The, 7.11.1930, 6.11.1931, 4.11.1932, 12.1.1934, 15.2.1935, 13.3.1942, 27.7.1945, 5.2.1965

Automobil, July 1987

Automobile, The, Karl Ludvigsen, 'Type 87 Tatra,' Vol 28, no 9, November 2010

Automobile Engineer, The, November 1930, April 1934, November 1934, April 1939

Automobile Quarterly, B P B De Dubé, 'The Constant Czech,' Volume VII, no 3, Griffith Borgeson, 'In the Name of the People: Origins of the VW Beetle,' Volume XVIII, no 4

BIOS number 19/20: Report on Rear-engined V8 Tatra Car Type 87, H A Dean, Passenger Vehicle Experimental Engineer, Vauxhall Motors Ltd, 15.7.1946

Blätter für Technikgeschichte, 'Leben und Werk des Automobilpioniers Dr tech hc Hans Ledwinka,' Springer Verlag, Wien 1980, 39/40 Heft

Blueprint, November 1987, March 1990

Car and Driver, April 1962

Classic and Sports Car, J McLellan, 'Curtain Raiser,' May 1983, D Armstrong, 'Czech Mates,' January 1987, E Lister, 'Avant Guard,' July 1987, September 1987, October 1987, April 1993, February 2015

Classic Cars, B Palmer, 'Command Performance,' October 1988, August 2000, May 2010

Club der Tatra-Freunde Mitteilungen, 1/1986, 8/1986, 12/1986, 4/1987, 12/1987, 5/1988, 9/1988, 1/1989, 5/1989

Československý Motorista , 24.3.1934

Fanmail, Tatra-Register UK, nos 19-54, 2000-2013

Fast Lane, September 1987

Magnus, Ivan Margolius, 'Comeback,' no 2, 2011

Motor, The, 15.8.1933, 10.10.1933, 12.1.1934, 13.3.1934, 3.4.1934, 29.5.1934, 23.10.1934, 19.9.1951, 1.8.1956, 27.3.1957, 11.6.1958, 15.4.1967

Motor Revue, 5.7.1934

Novojičínský deník, 26.10.2014

Omnia, A Caputo, 'Une Voiture d'avant-garde La Tatra 77,' Novembre 1934

On Four Wheels, Volume 7, part 116, London: Orbis, 1978

Ottagono, March 1982

Performance Tuning, March 1989

Road & Track, C G Proche, 'The incredible Tatra,' June 1960, R Thursby, '1939 Tatra 87,' April 1987

Ruoteclassiche, P Casucci, 'Tatra, con tanti anni d'anticipo,' February 1988

Society of Automotive Engineers, Karl Ludvigsen, 'The Time Tunnel – An Historical Survey of Automotive Aerodynamics,' 1978

Svět Motorů, 1951, Volume V, number 102

Tatra, Podnikový zpravodaj, number 10, 'Tradice/Pokrok/ Prosperita,' Kopřivnice 1990, Tatra driver manuals, workshop manuals, handbooks, car brochures, advertising material

Thoroughbred & Classic Cars, B Palmer, 'Forgotten Genius,' June 1983

Truck & Driver, April 1988

World Architecture, Ivan Margolius, 'Streamliners,' no 39

ACKNOWLEDGEMENTS

We would like to thank many people who participated in the realisation of the first and second editions, and are especially proud of making many friends through mutual enthusiasm and admiration for the Tatra marque. Primarily we continue to be grateful to Prof Dr techn Erich Ledwinka and Prof Dr Ivan Sviták for their advice and for supplying their family records, documents and photographs; to Norman Foster for writing a new foreword; to Lumír Kaválek, Karel Rosenkranz and Radim Zátopek from Tatra Museum Kopřivnice for supplying information from Tatra archives, and giving permission to reproduce from the archives; Tatra oborový podnik, Tatra a s, Tatra Trucks a s and the National Technical Museum in Prague for their permission to reproduce from their publications. We have been very fortunate to be lent or given a number of previously unpublished photographs, information and brochures by Gary Cullen, Dr Friedrich Düring, the former president of the Tatra-Freunde International, Wolfgang Schmarbeck, Dr Jan Tulis, Kees Smit, Pavel Kasík, Marián Šuman-Hreblay, David Pounder, Simon Blakeney-Edwards of Edwards Motorsport, and Nick Florian. Further thanks go to Daniel Margolius, Jan Margolius, Heda Margolius Kovály, Sheila Bates and Karen Ehlers for helping with word processing, corrections and translations; Amos Bires Sivan, June Rochester, David Horgan, Morag Smith of Ludvigsen Associates Ltd and Chris Leftley of the RAC library for their picture research; Amanda Bates for preparing the line-shot illustrations; Roy White for giving up some of his valuable time to draw a picture especially for this book; Paul Flancbaum of The Budd Company for supplying information on Joseph Ledwinka; and Gerry Killey and other members of the Tatra-Freunde International for their comments and photographs. We also wish to thank Dr Jan Hozák, Hampton C Wyat, Paul Schilperoord, David Pasek, Jeff Lane, David Yando, Geoffrey Goldberg, Bill Kreiner, Jan Němeček, Michal Froněk, Stanislav Karban, Zdeněk Lukeš, Tatiana Dacková, Robert Keil, Delwyn Mallett, Ian Tisdale, Fred Kuipers, Dave Richards, Dr Jiří M Pechan, David J Russel, Jiří Pollak, Patrick Granger, Paul Markham, Cees Koel, Peter Frost, Paul Wilson, Simon Redrup, Peter Visser, Klaus Buschbaum, Josef Šmarda, Václav Kvasnička, Dr Jan Králík, Petr Kožíšek and members of the Tatra Register UK for their valuable advice, comments, photographs and support. Finally we wish to thank Rod Grainger and his team at Veloce Publishing for their enthusiastic interest and perceptive attitude in accepting this new edition for publication.

Every reasonable effort has been made to identify owners of copyright of the plates, photographs and illustrations. Errors or omissions will be corrected in subsequent editions. Photographs and illustrations are reproduced with acknowledgements to the following:

Authors' archives, Erich Ledwinka, Ivan Sviták, Friedrich Düring, Tatra oborový podnik, Tatra a s, Tatra Trucks a s, Tatra Museum Kopřivnice, NTM Prague, Belli, Steyr-Daimler-Puch AG, Ludvigsen Associates and Ludvigsen Library, Vauxhall Motors Ltd, Deutsches Museum Archives, ETH-Bibliothek Hochschularchiv, Wolfgang Schmarbeck, Volkswagen AG Corporate History Department, The Budd Company, *Automobile Quarterly*, Pavel Kasík, Karel Thér, Dalibor Lupík, Jan Tulis, Karel Rosenkranz, Andrew Mahaddie, Rudolf Margolius, Binky Nixon, Gary Cullen, David Pounder, Studio Olgoj Chorchoj, Klaus Buschbaum, Photo Art Andreas Moosbrugger, David J Russel, Marián Šuman-Hreblay, Paul Schilperoord, Peter Visser, Josef Krümpelbeck, Peter Frost, Simon Redrup, Simon Blakeney-Edwards, Petr Kožíšek, Nigel Young, Ivan Hradil, Ian Tisdale, Werner Ledwinka, Tom Blikslager, Motor Presse Stuttgart, LAT Photographic Archives, David Yando, Lane Motor Museum.

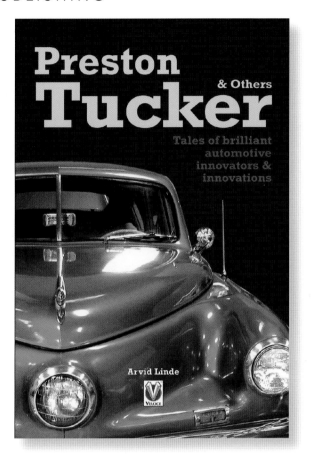

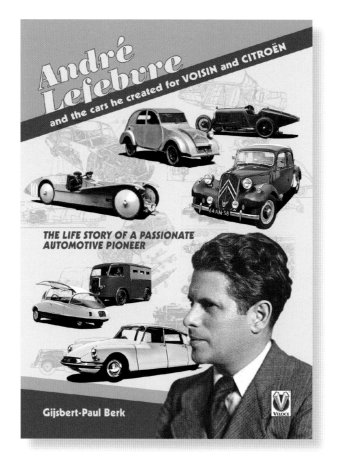

André Lefebvre

and the cars he created for VOISIN and CITROËN

THE LIFE STORY OF A PASSIONATE AUTOMOTIVE PIONEER

Gijsbert-Paul Berk

Now in paperback. This biography of André Lefebvre gives a revealing insight to the work of a practically unknown aeronautic engineer. Responsible for the minimalist 2CV and the Citroën DS – the sensation of the automotive world in 1955 – Lefebvre remains an icon of original automobile engineering and avant-garde design to this day.

ISBN: 978-1-845842-44-4
Paperback • 23.8x17cm • £19.99* UK/$34.95* USA • 144 pages • 154 colour and b&w pictures

For more info on Veloce titles, visit our website at www.veloce.co.uk • email: info@veloce.co.uk • Tel: +44(0)1305 260068
* prices subject to change, p&p extra

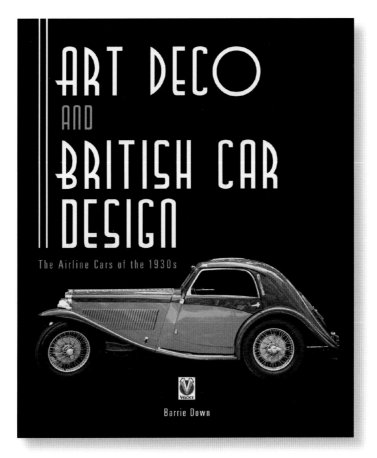

ART DECO
AND
BRITISH CAR DESIGN

The Airline Cars of the 1930s

Barrie Down

The Art Deco movement influenced many different industries in the 1930s, and the British motor industry was no exception. Featuring a comprehensive examination of Art Deco styling elements, and a beautifully illustrated portrayal of British streamlined production cars, this is a unique account of a radical era in automotive design.

ISBN: 978-1-845845-22-3
Paperback • 25x20.7cm • £19.99* UK/$34.95* USA • 144 pages • 215 colour and b&w pictures

For more info on Veloce titles, visit our website at www.veloce.co.uk • email: info@veloce.co.uk • Tel: +44(0)1305 260068
* prices subject to change, p&p extra

BUGATTI
Type 57 Grand Prix
– A Celebration

Neil Max Tomlinson

A comprehensive, radical look at the history and development of the Type 57 Grand Prix Bugattis. New material challenges traditional beliefs about these historic cars, and rejects some long-standing conventions. Myths are explored and truths are revealed in this book celebrating all aspects of these remarkable cars and their creators.

ISBN: 978-1-845847-89-0
Hardback • 24.8x24.8cm • £50* UK/$85* USA • 176 pages • 158 colour and b&w pictures

For more info on Veloce titles, visit our website at www.veloce.co.uk • email: info@veloce.co.uk • Tel: +44(0)1305 260068
* prices subject to change, p&p extra